Studying Culture

An Introductory Reader

Ann Gray

Lecturer in Cultural Studies,
University of Birmingham

and

Jim McGuigan

Principal Lecturer in Communication Studies
and Cultural Policy, Coventry University

Edward Arnold

A division of Hodder & Stoughton

LONDON   NEW YORK   AUCKLAND

To Lesley and Nick

© 1993 *Selection and editorial matter Ann Gray and Jim McGuigan*

First published in Great Britain 1993

Distributed in the USA by Routledge, Chapman and Hall, Inc.
29 West 35th Street, New York, NY 10001

British Library Cataloguing in Publication Data
Gray, Ann
 Studying Culture: Introductory Reader
 I. Title II. McGuigan, Jim
 306.07

ISBN 0-340-55628-5

Typeset in Great Britain by Hewer Text Composition Services,
Edinburgh
Printed and bound in Great Britain for Edward Arnold,
a division of Hodder and Stoughton Limited,
Mill Road, Dunton Green, Sevenoaks, Kent TN13 2YA by
Biddles Ltd, Guildford and King's Lynn.

Acknowledgements

When we decided to construct a reader in Cultural Studies we knew it would be fun. Making such a compilation of selected texts has an affinity with picking a list of favourite records, novels, films or whatever. Yet, little did we imagine how difficult and occasionally tortuous a project we had embarked upon. We have chopped and changed the selection so many times that we have now lost count of quite how many times. Also, when for one reason or another a piece had to be removed we found it impossible to merely slot in a substitute; the unbalancing effect was normally too great. In the end, however, we believe that the selection of writings presented here constitutes a fair representation of cultural studies, and possibly a better one than all the previous selections that we had to discard or modify drastically, which is not to say it is definitive: that would be impossible in any event. Some of the items are cut for reasons of space or in order to bring out the argument more sharply. These cuts are marked by the convention of [. . .]. We apologise to those authors who may feel this has distorted their work. It is, of course, to the authors we have drawn upon that we owe the greatest acknowledgement, all of whom have taught us something and whose works, we believe, exemplify the best of cultural studies. The particular selection of texts has been very much influenced by our learning from students, especially adult education students, initially at the Workers' Educational Association in Leeds and subsequently tutoring on the Open University's Popular Culture course in the mid-1980s. Our present students at the University of Birmingham and Coventry University have further demonstrated to us the value of material which is both accessible and challenging. We also thank our publishers, Lesley Riddle and Louise Thompson, for their endless patience and good humour.

A.G. & J.M.,
January 1993

The authors and publishers would like to thank the following for permission to use copyright material in this book:

Harper Collins Publishers Ltd for the extract from 'The rhetoric of the image' from *Image-Music-Text*, by R. Barthes, translated by S. Heath, (Fontana, 1977); Macmillan Press Ltd for Erica Carter, 'Alice in the consumer wonderland' from Angela McRobbie and Mica Nava (eds.), *Gender*

iii

and Generation (Macmillan, 1984); the author of Phil Cohen, 'Subcultural conflict and working-class community' reprinted from *Working Papers in Cultural Studies 2* (Centre for Contemporary Cultural Studies, University of Birmingham, Spring 1972); the author for Liz Curtis, 'Echoes of the present – the Victorian press and Ireland', from *Truth: the First Casualty* (Information on Ireland, 1978); Verso for Mike Davis, 'The view from futures past', from *City of Quartz – Excavating the Future of Los Angeles*, (Verso/NLB, London and New York, 1990), the authors and Broadcast for Richard Dyer, Terry Lovell and Jean McCrindle, 'Soap opera and women' reprinted from *Edinburgh International Television Festival 1977 – Official Programme* (Broadcast, 1977); Routledge for Nicholas Garnham, 'Concepts of culture' from *Cultural Studies*, Vol. 1, No. 1, Methuen & Co; Routledge for Marie Gillespie, 'Technology and tradition', from *Cultural Studies*, Vol. 3, No. 2.; Routledge for Paul Gilroy, 'Black and white on the dance floor' from *There Ain't No Black in the Union Jack* (Hutchinson, 1987); the Council of Europe for Stuart Hall, 'The television discourse – encoding and decoding', © Council of Europe, first published in *Education and Culture* No. 25, 1974; the author and the Institute of Contemporary Arts for Stuart Hall, 'Minimal selves', from *Identity: The Real Me – Postmodernism and the Question of Identity* (ICA Documents 6, 1987) pp. 44–6. © Stuart Hall and the ICA; Verso for Fredric Jameson, 'Postmodernism and consumer society', reprinted from E. Ann Kaplan (ed.), *Postmodernism and its Discontents* (Verso/NLB, London and New York, 1988) pp. 213–29 the author and *Marxism Today* for Doreen Massey, 'A global sense of place' first published in *Marxism Today*, June, 1991; the author for Kobena Mercer, 'Just looking for trouble – Robert Mapplethorpe and fantasies of race' reprinted from Lynne Segal and Mary McIntosh (eds.), *Sex Exposed – Sexuality and the Pornography Debate* (Virago, 1992); Australian Journal of Communication for Graham Murdock, 'Cultural studies at the crossroads' from *Australian Journal of Communication* No. 16 (December, 1989); 'The Institute of Race Relations for Jan Nederveen Pieterse, 'Fictions of Europe', from *Race and Class* Vol. 32, No. 3, (1991); the author for Bhikhu Parekh, 'Between holy text and moral void', reprinted from *New Statesman* (24 March 1989); Verso for Janice Radway, 'Reading *Reading the Romance*' (Introduction to the English edition of *Reading the Romance*, Verso/NLB, London and New York, 1987) pp. 1–18 Pantheon Books for the extract from *Orientalism* by Edward W. Said, © 1978 by Edward W. Said. Reprinted by permission of Pantheon Books, a division of Random House, Inc. Routledge for the extract from Edward W. Said, *Orientalism*, (Routledge and Kegan Paul, 1978); Merryn Williams for Raymond Williams, 'Culture is ordinary' reprinted from N. McKenzie (ed.), *Convictions* (MacGibbon and Kee, 1958); Marion Boyars Publishers Ltd for the extract from Judith Williamson, *Decoding Advertisements* (Marion Boyars, 1978); Open University Press for Paul Willis, 'Symbolic creativity' from *Common Culture*, (Open University Press, 1990).

Every effort has been made to trace copyright holders of material produced in this book. Any rights not acknowledged here will be acknowledged in subsequent printings if notice is given to the publisher.

Contents

Introduction

This book aims to introduce cultural studies by offering a particular selection of more or less 'classic' readings. Such an offering obliges the editors to address the question: 'what is cultural studies?' That is a perfectly reasonable question to be posed by a newcomer to the field, and it is newcomers to the field who are inevitably positioned as the ideal readers of an introductory textbook. The book, however, also aims to address those already familiar with the field of study who may feel they have been journeying through a terrain for which there is no agreed map. Which is not, of course, to say there are no maps, the best known being Stuart Hall's original efforts (1980a and 1980b). Since Hall mapped out the field according to the distinction between the paradigms of 'culturalism' and 'structuralism', his own neo-Gramscian synthesis of 'hegemony theory' and a series of 'post-structuralist' variants, the field has expanded and become much more diverse than it was at the end of the 1970s (Grossberg, Nelson and Treichler, 1992).

Although the question as posed is reasonable, there is no easy or satisfactory way of answering it. It is one of those questions which tends to come up against evasions and, at best, to spawn other questions, questions that are much more pertinent than the desire to achieve comfort by fixing too precisely the coordinates of an unruly and rapidly developing field of study. We do not intend to evade the question but we also believe there is no single answer that would not do violence to the values of openness. Ours is a particular version by virtue of being a selection shaped by educational considerations derived from our own experiences of studying and teaching cultural studies over several years. We think this book can be useful to students and tutors by facilitating a provisional entry into the field.

There are some answers to the question, however, both narrow and broad. The narrowest answer depends upon prefixing 'cultural studies' with 'British' (Turner, 1990). It is true that the term 'cultural studies' became current in Britain during the late 1960s and early 1970s with specific reference to its institutional siting at Birmingham University: the Centre for Contemporary Cultural Studies, founded in 1964 by the Professor of English, Richard Hoggart, and over which Stuart Hall presided as Director in the 1970s. This Centre of international repute, now superseded by the Birmingham Department of Cultural Studies, drew upon a tradition of study which emerged in the post-Second World War period in British adult education (Williams, 1989). Out of the discipline of English, inspired by Raymond Williams (1958) and the little-recorded efforts of many other adult education tutors, important questions were being asked, mainly by working-class mature students, about the relations between 'culture' and 'society', which broke the bounds of traditional disciplines like literature and history and had a difficult and sometimes deeply troubled association with newer social scientific disciplines, most notably sociology.

For sociologists schooled in a positivistic mode, cultural studies seemed far too soft, concerned with the interpretation of meanings, reminiscent of literary criticism, but encroaching upon the grounds of the social: qualitative in its approach rather than 'scientifically' quantitative. Richard Hoggart's *The Uses of Literacy* (1957) 'read' everyday working-class life, customs and habits, as though they were literary texts, opening up the study of popular culture and applying the interpretive procedures of the humanities to the stuff of social science. In this sense, cultural studies had more in common with anthropology than with the survey research methods and statistical analyses of mainstream sociology. Its great precursor was Mass Observation, a movement of the 1930s and 1940s which sought to turn the anthropological gaze inwards from colonial subjects exclusively to register indigenous subjects (Jeffrey, 1978). Another significant precursor of cultural studies was George Orwell, who wrote about the English working class (*The Road to Wigan Pier*, 1937) and popular cultural artefacts, such as the 'vulgar' postcards of Donald McGill ('The Art of Donald McGill', 1942, reprinted in Orwell's *Collected Essays*, 1968). A further complementary strand was that of 'history from below', represented at the time most profoundly by Edward Thompson's *The Making of the English Working Class* (1963). These precursors and complementarities to cultural studies, as it was forming, are not anthologized in this book. To leave Hoggart and Thompson out is indeed strange. It is due to limitations of space and to the stronger claims, at present, of more immediately usable material for understanding contemporary cultural practices. We have included Raymond Williams's less well known essay from 1958 to represent this 'culturalist' current, 'Culture is ordinary', which in its polemical title encapsulates most sharply the cardinal impulse of what became understood as 'cultural studies' in Britain and in the English-speaking world generally, the stress on 'lived experience' and the recovery of 'the popular' from its denigration or sentimentalization by cultural elitists (McGuigan, 1992). We also believe that Williams is the single most important figure in the original formation of cultural studies, although Hall played a larger role in establishing it as a curriculum subject, particularly by fusing the British tradition of 'culturalism' with the French tradition of 'structuralism', represented initially in this anthology by Roland Barthes's essay from 1964, 'The rhetoric of the image'.

The linguistic turn in cultural studies during the 1970s, inspired by structural linguistics (Saussure, 1974), Levi-Strauss's (1968) structural anthropology and Barthes's (1972) semiological readings of contemporary popular culture, relates to the broader answer to what is cultural studies: seen in retrospect, something of an imperialistic project. This was not only associated with the pretensions of structuralism since 'culture' could be conceived from a historical materialist perspective, after economy and polity, as 'the third instance of the social whole' (Mulhern, 1980: 32), clustering together all sense-making practices. There is a consistency here with structuralism's systematic retotalization of academic enquiry in general and especially its promise to colonize the humanities and social sciences entirely with a universalistic method and the startling claims that language speaks us and, because everything is discursive, therefore, inseparable from the subterranean operations of language (Lane, 1970). This is not the context in which to evaluate the structuralist project and its legacy for cultural studies: briefly, the crucial point is that cultural studies, for a moment, seemed to be out to capture the whole field of 'the cultural', to hegemonize its own intellectual leadership. That rationalist takeover bid did not succeed. The traditional disciplines changed but were not displaced. Literary criticism, for example, became increasingly redefined according to the new literary theory (Eagleton, 1983) and, for another example, sociology took on board the cultural to a greater extent, particularly in the encounter with postmodernism towards the end of the 1980s (see, for instance, Lash, 1990). The resultant outcome of cultural studies's bid for hegemony, however, was to leave it peculiarly boundless. Unlike older disciplines, and some of the newer ones, proponents of cultural studies are reluctant to enclose their terms of reference with definitional precision: everything remains up for grabs. There is also an enormous resistance to the very idea of disciplinarity and its connotations of policing the borders of knowledge. Cultural studies, broadly speaking, can still be said, however, to be concerned with anything that is meaningful, usually seen in connection to power relations.

There is an additional way of trying to pin cultural studies down: institutional and, to some extent, spatial. Cultural studies crept in from the margins, accompanied by other subjects (communication, film, media studies), to become institutionalized within the academy and to spread, in one form or another, throughout the educational system. We now have undergraduate degrees variously named which either mark themselves out explicitly as cultural studies or which are in some implicitly cognate relationship to it. For instance, communication studies, which led the way at this level, is frequently all but cultural studies in name or includes the cultural studies 'perspective' as one amongst any number of disciplinary contributions to an umbrella subject. Many students reading this book will be on programmes of study not named cultural studies but for which the book is undoubtedly relevant. And, on the school curriculum, there are now numerous and varied courses in communication, cultural and media studies.

Cultural studies has latterly gone international. Its reception, especially in Australia and North America, decentred what was once a distinctly British field of study that had been obsessed, arguably, with the peculiarities of the British, bringing continental rationalist theory to bear upon localized empirical objects, for example, the succession of spectacular youth subcultures, one of Britain's major exports to the rest of the world. It is debatable whether cultural studies has become decentred or, instead, *recentred* in the United States's university system, as a recent symposium held at the University of Illinois, drawing together stars in the firmament, to ponder the past, present and future of cultural studies, would suggest (Grossberg, Nelson and Treichler, 1992). The claims of feminism, black politics, the discourses of 'the other', however, were already decentring British cultural studies politically from its narrowly national and social class preoccupations. These political interventions and their theoretical consequences have guided our selection of material. For American students, Patrick Brantlinger's *In Crusoe's Footprints* (1990) provides a useful articulation of cultural studies with American studies that may offset the necessarily British-rootedness of this particular collection.

This book, in effect, traces the developments outlined above, beginning with Raymond Williams's challenge to cultural elitism from within the tradition of 'English' criticism, and concluding with writings that illustrate the internationalization of cultural studies and the critical renewal of an intellectual field which is not contained by traditional disciplinary borders. Mike Davis's elegaic remarks on socialism in the desert outside Los Angeles, the city which epitomizes utopian and dystopian imbrications in the modern world, are followed by Jan Nederveen Pieterse's critique of 'European' rhetoric in an old world riven by racial and ethnic conflicts. The final piece, by Doreen Massey, a geographer, discusses the relations between the global and the local, thus focussing attention on the contemporary politics of place in a complex and rapidly changing world.

By tracking through a dense forest of theoretical perspectives and analytical applications, not all of them compatible with one another, we aim to provide a sense of what cultural studies has been and might yet become. The selection slightly marginalizes the textual in favour of the lived. This reflects both the availability of other readers, particularly concerned with visual and literary media, which foreground the textual (supplemented by the psychoanalytic) and do not need yet further replication, for the time being at least, and our own predilections, which are more ethnographically-inclined and policy-oriented. The book represents, then, a comparatively sociological 'take' on cultural studies, though probably unrecognizably so to many sociologists. It may, therefore, be more accurate to describe this selection as one which foregrounds the social with the partial aim of redressing the balance in that direction.

References and further reading

Barthes, R. (1972) *Mythologies*, London: Paladin.
Brantlinger, P. (1990) *In Crusoe's Footprints—Cultural Studies in Britain and America*, London/New York: Routledge.
Eagleton, T. (1983) *Literary Theory—An Introduction*, Oxford: Basil Blackwell.
Grossberg, L., Nelson, C. and Treichler, P. (eds.) (1992) *Cultural Studies*, London/New York: Routledge.
Hall, S. (1980a) 'Cultural studies—two paradigms', *Media, Culture & Society*, vol. 2, no. 2, London: Sage.
Hall, S. (1980b) 'Cultural studies and the centre—some problematics and problems' in Hall, S., Hobson, D., Lowe, A. and Willis, P. (eds.), *Culture, Media, Language*, London: Hutchinson.
Hoggart, R. (1957) *The Uses of Literacy*, London: Chatto & Windus.

Jeffrey, T. (1978) *Mass Observation—A Short History*, Birmingham CCCS
  Occasional Paper.
Lane, M., ed. (1970) *Structuralism—A Reader*, London: Jonathan Cape.
Lash, S. (1990) *Sociology of Postmodernism*, London/New York: Routledge.
Levi-Strauss, C. (1968) *Structural Anthropology*, London: Allen Lane, the
  Penguin Press.
McGuigan, J. (1992) *Cultural Populism*, London/New York: Routledge.
Mulhern, F. (1980) 'Notes on culture and cultural struggle', *Screen Education* no.
  34, London: Society for Education in Film and Television.
Saussure, F. de (1974) *Course in General Linguistics*, London: Fontana.
Thompson, E.P. (1963) *The Making of the English Working Class*, London: Victor
  Gollancz.
Turner, B. (1990) *British Cultural Studies—An Introduction*, London: Unwin
  Hyman.
Williams, R. (1958) *Culture and Society*, London: Chatto & Windus.
Williams, R. (1989) *The Politics of Modernism*, London: Verso.

Editors' note

In some of the earlier pieces in this Reader the term 'man' is used to refer to both men and women in a manner common until feminism's questioning of patriarchal language impacted upon academic discourse. The problem is signalled now rather than marked in every instance.

Section I

Some foundations

Reference has already been made to the problems of definition in relation to cultural studies and the same can be said of any attempt to construct a history of a field of study, which the term 'foundations' would seem to imply. It is true that there could be many different histories accounting for the development of cultural studies but the most common one begins with the 'triumvirate' of Richard Hoggart, Raymond Williams and Edward Thompson, more remarkable for their differences than this traditional grouping would imply but who, writing in the late 1950s in Britain, shared at the very least a common questioning of academic values and disciplines, in particular those entrenched within English and History. However, our selection here is less concerned with constructing a coherent or chronological narrative through cultural studies, but rather seeks to indicate a number of interventions, often from the margins, which at their best cause disjunctures and dislocations in the development of the field of study.

Writing in 1958, **Raymond Williams** insisted that 'Culture is ordinary' and forced the first important shift into a new way of thinking about the symbolic dimensions of our lives. Thus, 'culture' is wrested from that privileged space of artistic production and specialist knowledge, into the lived experience of the everyday.

In following with **Roland Barthes**'s 'Rhetoric of the image', originally published in France in 1964, we are recognizing the impact of the body of work known as 'structuralism' in the development of cultural studies, although its impact reverberated through many disciplines. Structuralism and, particularly in this instance, semiology, was seen to offer the potential for a rigorous mode of analysis, especially of the visual image, but also of other texts and social practices. This was an analysis which, with its emphasis on the underlying structures of texts and practices, was seen to provide a necessary distance which the more experiential and humanistic versions of cultural studies lacked.

Although semiotics offered a method of textual analysis, attempts were made to go beyond this limited focus. The essay by **Stuart Hall** provides

1

a model for understanding the textual construction of meaning *and* the practice of reading, or decoding, the text. This model was taken up most notably by David Morley in his study of the popular magazine programme, *Nationwide* (Morley 1980). Here Hall introduces a sociological dimension to the question of 'reading' (a term used in relation to all texts) and this piece also serves to place television as a key object of study.

This focus is returned to and expanded in the paper presented to the Edinburgh International Television Festival in 1977 by **Richard Dyer**, **Terry Lovell** and **Jean McCrindle** on women's viewing of and representation in the soap opera genre, which insists that popular television should be taken seriously and further demands that genres specifically addressed to a female audience should be critically examined. This was an important intervention from which followed a number of studies of soap opera in particular (Dyer et al. 1981; Brunsdon 1981; Hobson 1982; Modleski 1982; Allen 1985; Ang 1985; Geraghty 1990), and also of female genres more generally and the female audience. The theme of soap opera and women provided an important bridge between the sociologically based media studies and feminist work within film theory, producing fruitful attempts to work with often incompatible theoretical frameworks (Kuhn 1984; Mattelart 1986; Brunsdon 1986; Gamman and Marshment 1988; Pibram 1988; Taylor 1989; Seiter et al. 1989; Brown 1990.)

Edward Said's ground-breaking book *Orientalism*, the introduction to which is printed here, opens up a very different set of questions, those of 'race' and ethnicity which were being raised elsewhere in a range of contexts, but more broadly, using a Foucauldian framework, he points to the operations of power in the Eurocentric constructions of the 'Orient' across many sites of knowledge production. The consequences of these dense accumulations of 'referential power' constituting myths of the Orient in the culture at large were never more sharply focussed than during the Gulf War of 1991 when the global dimensions of 'race' and 'otherness' and the crippling consequences of Orientalism were exposed in all public, and many private, discursive sites (Kabbani 1986; Norris 1992.)

The inclusion of **Nicholas Garnham**'s paper presented to the Greater London Council in 1983 is to introduce an often neglected dimension of culture within the field of mainstream cultural studies. That is the constitution and formation of the cultural industries, the intensification of cultural distribution, and therefore access to audiences, and what contribution cultural studies can offer to policy making. This important level of analysis is rendered absent in most studies of cultural consumption.

Janice Radway's introduction to the British publication of her influential work *Reading the Romance* usefully reminds us of the importance of the context of intellectual production whilst outlining her study of American romance readers as an 'interpretive community'. Whilst Radway's auto-critique is important (see also Radway 1988), *Reading the Romance* remains as one of the few examples of a multi-layered analysis of a hugely popular fictional genre and its readers.

This section ends with a note of caution and critique from **Graham Murdock** in which he registers a problem for the future of cultural studies. The metaphor of the 'Crossroads' is nicely ironic in its allusion to the highly popular and much analysed British soap opera of the same name given his critique of the tendencies in recent work within cultural studies; that of populism and a critical pluralism; its British focus and its tendency to ignore questions of political economy. What he, and others, have signalled is the danger in the slippage from 'ordinariness' to 'banality' (Morris 1988) in cultural studies, and the need to constantly reflect on our frameworks and objects of study.

References and further reading

Allen, R. (1985) *Speaking of Soap Operas*, Chapel Hill: University of North Carolina Press.

Ang, I. (1985) *Watching Dallas: Soap Opera and the Melodramatic Imagination*, London: Methuen.

Brown, M.E. (1990) *Television and Women's Culture*, London: Sage.

Brunsdon, C. (1981) 'Crossroads: notes on soap opera' in *Screen*, vol. 22, no. 4.

Brunsdon, C. (ed.) (1986) *Films for Women*, London: British Film Institute.

Dyer, R., Geraghty, C., Lovell, T., Jordan, M., Paterson, R. and Stewart, J. (1981) *Coronation Street*, London: British Film Institute.

Gamman, L., and Marshmant, M. (eds.) (1988) *The Female Gaze: Women as Viewers of Popular Culture*, London: The Women's Press.

Geraghty, C. (1990) *Women and Soap Opera*, Oxford: Polity Press.

Hobson, D. (1982) *Crossroads: the Drama of a Soap Opera*, London: Methuen.

Kabbani, R. (1986) *Europe's Myths of Orient*, London: Pandora.

Kuhn, A. (1982) *Women's Pictures: Feminism and Cinema*, London: Routledge & Kegan Paul.

Kuhn, A. (1984) 'Women's genres' in *Screen*, vol. 25, no. 1.

Mattelart, M. (1981) *Women, Media, Crisis*, London: Comedia.

Modleski, T. (1982) *Loving with a Vengeance*, Hamden (Connecticut): Shoestring Press.

Morley, D. (1980) *The Nationwide Audience*, London: British Film Institute.

Morley, D. (1986) *Family Television*, London: Comedia.

Morris, M. (1988) 'Banality in cultural studies' in *Block*, no. 14.

Norris, C. (1992) *Uncritical Theory—Postmodernism, Intellectuals and the Gulf War*, London: Lawrence & Wishart.

Pibram, E.D. (ed.) (1988) *Female Spectators*, London: Verso.

Radway, J. (1988) 'Reception study: ethnography and the problem of dispersed audience, and nomadic subjects' in *Cultural Studies*, vol. 2, no. 3, October.

Seiter, E., Borchers, H., Kreutzner, G. and Warth, E.M. (eds.) (1989) *Remote Control: TV Audiences and Cultural Power*, London: Routledge.

Taylor, H. (1989) *Scarlett's Women: Gone with the Wind and its Female Fans*, London: Virago.

Williams, R. (1965) *The Long Revolution*, Harmondsworth: Penguin.

Williams, R. (1974) *Television: Technology and Cultural Form*, London: Fontana.

Williams, R. (1976) *Keywords: A Vocabulary of Culture and Society*, London: Fontana.

Williams, R. (1980) *Problems in Materialism and Culture: Selected Essays*, London: New Left Review.

Williams, R. (1981) *Politics and Letters: Interviews with New Left Review*, London: Verso.

Williams, R. (1983) *Towards 2000*, London: Chatto & Windus.

1

Culture is ordinary

Raymond Williams

Originally published in N. McKenzie (ed.): *Convictions* (MacGibbon and Kee, 1958); reprinted in R. Williams: *Resources of Hope* (Verso, 1989).

The bus stop was outside the cathedral. I had been looking at the Mappa Mundi, with its rivers out of Paradise, and at the chained library, where a party of clergymen had got in easily, but where I had waited an hour and cajoled a verger before I even saw the chains. Now, across the street, a cinema advertised the *Six-Five Special* and a cartoon version of *Gulliver's Travels*. The bus arrived, with a driver and a conductress deeply absorbed in each other. We went out of the city, over the old bridge, and on through the orchards and the green meadows and the fields red under the plough. Ahead were the Black Mountains, and we climbed among them, watching the steep fields end at the grey walls, beyond which the bracken and heather and whin had not yet been driven back. To the east, along the ridge, stood the line of grey Norman castles; to the west, the fortress wall of the mountains. Then, as we still climbed, the rock changed under us. Here, now, was limestone, and the line of the early iron workings along the scarp. The farming valleys, with their scattered white houses, fell away behind. Ahead of us were the narrower valleys: the steel-rolling mill, the gasworks, the grey terraces, the pitheads. The bus stopped, and the driver and conductress got out, still absorbed. They had done this journey so often, and seen all its stages. It is a journey, in fact, that in one form or another we have all made.

I was born and grew up halfway along that bus journey. Where I lived is still a farming valley, though the road through it is being widened and straightened, to carry the heavy lorries to the north. Not far away, my grandfather, and so back through the generations, worked as a farm labourer until he was turned out of his cottage and, in his fifties, became a roadman. His sons went at thirteen or fourteen on to the farms, his daughters into service. My father, his third son, left the farm at fifteen to be a boy porter on the railway, and later became a signalman, working in a box in this valley until he died. I went up the road to the village school, where a curtain divided the two classes—Second to eight or nine, First to fourteen. At eleven I went to the local grammar school, and later to Cambridge.

Culture is ordinary: that is where we must start. To grow up in that country was to see the shape of a culture, and its modes of change. I could

5

stand on the mountains and look north to the farms and the cathedral, or south to the smoke and the flare of the blast furnace making a second sunset. To grow up in that family was to see the shaping of minds: the learning of new skills, the shifting of relationships, the emergence of different language and ideas. My grandfather, a big hard labourer, wept while he spoke, finely and excitedly, at the parish meeting, of being turned out of his cottage. My father, not long before he died, spoke quietly and happily of when he had started a trade-union branch and a Labour Party group in the village, and, without bitterness, of the 'kept men' of the new politics. I speak a different idiom, but I think of these same things.

Culture is ordinary: that is the first fact. Every human society has its own shape, its own purposes, its own meanings. Every human society expresses these, in institutions, and in arts and learning. The making of a society is the finding of common meanings and directions, and its growth is an active debate and amendment under the pressures of experience, contact, and discovery, writing themselves into the land. The growing society is there, yet it is also made and remade in every individual mind. The making of a mind is, first, the slow learning of shapes, purposes, and meanings, so that work, observation and communication are possible. Then, second, but equal in importance, is the testing of these in experience, the making of new observations, comparisons, and meanings. A culture has two aspects: the known meanings and directions, which its members are trained to; the new observations and meanings, which are offered and tested. These are the ordinary processes of human societies and human minds, and we see through them the nature of a culture: that it is always both traditional and creative; that it is both the most ordinary common meanings and the finest individual meanings. We use the word culture in these two senses: to mean a whole way of life—the common meanings; to mean the arts and learning—the special processes of discovery and creative effort. Some writers reserve the word for one or other of these senses; I insist on both, and on the significance of their conjunction. The questions I ask about our culture are questions about our general and common purposes, yet also questions about deep personal meanings. Culture is ordinary, in every society and in every mind.

Now there are two senses of culture—two colours attached to it—that I know about but refuse to learn. The first I discovered at Cambridge, in a teashop. I was not, by the way, oppressed by Cambridge. I was not cast down by old buildings, for I had come from a country with twenty centuries of history written visibly into the earth: I liked walking through a Tudor court, but it did not make me feel raw. I was not amazed by the existence of a place of learning; I had always known the cathedral, and the bookcases I now sit to work at in Oxford are of the same design as those in the chained library. Nor was learning, in my family, some strange eccentricity; I was not, on a scholarship in Cambridge, a new kind of animal up a brand-new ladder. Learning was ordinary; we learned where we could. Always, from those scattered white houses, it had made sense to go out and become a scholar or a poet or a teacher. Yet few of us could be spared from the immediate work; a price had been set on this kind of learning, and it was more, much more, than we could individually pay. Now, when we could pay in common, it was a good, ordinary life.

I was not oppressed by the university, but the teashop, acting as if it were one of the older and more respectable departments, was a different matter. Here was culture, not in any sense I knew, but in a special sense: the outward and emphatically visible sign of a special kind of people, cultivated people. They were not, the great majority of them, particularly learned; they practised few arts; but they had it, and they showed you they had it. They are still there, I suppose, still showing it, though even they must be hearing rude noises from outside, from a few scholars and writers they call—how comforting a label is!—angry young men. As a matter of fact there is no need to be rude. It is simply that if that is culture, we don't want it; we have seen other people living.

But of course it is not culture, and those of my colleagues who, hating the teashop, make culture, on its account, a dirty word, are mistaken. If the people in the teashop go on insisting that culture is their trivial differences of behaviour, their trivial variations of speech habit, we cannot stop them, but we can ignore them. They are not that important, to take culture from where it belongs.

Yet, probably also disliking the teashop, there were writers I read then, who went into the same category in my mind. When I now read a book such as Clive Bell's *Civilisation*, I experience not so much disagreement as stupor. What kind of life can it be, I wonder, to produce this extraordinary fussiness, this extraordinary decision to call certain things culture and then separate them, as with a park wall, from ordinary people and ordinary work? At home we met and made music, listened to it, recited and listened to poems, valued fine language. I have heard better music and better poems since; there is the world to draw on. But I know, from the most ordinary experience, that the interest is there, the capacity is there. Of course, farther along that bus journey, the old social organization in which these things had their place has been broken. People have been driven and concentrated into new kinds of work, new kinds of relationship; work, by the way, which built the park walls, and the houses inside them, and which is now at last bringing, to the unanimous disgust of the teashop, clean and decent and furnished living to the people themselves. Culture is ordinary: through every change let us hold fast to that.

The other sense, or colour, that I refuse to learn, is very different. Only two English words rhyme with culture, and these, as it happens, are sepulture and vulture. We don't yet call museums or galleries or even universities culture-sepultures, but I hear a lot, lately, about culture-vultures (man must rhyme), and I hear also, in the same North Atlantic argot, of do-gooders and highbrows and superior prigs. Now I don't like the teashop, but I don't like this drinking-hole either. I know there are people who are humourless about the arts and learning, and I know there is a difference between goodness and sanctimony. But the growing implications of this spreading argot—the true cant of a new kind of rogue—I reject absolutely. For, honestly, how can anyone use a word like 'do-gooder' with this new, offbeat complacency? How can anyone wither himself to a state where he must use these new flip words for any attachment to learning or the arts?

It is plain that what may have started as a feeling about hypocrisy, or about pretentiousness (in itself a two-edged word), is becoming a guilt-ridden tic at the mention of any serious standards whatever. And the word 'culture' has been heavily compromised by this conditioning: Goering reached for his gun; many reach for their chequebooks; a growing number, now, reach for the latest bit of argot.

'Good' has been drained of much of its meaning, in these circles, by the exclusion of its ethical content and emphasis on a purely technical standard; to do a good job is better than to be a do-gooder. But do we need reminding that any crook can, in his own terms, do a good job? The smooth reassurance of technical efficiency is no substitute for the whole positive human reference. Yet men who once made this reference, men who were or wanted to be writers or scholars, are now, with every appearance of satisfaction, advertising men, publicity boys, names in the strip newspapers. These men were given skills, given attachments, which are now in the service of the most brazen money-grabbing exploitation of the inexperience of ordinary people. And it is these men—this new, dangerous class—who have invented and disseminated the argot, in an attempt to influence ordinary people—who because they do real work have real standards in the fields they know—against real standards in the fields these men knew and have abandoned. The old cheapjack is still there in the market, with the country boys' half-crowns on his reputed packets of gold rings or watches. He thinks of his victims as a slow, ignorant crowd, but they live, and farm, while he coughs behind his portable stall. The new cheapjack is in offices with contemporary *décor*, using scraps of linguistics, psychology and sociology to influence what he thinks of as the mass mind. He too, however, will have to pick up and move on, and meanwhile we are not to be influenced by his argot; we can simply refuse to learn it. Culture is ordinary. An interest in learning or the arts is simple, pleasant and natural. A desire to know what is best, and to do what is good, is the whole positive nature of man. We are not to be scared from these things by noises. There are many versions of what is wrong with our culture. So far I have tried only to clear away the detritus which makes it difficult for us to think seriously about it at all. When I got to Cambridge I encountered two serious influences which have left a very deep impression on my mind. The first was Marxism, the second the teaching of Leavis. Through all subsequent disagreement I retain my respect for both.

The Marxists said many things, but those that mattered were three. First, they said that a culture must be finally interpreted in relation to its underlying system of production. I have argued this theoretically elsewhere*—it is a more difficult idea than it looks—but I still accept its emphasis. Everything I had seen, growing up in that border country, had led me towards such an emphasis: a culture is a whole way of life, and the arts are part of a social organization which economic change clearly radically affects. I did not have to be taught dissatisfaction with the existing economic system, but the subsequent questions about our culture were, in these terms, vague. It was said that it was a class-dominated culture, deliberately

* *Culture and Society* (1958).

restricting a common inheritance to a small class, while leaving the masses ignorant. The fact of restriction I accepted—it is still very obvious that only the *deserving* poor get much educational opportunity, and I was in no mood, as I walked about Cambridge, to feel glad that I had been thought deserving; I was no better and no worse than the people I came from. On the other hand, just because of this, I got angry at my friends' talk about the ignorant masses: one kind of Communist has always talked like this, and has got his answer, at Poznan and Budapest, as the imperialists, making the same assumption, were answered in India, in Indo-China, in Africa. There is an English bourgeois culture, with its powerful educational, literary and social institutions, in close contact with the actual centres of power. To say that most working people are excluded from these is self-evident, though the doors, under sustained pressure, are slowly opening. But to go on to say that working people are excluded from English culture is nonsense; they have their own growing institutions, and much of the strictly bourgeois culture they would in any case not want. A great part of the English way of life, and of its arts and learning, is not bourgeois in any discoverable sense. There are institutions, and common meanings, which are in no sense the sole product of the commercial middle class, and there are art and learning, a common English inheritance, produced by many kinds of men, including many who hated the very class and system which now take pride in consuming it. The bourgeoisie has given us much, including a narrow but real system of morality; that is at least better than its court predecessors. The leisure which the bourgeoisie attained has given us much of cultural value. But this is not to say that contemporary culture is bourgeois culture: a mistake that everyone, from Conservatives to Marxists, seems to make. There is a distinct working-class way of life, which I for one value—not only because I was bred in it, for I now, in certain respects, live differently. I think this way of life, with its emphases of neighbourhood, mutual obligation, and common betterment, as expressed in the great working-class political and industrial institutions, is in fact the best basis for any future English society. As for the arts and learning, they are in a real sense a national inheritance, which is, or should be, available to everyone. So when the Marxists say that we live in a dying culture, and that the masses are ignorant, I have to ask them, as I asked them then, where on earth they have lived. A dying culture, and ignorant masses, are not what I have known and see.

What I had got from the Marxists then, so far, was a relationship between culture and production, and the observation that education was restricted. The other things I rejected, as I rejected also their third point, that since culture and production are related, the advocacy of a different system of production is in some way a cultural directive, indicating not only a way of life but new arts and learning. I did some writing while I was, for eighteen months, a member of the Communist Party, and I found out in trivial ways what other writers, here and in Europe, have found out more gravely: the practical consequences of this kind of theoretical error. In this respect, I saw the future, and it didn't work. The Marxist interpretation of culture can never be accepted while it retains, as it need not retain, this directive element, this insistence that if you honestly want socialism you must write, think, learn in certain prescribed ways. A culture is common meanings, the product of a whole people, and offered individual meanings, the product of a man's whole committed personal and social experience. It is stupid and arrogant to suppose that any of these meanings can in any way be prescribed; they are made by living, made and remade, in ways we cannot know in advance. To try to jump the future, to pretend that in some way you *are* the future, is strictly insane. Prediction is another matter, an offered meaning, but the only thing we can say about culture in an England that has socialized its means of production is that all the channels of expression and communication should be cleared and open, so that the whole actual life, that we cannot know in advance, that we can know only in part even while it is being lived, may be brought to consciousness and meaning.

Leavis has never liked Marxists, which is in one way a pity, for they know more than he does about modern English society, and about its immediate history. He, on the other hand, knows more than any Marxist I have met about the real relations between art and experience. We have all learned from him in this, and we have also learned his version of what is wrong with English culture. The diagnosis is radical, and is rapidly becoming orthodox. There was an old, mainly agricultural England, with a traditional culture of great value. This has been replaced by a modern, organized, industrial state, whose characteristic institutions deliberately cheapen our natural human responses, making art and literature into desperate survivors and witnesses, while a new mechanized vulgarity sweeps into the centres of power. The only defence is in education, which will at least keep certain things alive, and which will also, at least in a minority, develop ways of thinking and feeling which are competent to understand what is happening and to maintain the finest individual values. I need not add how widespread this diagnosis has become, though little enough acknowledgement is still made to Leavis himself. For my own part, I was deeply impressed by it; deeply enough for my ultimate rejection of it to be a personal crisis lasting several years.

For, obviously, it seemed to fit a good deal of my experience. It did not tell me that my father and grandfather were ignorant wage-slaves; it did not tell me that the smart, busy, commercial culture (which I had come to as a stranger, so much so that for years I had violent headaches whenever I passed through London and saw underground advertisements and evening newspapers) was the thing I had to catch up with. I even made a fool of myself, or was made to think so, when after a lecture in which the usual point was made that 'neighbour' now does not mean what it did to Shakespeare, I said—imagine!—that to me it did. (When my father was dying this year, one man came in and dug his garden; another loaded and delivered a lorry of sleepers for firewood; another came and chopped the sleepers into blocks; another—I don't know who, it was never said—left a sack of potatoes at the back door; a woman came in and took away a basket of washing.) But even this was explicable; I came from a bit of the old society, but my future was Surbiton (it took me years to find Surbiton, and have a good look at it, but it's served a good many as a symbol—without having lived there I couldn't say whether rightly). So there I was, and it all seemed to fit.

Yet not all. Once I got away, and thought about it, it didn't really fit properly. For one thing I knew this: at home we were glad of the Industrial Revolution, and of its consequent social and political changes. True, we lived in a very beautiful farming valley, and the valleys beyond the limestone we could all see were ugly. But there was one gift that was overriding, one gift which at any price we would take, the gift of power that is everything to men who have worked with their hands. It was slow in coming to us, in all its effects, but steam power, the petrol engine, electricity, these and their host of products in commodities and services, we took as quickly as we could get them, and were glad. I have seen all these things being used, and I have seen the things they replaced. I will not listen with patience to any acid listing of them—you know the sneer you can get into plumbing, baby Austins, aspirin, contraceptives, canned food. But I say to these Pharisees: dirty water, an earth bucket, a four-mile walk each way to work, headaches, broken women, hunger and monotony of diet. The working people, in town and country alike, will not listen (and I support them) to any account of our society which supposes that these things are not progress: not just mechanical, external progress either, but a real service of life. Moreover, in the new conditions, there was more real freedom to dispose of our lives, more real personal grasp where it mattered, more real say. Any account of our culture which explicitly or implicitly denies the value of an industrial society is really irrelevant; not in a million years would you make us give up this power.

So then the social basis of the case was unacceptable, but could one, trying to be a writer, a scholar, a teacher, ignore the indictment of the new cultural vulgarity? For the plumbing and the tractors and the medicines could one ignore the strip newspapers, the multiplying cheapjacks, the raucous triviality? As a matter of priorities, yes, if necessary; but was the cheapening of response really a consequence of the cheapening of power? It looks like it, I know, but is this really as much as one can say? I believe the central problem of our society, in the coming half-century, is the use of our new resources to make a good common culture; the means to a good, abundant economy we already understand. I think the good common culture can be made, but before we can be serious about this, we must rid ourselves of a legacy from our most useful critics—a legacy of two false equations, one false analogy, and one false proposition.

The false proposition is easily disposed of. It is a fact that the new power brought ugliness: the coal brought dirt, the factory brought overcrowding, communications brought a mess of wires. But the proposition that ugliness is a price we pay, or refuse to pay, for economic power need no longer be true. New sources of power, new methods of production, improved systems of transport and communication can, quite practically, make England clean and pleasant again, and with much more power, not less. Any new ugliness is the product of stupidity, indifference, or simply incoordination; these things will be easier to deal with than when power was necessarily noisy, dirty, and disfiguring.

The false equations are more difficult. One is the equation between popular education and the new commercial culture: the latter proceeding inevitably from the former. Let the masses in, it is said, and this is what you inevitably get. Now the question is obviously difficult, but I can't accept this equation, for two reasons. The first is a matter of faith: I don't believe that the ordinary people in fact resemble the normal description of the masses, low and trivial in taste and habit. I put it another way: that there are in fact no masses, but only ways of seeing people as masses. With the coming of industrialism, much of the old social organization broke down and it became a matter of difficult personal experience that we were constantly seeing people we did not know, and it was tempting to mass them, as 'the others', in our minds. Again, people were physically massed, in the industrial towns, and a new class structure (the names of our social classes, and the word 'class' itself in this sense, date only from the Industrial Revolution) was practically imposed. The improvement in communications, in particular the development of new forms of multiple transmission of news and entertainment, created unbridgeable divisions between transmitter and audience, which again led to the audience being interpreted as an unknown mass. Masses became a new word for mob: the others, the unknown, the unwashed, the crowd beyond one. As a way of knowing other people, this formula is obviously ridiculous, but, in the new conditions, it seemed an effective formula—the only one possible. Certainly it was the formula that was used by those whose money gave them access to the new communication techniques; the lowness of taste and habit, which human beings assign very easily to other human beings, was assumed, as a bridge. The new culture was built on this formula, and if I reject the formula, if I insist that this lowness is not inherent in ordinary people, you can brush my insistence aside, but I shall go on holding to it. A different formula, I know from experience, gets a radically different response.

My second reason is historical: I deny, and can prove my denial, that popular education and commercial culture are cause and effect. I have shown elsewhere that the myth of 1870—the Education Act which is said to have produced, as its children grew up, a new cheap and nasty press—is indeed myth. There was more than enough literacy, long before 1870, to support a cheap press, and in fact there were cheap and really bad newspapers selling in great quantities before the 1870 Act was heard of. The bad new commercial culture came out of the social chaos of industrialism, and out of the success, in this chaos, of the 'masses' formula, not out of popular education. Northcliffe did few worse things than start this myth, for while the connection between bad culture and the social chaos of industrialism is significant, the connection between it and popular education is vicious. The Northcliffe Revolution, by the way, was a radical change in the financial structure of the press, basing it on a new kind of revenue—the new mass advertising of the 1890s—rather than the making of a cheap popular press, in which he had been widely and successfully preceded. But I tire of making these points. Everyone prefers to believe Northcliffe. Yet does nobody, even a Royal Commission, read the most ordinarily accessible newspaper history? When people do read the history, the false equation between popular education and commercial culture will disappear for ever. Popular education came out of the other camp, and has had quite opposite effects.

The second false equation is this: that the observable badness of so much widely distributed popular culture is a true guide to the state of mind and feeling, the essential quality of living of its consumers. Too many good men have said this for me to treat it lightly, but I still, on evidence, can't accept it. It is easy to assemble, from print and cinema and television, a terrifying and fantastic congress of cheap feelings and moronic arguments. It is easy to go on from this and assume this deeply degrading version of the actual lives of our contemporaries. Yet do we find this confirmed, when we meet people? This is where 'masses' comes in again, of course: the people *we* meet aren't vulgar, but God, think of Bootle and Surbiton and Aston! I haven't lived in any of those places; have you? But a few weeks ago I was in a house with a commercial traveller, a lorry driver, a bricklayer, a shopgirl, a fitter, a signalman, a nylon operative, a domestic help (perhaps, dear, she is your very own treasure). I hate describing people like this, for in fact they were my family and family friends. Now they read, they watch, this work we are talking about; some of them quite critically, others with a good deal of pleasure. Very well, I read different things, watch different entertainments, and I am quite sure why they are better. But could I sit down in that house and make this equation we are offered? Not, you understand, that shame was stopping me; I've learned, thank you, how to behave. But talking to my family, to my friends, talking, as we were, about our own lives, about people, about feelings, could I in fact find this lack of quality we are discussing? I'll be honest—I looked; my training has done that for me. I can only say that I found as much natural fineness of feeling, as much quick discrimination, as much clear grasp of ideas within the range of experience as I have found anywhere. I don't altogether understand this, though I am not really surprised. Clearly there is something in the psychology of print and image that none of us has yet quite grasped. For the equation looks sensible, yet when you test it, in experience—and there's nowhere else you can test it—it's wrong. I can understand the protection of critical and intelligent reading: my father, for instance, a satisfied reader of the *Daily Herald*, got simply from reading the company reports a clear idea, based on names, of the rapid development of combine and interlocking ownership in British industry, which I had had made easy for me in two or three academic essays; and he had gone on to set these facts against the opinions in a number of articles in the paper on industrial ownership. That I understand; that is simply intelligence, however partly trained. But there is still this other surprising fact: that people whose quality of personal living is high are apparently satisfied by a low quality of printed feeling and opinion. Many of them still live, it is true, in a surprisingly enclosed personal world, much more so than mine, and some of their personal observations are the finer for it. Perhaps this is enough to explain it, but in any case, I submit, we need a new equation, to fit the observable facts.

Now the false analogy, that we must also reject. This is known, in discussions of culture, as a 'kind of Gresham's Law'. Just as bad money will drive out good, so bad culture will drive out good, and this, it is said, has in fact been happening. If you can't see, straight away, the defect of the analogy, your answer, equally effective, will have to be historical. For in fact, of course, it has not been happening. There is more, much more bad culture about; it is easier, now, to distribute it, and there is more leisure to receive it. But test this in any field you like, and see if this has been accompanied by a shrinking consumption of things we can all agree to be good. The editions of good literature are very much larger than they were; the listeners to good music are much more numerous than they were; the number of people who look at good visual art is larger than it has ever been. If bad newspapers drive out good newspapers, by a kind of Gresham's Law, why is it that, allowing for the rise in population, *The Times* sells nearly three times as many copies as in the days of its virtual monopoly of the press, in 1850? It is the law I am questioning, not the seriousness of the facts as a whole. Instead of a kind of Gresham's Law, keeping people awake at nights with the now orthodox putropian nightmare, let us put it another way, to fit the actual facts: we live in an expanding culture, and all the elements in this culture are themselves expanding. If we start from this, we can then ask real questions: about relative rates of expansion; about the social and economic problems raised by these; about the social and economic answers. I am working now on a book* to follow my *Culture and Society*, trying to interpret, historically and theoretically, the nature and conditions of an expanding culture of our kind. I could not have begun this work if I had not learned from the Marxists and from Leavis; I cannot complete it unless I radically amend some of the ideas which they and others have left us.   [. . .]

* *The Long Revolution* (1961).

2

The rhetoric of the image

Roland Barthes

French original, 'Rhetorique de l'image', *Communications* 1, 1964; English translation by Stephen Heath in R. Barthes: *Image—Music—Text* (Fontana, 1977).

According to an ancient etymology, the word *image* should be linked to the root *imitari*. Thus we find ourselves immediately at the heart of the most important problem facing the semiology of images: can analogical representation (the 'copy') produce true systems of signs and not merely simple agglutinations of symbols? Is it possible to conceive of an analogical 'code' (as opposed to a digital one)? We know that linguists refuse the status of language to all communication by analogy—from the 'language' of bees to the 'language' of gesture—the moment such communications are not doubly articulated, are not founded on a combinatory system of digital units as phonemes are. Nor are linguists the only ones to be suspicious as to the linguistic nature of the image; general opinion too has a vague conception of the image as an area of resistance to meaning—this is the name of a certain mythical idea of Life: the image is re-presentation, which is to say ultimately resurrection, and, as we know, the intelligible is reputed antipathetic to lived experience. Thus from both sides the image is felt to be weak in respect of meaning: there are those who think that the image is an extremely rudimentary system in comparison with language and those who think that signification cannot exhaust the image's ineffable richness. Now even—and above all if—the image is in a certain manner the *limit* of meaning, it permits the consideration of a veritable ontology of the process of signification. How does meaning get into the image? Where does it end? And if it ends, what is there *beyond*? Such are the questions that I wish to raise by submitting the image to a spectral analysis of the messages it may contain. We will start by making it considerably easier for ourselves: we will only study the advertising image. Why? Because in advertising the signification of the image is undoubtedly intentional; the signifieds of the advertising message are formed *a priori* by certain attributes of the product and these signifieds have to be transmitted as clearly as possible. If the image contains signs, we can be sure that in advertising these signs are full, formed with a view to the optimum reading: the advertising image is *frank*, or at least emphatic.

The three messages

Here we have a Panzani advertisement: some packets of pasta, a tin, a
sachet, some tomatoes, onions, peppers, a mushroom, all emerging from
a half-open string-bag, in yellows and greens on a red background.* Let
us try to 'skim off' the different messages it contains.

The image immediately yields a first message whose substance is
linguistic; its supports are the caption, which is marginal, and the labels,
these being inserted into the natural disposition of the scene, '*en abyme*'. The
code from which this message has been taken is none other than that of the
French language; the only knowledge required to dicipher it is a knowledge
of writing and French. In fact, this message can itself be further broken
down, for the sign *Panzani* gives not simply the name of the firm but also,

---

* The *description* of the photograph is given here with prudence, for it already constitutes
a metalanguage. The reader is asked to refer to the reproduction.

by its assonance, an additional signified, that of 'Italianicity'. The linguistic message is thus twofold (at least in this particular image): denotational and connotational. Since, however, we have here only a single typical sign,* namely that of articulated (written) language, it will be counted as one message.

Putting aside the linguistic message, we are left with the pure image (even if the labels are part of it, anecdotally). This image straightaway provides a series of discontinuous signs. First (the order is unimportant as these signs are not linear), the idea that what we have in the scene represented is a return from the market. A signified which itself implies two euphoric values: that of the freshness of the products and that of the essentially domestic preparation for which they are destined. Its signifier is the half-open bag which lets the provisions spill out over the table, 'unpacked'. To read this first sign requires only a knowledge which is in some sort implanted as part of the habits of a very widespread culture where 'shopping around for oneself' is opposed to the hasty stocking up (preserves, refrigerators) of a more 'mechanical' civilization. A second sign is more or less equally evident; its signifier is the bringing together of the tomato, the pepper and the tricoloured hues (yellow, green, red) of the poster; its signified is Italy or rather *Italianicity*. This sign stands in a relation of redundancy with the connoted sign of the linguistic message (the Italian assonance of the name *Panzani*) and the knowledge it draws upon is already more particular; it is a specifically 'French' knowledge (an Italian would barely perceive the connotation of the name, no more probably than he would the Italianicity of tomato and pepper), based on a familiarity with certain tourist stereotypes. Continuing to explore the image (which is not to say that it is not entirely clear at the first glance), there is no difficulty in discovering at least two other signs: in the first, the serried collection of different objects transmits the idea of a total culinary service, on the one hand as though Panzani furnished everything necessary for a carefully balanced dish and on the other as though the concentrate in the tin were equivalent to the natural produce surrounding it; in the other sign, the composition of the image, evoking the memory of innumerable alimentary paintings, sends us to an aesthetic signified: the '*nature morte*' or, as it is better expressed in other languages, the 'still life'†; the knowledge on which this sign depends is heavily cultural. It might be suggested that, in addition to these four signs, there is a further information pointer, that which tells us that this is an advertisement and which arises both from the place of the image in the magazine and from the emphasis of the labels (not to mention the caption). This last information, however, is co-extensive with the scene; it eludes signification insofar as the advertising nature of the image is essentially functional: to utter something is not necessarily to declare *I am speaking*, except in a deliberately reflexive system such as literature.

Thus there are four signs for this image and we will assume that they

---

* By *typical sign* is meant the sign of a system insofar as it is adequately defined by its substance: the verbal sign, the iconic sign, the gestural sign are so many typical signs.
† In French, the expression *nature morte* refers to the original presence of funereal objects, such as a skull, in certain pictures.

form a coherent whole (for they are all discontinuous), require a generally cultural knowledge, and refer back to signifieds each of which is global (for example, *Italianicity*), imbued with euphoric values. After the linguistic message, then, we can see a second, iconic message. Is that the end? If all these signs are removed from the image, we are still left with a certain informational matter; deprived of all knowledge, I continue to 'read' the image, to 'understand' that it assembles in a common space a number of identifiable (nameable) objects, not merely shapes and colours. The signifieds of this third message are constituted by the real objects in the scene, the signifiers by these same objects photographed, for, given that the relation between thing signified and image signifying in analogical representation is not 'arbitrary' (as it is in language), it is no longer necessary to dose the relay with a third term in the guise of the psychic image of the object. What defines the third message is precisely that the relation between signified and signifier is quasi-tautological; no doubt the photograph involves a certain arrangement of the scene (framing, reduction, flattening) but this transition is not a *transformation* (in the way a coding can be); we have here a loss of the equivalence characteristic of true sign systems and a statement of quasi-identity. In other words, the sign of this message is not drawn from an institutional stock, is not coded, and we are brought up against the paradox (to which we will return) of a *message without a code*. This peculiarity can be seen again at the level of the knowledge invested in the reading of the message; in order to 'read' this last (or first) level of the image, all that is needed is the knowledge bound up with our perception. That knowledge is not nil, for we need to know what an image is (children only learn this at about the age of four) and what a tomato, a string-bag, a packet of pasta are, but it is a matter of an almost anthropological knowledge. This message corresponds, as it were, to the letter of the image and we can agree to call it the literal message, as opposed to the previous symbolic message.

If our reading is satisfactory, the photograph analysed offers us three messages: a linguistic message, a coded iconic message, and a non-coded iconic message. The linguistic message can be readily separated from the other two, but since the latter share the same (iconic) substance, to what extent have we the right to separate them? It is certain that the distinction between the two iconic messages is not made spontaneously in ordinary reading: the viewer of the image receives *at one and the same time* the perceptual message and the cultural message, and it will be seen later that this confusion in reading corresponds to the function of the mass image (our concern here). The distinction, however, has an operational validity, analogous to that which allows the distinction in the linguistic sign of a signifier and a signified (even though in reality no one is able to separate the 'word' from its meaning except by recourse to the metalanguage of a definition). If the distinction permits us to describe the structure of the image in a simple and coherent fashion and if this description paves the way for an explanation of the role of the image in society, we will take it to be justified. The task now is thus to reconsider each type of message so as to explore it in its generality, without losing sight of our aim of understanding the overall structure of the image, the final interrelationship of the three messages. Given that what is in question is not a 'naive' analysis but a structural description,* the order of the messages will be modified a little by the inversion of the cultural message and the literal message; of the two iconic messages, the first is in some sort imprinted on the second: the literal message appears as the *support* of the 'symbolic' message. Hence, knowing that a system which takes over the signs of another system in order to make them its signifiers is a system of connotation,[†] we may say immediately that the literal image is *denoted* and the symbolic image *connoted*. Successively, then, we shall look at the linguistic message, the denoted image, and the connoted image.

The linguistic message

Is the linguistic message constant? Is there always textual matter in, under, or around the image? In order to find images given without words, it is doubtless necessary to go back to partially illiterate societies, to a sort of pictographic state of the image. From the moment of the appearance of the book, the linking of text and image is frequent, though it seems to have been little studied from a structural point of view. What is the signifying structure of 'illustration'? Does the image duplicate certain of the informations given in the text by a phenomenon of redundancy or does the text add a fresh information to the image? The problem could be posed historically as regards the classical period with its passion for books with pictures (it was inconceivable in the eighteenth century that editions of La Fontaine's *Fables* should not be illustrated) and its authors such as Menestrier who concerned themselves with the relations between figure and discourse.[‡] Today, at the level of mass communications, it appears that the linguistic message is indeed present in every image: as title, caption, accompanying press article, film dialogue, comic strip balloon. Which shows that it is not very accurate to talk of a civilization of the image—we are still, and more than ever, a civilization of writing,[§] writing and speech continuing to be the full terms of the informational structure. In fact, it is simply the presence of the linguistic message that counts, for neither its position nor its length seem to be pertinent (a long text may only comprise a single global signified, thanks to connotation, and it is this signified which is put in relation with the image). What are the functions of the linguistic message with regard to the (twofold) iconic message? There appear to be two: *anchorage* and *relay*.

As will be seen more clearly in a moment, all images are polysemous; they imply, underlying their signifiers, a 'floating chain' of signifieds, the reader able to choose some and ignore others. Polysemy poses a question

---

* 'Naive' analysis is an enumeration of elements, structural description aims to grasp the relation of these elements by virtue of the principle of the solidarity holding between the terms of a structure: if one term changes, so also do the others.
[†] Cf. R. Barthes, *Eléments de sémiologie, Communications* 4, 1964, p. 130 (trans. *Elements of Semiology*, London 1967 and New York 1968, pp. 89–92).
[‡] Menestrier, *L'Art des emblèmes*, 1684.
[§] Images without words can certainly be found in certain cartoons, but by way of a paradox; the absence of words always covers an enigmatic intention.

of meaning and this question always comes through as a dysfunction, even if this dysfunction is recuperated by society as a tragic (silent, God provides no possibility of choosing between signs) or a poetic (the panic 'shudder of meaning' of the Ancient Greeks) game; in the cinema itself, traumatic images are bound up with an uncertainty (an anxiety) concerning the meaning of objects or attitudes. Hence in every society various techniques are developed intended to *fix* the floating chain of signifieds in such a way as to counter the terror of uncertain signs; the linguistic message is one of these techniques. At the level of the literal message, the text replies—in a more or less direct, more or less partial manner—to the question: *what is it?* The text helps to identify purely and simply the elements of the scene and the scene itself; it is a matter of a denoted description of the image (a description which is often incomplete), or, in Hjelmslev's terminology, of an *operation* (as opposed to connotation).* The denominative function corresponds exactly to an *anchorage* of all the possible (denoted) meanings of the object by recourse to a nomenclature [. . .]. When it comes to the 'symbolic message', the linguistic message no longer guides identification but interpretation, constituting a kind of vice which holds the connoted meanings from proliferating, whether towards excessively individual regions (it limits, that is to say, the projective power of the image) or towards dysphoric values. An advertisement (for *d'Arcy* preserves) shows a few fruits scattered around a ladder; the caption (*'as if from your own garden'*) banishes one possible signified (parsimony, the paucity of the harvest) because of its unpleasantness and orientates the reading towards a more flattering signified (the natural and personal character of fruit from a private garden); it acts here as a counter-taboo, combating the disagreeable myth of the artificial usually associated with preserves. Of course, elsewhere than in advertising, the anchorage may be ideological and indeed this is its principal function; the text *directs* the reader through the signifieds of the image, causing him to avoid some and receive others; by means of an often subtle *dispatching*, it remote-controls him towards a meaning chosen in advance. In all these cases of anchorage, language clearly has a function of elucidation, but this elucidation is selective, a metalanguage applied not to the totality of the iconic message but only to certain of its signs. The text is indeed the creator's (and hence society's) right of inspection over the image; anchorage is a control, bearing a responsibility—in the face of the projective power of pictures—for the use of the message. With respect to the liberty of the signifieds of the image, the text has thus a *repressive* value† and we can see that it is at this level that the morality and ideology of a society are above all invested.

* *Eléments de sémiologie*, pp. 131–2 (trans. pp. 90–4).
† This can be seen clearly in the paradoxical case where the image is constructed according to the text and where, consequently, the control would seem to be needless. An advertisement which wants to communicate that in such and such a coffee the aroma is 'locked in' the product in powder form and that it will thus be wholly there when the coffee is used depicts above this proposition a tin of coffee with a chain and padlock round it. Here, the linguistic metaphor ('locked in') is taken literally (a well-known poetic device); in fact, however, it is the image which is read first and the text from which the image is constructed becomes in the end the simple choice of one signified among others. The repression is present again in the circular movement as a banalization of the message.

Anchorage is the most frequent function of the linguistic message and is commonly found in press photographs and advertisements. The function of relay is less common (at least as far as the fixed image is concerned); it can be seen particularly in cartoons and comic strips. Here text (most often a snatch of dialogue) and image stand in a complementary relationship; the words, in the same way as the images, are fragments of a more general syntagm and the unity of the message is realized at a higher level, that of the story, the anecdote, the diegesis (which is ample confirmation that the diegesis must be treated as an autonomous system).* While rare in the fixed image, this relay-text becomes very important in film, where dialogue functions not simply as elucidation but really does advance the action by setting out, in the sequence of messages, meanings that are not to be found in the image itself. Obviously, the two functions of the linguistic message can co-exist in the one iconic whole, but the dominance of the one or the other is of consequence for the general economy of a work. When the text has the diegetic value of relay, the information is more costly, requiring as it does the learning of a digital code (the system of language); when it has a substitute value (anchorage, control), it is the image which detains the informational charge and, the image being analogical, the information is then 'lazier': in certain comic strips intended for 'quick' reading the diegesis is confided above all to the text, the image gathering the attributive informations of a paradigmatic order (the stereotyped status of the characters); the costly message and the discursive message are made to coincide so that the hurried reader may be spared the boredom of verbal 'descriptions', which are entrusted to the image, that is to say to a less 'laborious' system.

The denoted image

We have seen that in the image properly speaking, the distinction between the literal message and the symbolic message is operational; we never encounter (at least in advertising) a literal image in a pure state. Even if a totally 'naive' image were to be achieved, it would immediately join the sign of naivety and be completed by a third—symbolic—message. Thus the characteristics of the literal message cannot be substantial but only relational. It is first of all, so to speak, a message by eviction, constituted by what is left in the image when the signs of connotation are mentally deleted (it would not be possible actually to remove them for they can impregnate the whole of the image, as in the case of the 'still life composition'). This evictive state naturally corresponds to a plenitude of virtualities: it is an absence of meaning full of all the meanings. Then again (and there is no contradiction with what has just been said), it is a sufficient message, since it has at least one meaning at the level of the identification of the scene represented; the letter of the image corresponds in short to the first degree of intelligibility (below which the reader would perceive only lines, forms, and colours), but this intelligibility remains virtual by reason

* Cf. Claude Bremond, 'Le message narratif', *Communications* 4, 1964.

of its very poverty, for everyone from a real society always disposes of a knowledge superior to the merely anthropological and perceives more than just the letter. Since it is both evictive and sufficient, it will be understood that from an aesthetic point of view the denoted image can appear as a kind of Edenic state of the image; cleared utopianically of its connotations, the image would become radically objective, or, in the last analysis, innocent.

This utopian character of denotation is considerably reinforced by the paradox already mentioned, that the photograph (in its literal state), by virtue of its absolutely analogical nature, seems to constitute a message without a code. Here, however, structural analysis must differentiate, for of all the kinds of image only the photograph is able to transmit the (literal) information without forming it by means of discontinuous signs and rules of transformation. The photograph, message without a code, must thus be opposed to the drawing which, even when denoted, is a coded message. The coded nature of the drawing can be seen at three levels. Firstly, to reproduce an object or a scene in a drawing requires a set of *rule-governed* transpositions; there is no essential nature of the pictorial copy and the codes of transposition are historical (notably those concerning perspective). Secondly, the operation of the drawing (the coding) immediately necessitates a certain division between the significant and the insignificant: the drawing does not reproduce *everything* (often it reproduces very little), without its ceasing, however, to be a strong message; whereas the photograph, although it can choose its subject, its point of view and its angle, cannot intervene *within* the object (except by trick effects). In other words, the denotation of the drawing is less pure than that of the photograph, for there is no drawing without style. Finally, like all codes, the drawing demands an apprenticeship (Saussure attributed a great importance to this semiological fact). Does the coding of the denoted message have consequences for the connoted message? It is certain that the coding of the literal prepares and facilitates connotation since it at once establishes a certain discontinuity in the image: the 'execution' of a drawing itself constitutes a connotation. But at the same time, insofar as the drawing displays its coding, the relationship between the two messages is profoundly modified: it is no longer the relationship between a nature and a culture (as with the photograph) but that between two cultures; the 'ethic' of the drawing is not the same as that of the photograph.

In the photograph—at least at the level of the literal message—the relationship of signifieds to signifiers is not one of 'transformation' but of 'recording', and the absence of a code clearly reinforces the myth of photographic 'naturalness': the scene *is there*, captured mechanically, not humanly (the mechanical is here a guarantee of objectivity). Man's interventions in the photograph (framing, distance, lighting, focus, speed) all effectively belong to the plane of connotation; it is as though in the beginning (even if utopian) there were a brute photograph (frontal and clear) on which man would then lay out, with the aid of various techniques, the signs drawn from a cultural code. Only the opposition of the cultural code and the natural non-code can, it seems, account for the specific character of the photograph and allow the assessment of the anthropological revolution it represents in man's history. The type of consciousness the photograph involves is indeed truly unprecedented, since it establishes not a consciousness of the *being-there* of the thing (which any copy could provoke) but an awareness of its *having-been-there*. What we have is a new space-time category: spatial immediacy and temporal anteriority, the photograph being an illogical conjunction between the *here-now* and the *there-then*. It is thus at the level of this denoted message or message without code that the *real unreality* of the photograph can be fully understood: its unreality is that of the *here-now*, for the photograph is never experienced as illusion, is in no way a *presence* (claims as to the magical character of the photographic image must be deflated); its reality that of the *having-been-there*, for in every photograph there is the always stupefying evidence of *this is how it was*, giving us, by a precious miracle, a reality from which we are sheltered. This kind of temporal equilibrium (*having-been-there*) probably diminishes the projective power of the image (very few psychological tests resort to photographs while many use drawings): the *this was so* easily defeats the *it's me*. If these remarks are at all correct, the photograph must be related to a pure spectatorial consciousness and not to the more projective, more 'magical' fictional consciousness on which film by and large depends. This would lend authority to the view that the distinction between film and photograph is not a simple difference of degree but a radical opposition. Film can no longer be seen as animated photographs: the *having-been-there* gives way before a *being-there* of the thing; which omission would explain how there can be a history of the cinema, without any real break with the previous arts of fiction, whereas the photograph can in some sense elude history (despite the evolution of the techniques and ambitions of the photographic art) and represent a 'flat' anthropological fact, at once absolutely new and definitively unsurpassable, humanity encountering for the first time in its history *messages without a code*. Hence, the photograph is not the last (improved) term of the great family of images; it corresponds to a decisive mutation of informational economies.

At all events, the denoted image, to the extent to which it does not imply any code (the case with the advertising photograph), plays a special role in the general structure of the iconic message which we can begin to define (returning to this question after discussion of the third message): the denoted image naturalizes the symbolic message, it innocents the semantic artifice of connotation, which is extremely dense, especially in advertising. Although the *Panzani* poster is full of 'symbols', there nonetheless remains in the photograph, insofar as the literal message is sufficient, a kind of natural *being-there* of objects: nature seems spontaneously to produce the scene represented. A pseudo-truth is surreptitiously substituted for the simple validity of openly semantic systems; the absence of code disintellectualizes the message because it seems to found in nature the signs of culture. This is without doubt an important historical paradox: the more technology develops the diffusion of information (and notably of images), the more it provides the means of masking the constructed meaning under the appearance of the given meaning.

Rhetoric of the image

It was seen that the signs of the third message (the 'symbolic' message, cultural or connoted) were discontinuous. Even when the signifier seems to extend over the whole image, it is nonetheless a sign separated from the others: the 'composition' carries an aesthetic signified, in much the same way as intonation although suprasegmental is a separate signifier in language. Thus we are here dealing with a normal system whose signs are drawn from a cultural code (even if the linking together of the elements of the sign appears more or less analogical). What gives this system its originality is that the number of readings of the same lexical unit or *lexia* (of the same image) varies according to individuals. In the *Panzani* advertisement analysed, four connotative signs have been identified; probably there are others (the net bag, for example, can signify the miraculous draught of fishes, plenty, etc.). The variation in readings is not, however, anarchic; it depends on the different kinds of knowledge—practical, national, cultural, aesthetic—invested in the image and these can be classified, brought into a typology. It is as though the image presented itself to the reading of several different people who can perfectly well co-exist in a single individual: *the one lexia mobilizes different lexicons*. What is a lexicon? A portion of the symbolic plane (of language) which corresponds to a body of practices and techniques.* This is the case for the different readings of the image: each sign corresponds to a body of 'attitudes'—tourism, housekeeping, knowledge of art—certain of which may obviously be lacking in this or that individual. There is a plurality and a co-existence of lexicons in one and the same person, the number and identity of these lexicons forming in some sort a person's *idiolect*.† The image, in its connotation, is thus constituted by an architecture of signs drawn from a variable depth of lexicons (of idiolects); each lexicon, no matter how 'deep', still being coded, if, as is thought today, the *psyche* itself is articulated like a language; indeed, the further one 'descends' into the psychic depths of an individual, the more rarified and the more classifiable the signs become—what could be more systematic than the readings of Rorschach tests? The variability of readings, therefore, is no threat to the 'language' of the image if it be admitted that that language is composed of idiolects, lexicons and subcodes. The image is penetrated through and through by the system of meaning, in exactly the same way as man is articulated to the very depths of his being in distinct languages. The language of the image is not merely the totality of utterances emitted (for example at the level of the combiner of the signs or creator of the message), it is also the totality of utterances received:‡ the language must include the 'surprises' of meaning.

* Cf. A.J. Greimas, 'Les problèmes de la description mécanographique', *Cahiers de Lexicologie*, 1, 1959, p. 63.
† Cf. *Eléments de sémiologie*, p. 96 (trans. pp. 21–2).
‡ In the Saussurian perspective, speech (utterances) is above all that which is emitted, drawn from the language-system (and constituting it in return). It is necessary today to enlarge the notion of language (*langue*), especially from the semantic point of view: language is the 'totalizing abstraction' of the messages emitted *and received*.

Another difficulty in analysing connotation is that there is no particular analytical language corresponding to the particularity of its signifieds—how are the signifieds of connotation to be named? For one of them we ventured the term *Italianicity*, but the others can only be designated by words from ordinary language (*culinary preparation, still life, plenty*); the metalanguage which has to take charge of them at the moment of the analysis is not specialized. This is a difficulty, for these signifieds have a particular semantic nature; as a seme of connotation, 'plenty' does not exactly cover 'plenty' in the denoted sense; the signifier of connotations (here the profusion and the condensation of the produce) is like the essential cipher of all possible plenties, of the purest idea of plenty. The denoted word never refers to an essence for it is always caught up in a contingent utterance, a continuous syntagm (that of verbal discourse), oriented towards a certain practical transitivity of language; the seme 'plenty', on the contrary, is a concept in a pure state, cut off from any syntagm, deprived of any context and corresponding to a sort of theatrical state of meaning, or, better (since it is a question of a sign without a syntagm), to an *exposed* meaning. To express these semes of connotation would therefore require a special metalanguage and we are left with barbarisms of the *Italianicity* kind as best being able to account for the signifieds of connotation, the suffix *-icity* deriving an abstract noun from the adjective: *Italianicity* is not Italy, it is the condensed essence of everything that could be Italian, from spaghetti to painting. By accepting to regulate artificially—and if needs be barbarously—the naming of the semes of connotation, the analysis of their form will be rendered easier.* These semes are organized in associative fields, in paradigmatic articulations, even perhaps in oppositions, according to certain defined paths or, as A.J. Greimas puts it, according to certain semic axes.† *Italianicity* belongs to a certain axis of nationalities, alongside Frenchicity, Germanicity or Spanishicity. The reconstitution of such axes —which may eventually be in opposition to one another—will clearly only be possible once a massive inventory of the systems of connotation has been carried out, an inventory not merely of the connotative system of the image but also of those of other substances, for if connotation has typical signifiers dependent on the different substances utilized (image, language, objects, modes of behaviour) it holds all its signifieds in common: the same signifieds are to be found in the written press, the image or the actor's gestures (which is why semiology can only be conceived in a so to speak total framework). This common domain of the signifieds of connotation is that of *ideology*, which cannot but be single for a given society and history, no matter what signifiers of connotation it may use.

To the general ideology, that is, correspond signifiers of connotation which are specified according to the chosen substance. These signifiers will be called *connotators* and the set of connotators a *rhetoric*, rhetoric thus appearing as the signifying aspect of ideology. Rhetorics inevitably vary by their substance (here articulated sound, there image, gesture or

---

* *Form* in the precise sense given it by Hjelmslev (cf. *Eléments de sémiologie*, p. 105 [trans. pp. 39–41]), as the functional organization of the signifieds among themselves.
† A.J. Greimas, *Cours de Sémantique*, 1964 (notes roneotyped by the Ecole Normale Supérieure de Saint-Cloud).

whatever) but not necessarily by their form; it is even probable that there exists a single rhetorical *form*, common for instance to dream, literature and image.* Thus the rhetoric of the image (that is to say, the classification of its connotators) is specific to the extent that it is subject to the physical constraints of vision (different, for example, from phonatory constraints) but general to the extent that the 'figures' are never more than formal relations of elements. This rhetoric could only be established on the basis of a quite considerable inventory, but it is possible now to foresee that one will find it in some of the figures formerly identified by the Ancients and the Classics;† the tomato, for example, signifies *Italianicity* by metonymy and in another advertisement the sequence of three scenes (coffee in beans, coffee in powder, coffee sipped in the cup) releases a certain logical relationship in the same way as an asyndeton. It is probable indeed that among the metabolas (or figures of the substitution of one signifier for another),‡ it is metonymy which furnishes the image with the greatest number of its connotators, and that among the parataxes (or syntagmatic figures), it is asyndeton which predominates.

The most important thing, however, at least for the moment, is not to inventorize the connotators but to understand that in the total image they constitute *discontinuous* or better still *scattered traits*. The connotators do not fill the whole of the lexia, reading them does not exhaust it. In other words (and this would be a valid proposition for semiology in general), not all the elements of the lexia can be transformed into connotators; there always remaining in the discourse a certain denotation without which, precisely, the discourse would not be possible. Which brings us back to the second message or denoted image. In the *Panzani* advertisement, the Mediterranean vegetables, the colour, the composition, the very profusion rise up as so many scattered blocks, at once isolated and mounted in a general scene which has its own space and, as was seen, its 'meaning': they are 'set' in a syntagm *which is not theirs and which is that of the denotation*. This last proposition is important for it permits us to found (retroactively) the structural distinction between the second or literal message and the third or symbolic message and to give a more exact description of the naturalizing function of the denotation with respect to the connotation. We can now understand that *it is precisely the syntagm of the denoted message which 'naturalizes' the system of the connoted message*. Or again: connotation is only system, can only be defined in paradigmatic terms; iconic denotation is only syntagm, associates elements without any system: the discontinuous connotators are connected, actualized, 'spoken' through the syntagm of the

* Cf. Emile Benveniste, 'Remarques sur la fonction du langage dans la découverte freudienne', *La Psychanalyse* 1, 1956, pp. 3–16 (reprinted in E. Benveniste, *Problèmes de linguistique générale*, Paris 1966, Chapter 7; translated as *Problems of General Linguistics*, Coral Gables, Florida 1971).
† Classical rhetoric needs to be rethought in structural terms (this is the object of a work in progress); it will then perhaps be possible to establish a general rhetoric or linguistics of the signifiers of connotation, valid for articulated sound, image, gesture, etc. See 'L'ancienne rhétorique (Aide-mémoire)', *Communications* 16, 1970.
‡ We prefer here to evade Jakobson's opposition between metaphor and metonymy for if metonymy by its origin is a figure of contiguity, it nevertheless functions finally as a substitute of the signifier, that is as a metaphor.

denotation, the discontinuous world of symbols plunges into the story of the denoted scene as though into a lustral bath of innocence.

It can thus be seen that in the total system of the image the structural functions are polarized: on the one hand there is a sort of paradigmatic condensation at the level of the connotators (that is, broadly speaking, of the symbols), which are strong signs, scattered, 'reified'; on the other a syntagmatic 'flow' at the level of the denotation—it will not be forgotten that the syntagm is always very close to speech, and it is indeed the iconic 'discourse' which naturalizes its symbols. Without wishing to infer too quickly from the image to semiology in general, one can nevertheless venture that the world of total meaning is torn internally (structurally) between the system as culture and the syntagm as nature: the works of mass communications all combine, through diverse and diversely successful dialectics, the fascination of a nature, that of story, diegesis, syntagm, and the intelligibility of a culture, withdrawn into a few discontinuous symbols which men 'decline' in the shelter of their living speech.

3

The television discourse—encoding and decoding

Stuart Hall

From *Education and Culture*, no. 25 (UNESCO, 1974).

The 'object' of production practices and structures in television is the production of a *message*: that is, a sign-vehicle, or rather sign-vehicles of a specific kind organized, like any other form of communication or language, through the operation of codes, within the syntagmatic chains of a discourse. The apparatus and structures of production issue, at a certain moment, in the form of a symbolic vehicle constituted within the rules of 'language'. It is in this 'phenomenal form' that the circulation of the 'product' takes place. Of course, the transmission of this symbolic vehicle also requires its material substratum—videotape, film, the transmitting and receiving apparatus, etc. But it is primarily in this symbolic form that the reception of the 'product', and its distribution between different segments of the audience, takes place. Once accomplished, the translation of that message into societal structures must be made again for the communication circuit to be completed. Thus, whilst in no way wanting to limit research to 'following only those leads which emerge from content analyses',[*] we must recognize that the symbolic form of the message has a privileged position in the communicative exchange: and that the moments of 'encoding' and 'decoding', though only 'relatively autonomous' in relation to the communicative process as a whole, are *determinate* moments. The raw historical event cannot in that form be transmitted by, say, a television newscast. It can only be signified within the aural–visual form of a televisual language. In the moment when the historical event passes under the sign of language, it is subject to all the complex formal 'rules' by which language signifies. To put it paradoxically, the event must become a 'story' before it can become a *communicative event*. In that moment of 'encoding', the formal sub-rules of language are 'in dominance', without, of course, subordinating out of existence the historical event so signified, or the historical consequences of the event having been signified in this way. The 'message-form' is the necessary form of the appearance of the event in its passage from source to receiver. Thus, the transposition into and out of the 'message-form' or the meaning-dimension (or mode of exchange of the

[*] Halloran, 'Understanding television'. *Screen Education* no. 14, Spring 1975.

message) is not a random 'moment', which we can take up or ignore for the sake of convenience or simplicity. The 'message-form' is a determinate moment, though, at another level, it comprises the surface-movements of the communications system only, and requires, at another stage of the analysis, to be integrated into the essential relations of communication of which it forms only a part.

From this general perspective, we may crudely characterize the communicative exchange as follows. The broadcasting organizations, with their institutional structures and networks of production, their organized routines and technical infrastructures, are required to produce the programme. Production, here, initiates the message. Production and reception of the television message are not identical, but they are related: they are differentiated moments within the totality formed by the communicative process as a whole.

Though we know the television programme is not a behavioural input, like a tap on the knee-cap, it seems to have been almost impossible for researchers to conceptualize the communicative process without lapsing back into one or other variant of low-flying behaviourism. Yet, by now, it should have been firmly established, as Gerbner has remarked, that representations of violence on the TV screen 'are not violence but messages about violence'.*

Take, for example, the simple-structure, early (and now children's) TV Western, modelled on the early Hollywood B-feature genre Western; with its clear-cut, good/bad Manichean moral universe, its clear social and moral designation of villain and hero, the clarity of its narrative line and development, its iconographical features, its clearly-registered climax in the violent shoot-out, chase, personal show-down, street or bar-room duel, etc. For long, on both British and American TV, this form constituted the predominant drama-entertainment genre. In quantitative terms, such films/programmes contained a high ratio of violent incidents, deaths, woundings, etc. Whole gangs of men, whole troops of Indians, went down nightly to their deaths. Researchers—Himmelweit among others—have, however, suggested that the structure of the early TV/B-feature Western was so clear-cut, its action so conventionalized, stylized, that most children (boys rather earlier than girls, an interesting finding in itself) soon learned to recognize and 'read' it like a 'game': a 'cowboys-and-Injuns' game. It was therefore further hypothesized that Westerns with this clarified structure were less likely to trigger the aggressive imitation of violent behaviour or other types of aggressive 'acting-out' than other types of programmes with a high violence ratio which were not stylized. But it is worth asking what this recognition of the Western as a 'symbolic game' means or implies: how does this transform our research conceptualizations and perspectives?

Conventionalizing the Western means that a set of extremely tightly-coded 'rules' exist whereby stories of a certain recognizable type, content and structure can be easily encoded within the Western form. What is more, these 'rules of encoding' were so diffused, so symmetrically shared

* Gerbner et al., Violence in TV Drama: A study of Trends & Symbolic Functions. Annenberg School, Univ. of Pennsylvania (1970).

as between producer and audience, that the 'message' was likely to be decoded in a manner highly symmetrical to that in which it had been encoded. This reciprocity of codes is, indeed, precisely what is entailed in the notion of stylization or 'conventionalization', and the persistence of such reciprocal codes over time is, of course, what defines or makes possible the existence of a *genre*. Such an account, then, takes the encoding/decoding moments properly into account, and the case appears an unproblematic one.

The violent element or string in the narrative structure of the simple-structure Western—shoot-out, brawl, ambush, bank-raid, fist-fight, wounding, duel or massacre—like any other semantic unit in a structured discourse, cannot signify anything on its own. It can only signify in terms of the structured meanings of the message as a whole. Further, its signification depends on its relation—or the sum of the relations of similarity and difference—with other elements or units. Burgelin* has long ago, and definitively, reminded us that the violent or wicked acts of a villain only mean something in relation to the presence/absence of good acts.

We must now add that the meaning of the violent act or episode cannot be fixed, single and unalterable, but must be capable of signifying different values depending on how and with what it is articulated. As the signifying element, among other elements, in a discourse, it remains *polysemic*. Indeed, the way it is structured in its combination with other elements serves to delimit its meanings within that specified field, and effects a 'closure', so that a *preferred meaning* or reading is suggested. There can never be only one single, univocal and determined meaning for such a lexical item; but, depending on how its integration within the code has been accomplished, its possible meanings will be organized within a scale which runs from *dominant* to *subordinate*. And this, of course, has consequences for the other—the reception—end of the communicative chain: there can be no law to ensure that the receiver will take the preferred or dominant meaning of an episode of violence in precisely the way in which it has been encoded by the producer.

The presence of the code has the effect of displacing the meaning of single episodes from one category to another. Thus, within the structure of the programme as a whole, the violent episode may contain a message or make a proposition, not about violence but about conduct, or even about professionalism, nor perhaps even about the relation of professionalism to character. And here we recall Robert Warshow's intuitive observation that, fundamentally, the Western is not 'about' violence but about codes of conduct . . .

Thus, drawing attention to the symbolic/linguistic/coded nature of communications, far from boxing us into the closed and formal universe of signs, precisely opens out into the area where cultural content, of the most resonant but 'latent' kind, is transmitted: and especially the manner in which the interplay of codes and content serves to *displace* meanings from one frame to another, and thus to bring to the surface in 'disguised'

* O. Burgelin, 'Structural Analysis & Mass Communications'. Studies in *Broadcasting*, no. 6. Nippon Hoso Kyokai (1968).

forms, the repressed contents of a culture.

Let us turn now to a different area of programming, and a different aspect of the operation of codes. The televisual sign is a peculiarly complex one, as we know. It is a visual sign with strong, supplementary aural–verbal support. It is one of the iconic signs, in Peirce's sense.

As Eco has convincingly argued, iconic signs 'look like objects in the real world', to put it crudely (e.g. the photograph or drawing of a /cow/, and the animal /cow/), because they 'reproduce the conditions of perception in the receiver'.* These conditions of 'recognition' in the viewer constitute some of the most fundamental perceptual codes which all culture-members share. Now, because these perceptual codes are so widely distributed, denotative visual signs probably give rise to less 'misunderstandings' than linguistic ones. A lexical inventory of the English language would throw up thousands of words which the ordinary speaker could not denotatively comprehend: but provided enough 'information' is given, culture-members would be able or be competent to decode, denotatively, a much wider range of visual signifiers. In this sense, and at the denotative level, the visual sign is probably a more universal one than the linguistic sign. Similarly, whereas, in societies like ours, linguistic competence is very unequally distributed as between different classes and segments of the population (predominantly, by the family and the education system), what we might call 'visual competence', at the denotative level, is more universally diffused. (It is worth reminding ourselves, of course, that it is not, in fact, 'universal', and that we are dealing with a spectrum: there are kinds of visual representation, short of the 'purely abstract', which create all kinds of visual puzzles for ordinary viewers: e.g. cartoons, certain kinds of diagrammatic representation, representations which employ unfamiliar conventions, types of photographic or cinematic cutting and editing, etc.). It is also true that the iconic sign may support 'misreadings' simply because it is so 'natural', so 'transparent'. Mistakes may arise here, not because we as viewers cannot literally decode the sign (it is perfectly obvious what it is a picture of), but because we are tempted, by its very 'naturalization' to 'misread' the image for the thing it signifies.† With this important proviso, however, we would be surprised to find that the majority of the television audience had much difficulty in literally or denotatively identifying what the visual signs they see on the screen refer to or signify. Whereas most people require a lengthy process of education in order to become relatively competent users of the language of their speech community, they seem to pick up its visual–perceptual codes at a very early age, without formal training, and are quickly competent in its use.

The visual sign is, however, also a *connotative sign*. And it is so pre-eminently within the discourses of modern mass communication. The level of connotation of the visual sign, of its contextual reference, of its position in the various associative fields of meanings, is precisely the point where the denoted sign intersects with the deep semantic structures

* U. Eco, (1965), 'Towards a semiotic inquiry into the television message', *Working Papers in Cultural Studies 3* (1972), Birmingham CCCS.
† Cf. S. Hall, 'Determinations . . .'. op. cit.

of a culture, and takes on an ideological dimension. In the advertising discourse, for example, we might say that there is almost no 'purely denotative' communication. Every visual sign in advertising 'connotes' a quality, situation, value or inference which is present as an implication or implied meaning, depending on the connotational reference. We are all probably familiar with Barthes's example of the /sweater/, which, in the rhetoric of advertising and fashion, always connotes, at least, 'a warm garment' or 'keeping warm', and thus by further connotative elaboration, 'the coming of winter' or 'a cold day'. In the specialized sub-codes of fashion, /sweater/ may connote 'a fashionable style of *haute-couture*', or, alternatively, 'an informal style of dress'. But, set against the right background, and positioned in the romantic sub-code, it may connote a 'long autumn walk in the woods'.* Connotational codes of this order are, clearly, structured enough to signify, but they are more 'open' or 'open-ended' than denotative codes. What is more, they clearly contract relations with the universe of ideologies in a culture, and with history and ethnography. These connotative codes are the 'linguistic' means by which the domains of social life, the segmentations of culture, power and ideology are made to signify. They refer to the 'maps of meaning' into which any culture is organized, and those 'maps of social reality' have the whole range of social meanings, practices and usages, power and interest 'written in' to them.

Literal or denotative 'errors' are relatively unproblematic. They represent a kind of noise in the channel. But 'misreadings' of a message at the connotative or contextual level are a different matter. They have, fundamentally, a societal, not a communicative, basis. They signify, at the 'message' level the structural conflicts, contradictions and negotiations of economic, political and cultural life. The first position we want to identify is that of the *dominant or hegemonic code*. (There are, of course, many different codes and sub-codes required to produce an event within the dominant code.) When the viewer takes the connoted meaning from, say, a television newscast or current affairs programme, full and straight, and decodes the message in terms of the reference-code in which it has been coded, we might say that the viewer is operating inside the dominant code. This is the ideal-typical case of 'perfectly transparent communication', or as close as we are likely to come to it 'for all practical purposes'.

Next (here we are amplifying Parkin's model), we would want to identify the *professional code*. The professional code is 'relatively independent' of the dominant code, in that it applies criteria and operations of its own, especially those of a technico–practical nature. The professional code, however, operates within the 'hegemony' of the dominant code. The hegemonic interpretations of the politics of Northern Ireland, or the Chilean coup or the Industrial Relations Bill are given by political elites: the particular choice of presentational occasions and formats, the selection of personnel, the choice of images, the 'staging' of debates, etc. are selected by the operation of the professional

---

* R. Barthes, 'Rhetoric of the Image', in WPCS 1, CCS, Birmingham (1971). A longer version of Barthes' article which is indicated in this reader.

code.* How the broadcasting professionals are able to operate with 'relatively autonomous' codes of their own, while acting in such a way as to reproduce (not without contradiction) the hegemonic signification of events, is a complex matter which cannot be further spelled out here. It must suffice to say that the professionals are linked with the defining elites not only by the institutional position of broadcasting itself as an 'ideological apparatus',† but more intimately by the structure of *access* (i.e., the systematic 'over-accessing' of elite personnel and 'definitions of the situation' in television). It may even be said that the professional codes serve to reproduce hegemonic definitions specifically by not overtly biasing their operations in their direction: ideological reproduction therefore takes place here inadvertently, unconsciously, 'behind men's backs'. Of course, conflicts, contradictions and even 'misunderstandings' regularly take place between the dominant and the professional significations and their signifying agencies.

The third position we would identify is that of the *negotiated code*. Majority audiences probably understand quite adequately what has been dominantly defined and professionally signified. The dominant definitions, however, are hegemonic precisely because they represent definitions of situations and events which are 'in dominance' and which are *global*. Dominant definitions connect events, implicitly or explicitly, to grand totalizations, to the great syntagmatic views-of-the-world: they take 'large views' of issues: they relate events to 'the national interest' or to the level of geopolitics, even if they make these connections in truncated, inverted or mystified ways. The definition of a 'hegemonic' viewpoint is (a) that it defines within its terms the mental horizon, the universe of possible meanings of a whole society or culture; and (b) that it carries with it the stamp of legitimacy—it appears coterminous with what is 'natural', 'inevitable', 'taken for granted' about the social order. Decoding within the *negotiated version* contains a mixture of adaptive and oppositional elements: it acknowledges the legitimacy of the hegomonic definitions to make the grand significations, while, at a more restricted, situational level, it makes its own ground-rules, it operates with 'exceptions' to the rule. It accords the privileged position to the dominant definition of events, whilst reserving the right to make a more negotiated application to 'local conditions', to its own more *corporate* situation. This negotiated version of the dominant ideology is thus shot through with contradictions, though these are only on certain occasions brought to full visibility. Negotiated codes operate through what we might call particular or situated logics: and these logics arise from the differential position of those who occupy this position in the spectrum, and from their differential and unequal relation to power.

The simplest example of a negotiated code is that which governs the response of a worker to the notion of an industrial relations bill limiting the right to strike, or to arguments for a wages freeze. At the level of the

* Cf. S. Hall, 'External/Internal Dialectic in Broadcasting', in Fourth Symposium on Broadcasting, Dept. of extra-mural studies, U. of Manchester (1972).
† Cf. L. Althusser, 'Ideological Stage Apparatuses', in Lenin & Philosophy, and other essays. *New Left Books* (1971).

national-interest economic debate, he may adopt the hegemonic definition, agreeing that 'we must all pay ourselves less in order to combat inflation', etc. This, however, may have little or no relation to his willingness to go on strike for better pay and conditions, or to oppose the industrial relations bill at the level of his shop-floor or union organization. We suspect that the great majority of so-called 'misunderstandings' arise from the disjunctures between hegemonic–dominant encodings and negotiated–corporate decodings. It is just these mismatches in the levels which most provoke defining elites and professionals to identify a 'failure in communications'. Finally, it is possible for a viewer perfectly to understand both the literal and connotative inflection given to an event, but to determine to decode the message in a globally contrary way. He detotalizes the message in the preferred code in order to retotalize the message within some alternative framework of reference. This is the case of the viewer who listens to a debate on the need to limit wages, but who 'reads' every mention of 'the national interest' as 'class interest'. He is operating with what we must call an *oppositional code*. One of the most significant political moments (they also coincide with crisis-points within the broadcasting organizations themselves for obvious reasons) is the point when events which are normally signified and decoded in a negotiated way begin to be given an oppositional reading.

The question of cultural policies now falls, awkwardly, into place. When dealing with social communications, it is extremely difficult to identify as a neutral, educational goal, the task of 'improving communications' or of 'making communications more effective', at any rate once one has passed beyond the strictly denotative level of the message. The educator or cultural policy-maker is performing one of his most partisan acts when he colludes with the resignification of real conflicts and contradictions as if they were simply kinks in the communicative chain. Denotative mistakes are not structurally significant. But connotative and contextual 'misunderstandings' are, or can be, of the highest structural significance. To interpret what are in fact essential elements in the systematic distortions of a socio-communications system as if they were merely technical faults in transmission is to misread a deep-structure process for a surface phenomenon. The decision to intervene in order to make the hegemonic codes of dominant elites more effective and transparent for the majority audience is not a technically neutral, but a political one. To 'misread' a political choice as a technical one represents a type of unconscious collusion with the dominant interests, a form of 'technological rationality' to which social science researchers are all too prone. Though the sources of such mystification are both social and structural, the actual process is greatly facilitated by the operation of discrepant codes. It would not be the first time that scientific researchers had 'unconsciously' played a part in the reproduction of hegemony, not by openly submitting to it, but simply by operating the 'professional bracket'.

4

Soap opera and women

Richard Dyer, Terry Lovell and Jean McCrindle

From *Edinburgh International Television Festival 1977—Official Programme* (Broadcast, 1977).

[. . .] We are not yet in a situation where all criticism assumes that the world of women is as important as the world of men, leave alone that the separation of the two worlds ought to be broken down; and until we are, polemical papers specifically about women and largely written by them have to be produced.

Why then turn to soap opera? We did begin to analyse the marginality or absence or distortion of women in high drama and this is still something that needs to be done. But we decided instead to look closely at the only form of television drama that has been traditionally defined as drama for women and about women and watched by women. As a major output on television, particularly commercial television (and the link with advertising and women as consumers is obvious), how does it define the experience that it offers to its female audience and what are the limits and possibilities of this kind of dramatic form from the point of view of a critical feminism? We are trying to analyse the ways in which representations of women in soap opera reproduce and reinforce the subordination of women in contemporary society and to explore possible strategies for women directors and writers struggling in their work against the prevailing sexism of the media.

'Coronation Street', which is the soap opera we have done most work on up to date, has become Granada's nostalgic look back to the 1950s before affluence and consumerist ethics corrupted working-class values of togetherness and community (Hilda Ogden is always being laughed at for her attempts to keep up to date with her interior decorating and getting the names of the trends wrong—'my murial'). Middle-class television directors, script writers and producers clearly find it much easier to identify with a supposedly more sympathetic working class than they can find around on the contemporary scene. This nostalgia for the past also affects the American series 'The Waltons', which, unlike 'Coronation Street', is trying to recreate not a working-class street, but a rural extended family living also before the days of affluence, in fact in the depression, and expressing strong family ideology to the point of throat-hurting efficacy. Granny looks like the picture on the oatcakes packet; mom is lovely, gentle, morally supportive, still loves dad and runs the large farm kitchen where the most important ritual of family life takes place—the evening meal. Dad works hard at his own business, helped by grandad, loves mom, calms her down if she gets upset by the children, is tolerant, wise and prepared to learn from the insufferable John Boy when American ideals of honesty and integrity are being undermined by unscrupulous politicians, etc., etc. It has the same nauseating message each week and yet each week this utopia exercises its charm over children and women and probably even some men. We are still trying to understand why and we deal with this aspect later in the paper.

Obviously very different representations of women are being shown if a comparison is made between 'Coronation Street' and 'The Waltons'. The first obvious fact about the women in 'Coronation Street' is how many of them are strong, independent women from whom much of the action is generated—Ena Sharples, Elsie, Bet, Rita, Annie Walker—only one of them has found a man to stay around and producer Bill Podmore says he is worried because marriage so easily diminishes characters in a serial.

But these women not only dominate much of the narrative, they also do not live in nuclear families and rarely have children living with them—hence a whole era that 'The Waltons' depends on for narrative momentum is missing on 'Coronation Street' since these are women without children. Presumably this is partly the problem of employing child actors over such long numbers of years and the family consequently has always to be the grown up family as in 'Crossroads' where they run the motel and garage, or else small babies can be occasionally shown of as they are always just about to go off to bed!

The other effect of the absence of children is that almost all the women in soap operas work outside the home; they work in service jobs—cleaning, typing, shop-keeping, waitressing, running the pub, motel, boutique, office. In fact work in these fictional worlds is not large-scale factory production where the sexual division of labour has condemned women to the most trivial, monotonous, unskilled, degraded, low-paid jobs—work for the scriptwriters of soap operas is petty bourgeois jobs for men and women alike with all the values that go with self-made, self-employed, hard-working, individualized workers. Mike Baldwin's machinists are made to look like selfish, grasping, parochial, demanding wage workers in comparison with his concern with 'the national interest' (in this case simply that he has another factory down South that he has to worry about). The Ogdens are the epitome of the feckless working class and the message about work that comes through is that it is your fault for being lazy and inadequate if you end up like Stan. Hence, the men and women of 'Coronation Street' are much more identified with their work than can be true for the majority of the audience who watch and this echoes the nostalgia of the programme for the days of a supposedly more humane and less alienating work ethic.

This is not to say that class difference is absent from 'Coronation Street' —Annie Walker talks posh, Hilda always has her hair in curlers, Ken Barlow wears middle-class clothes—but these differences are a source of humour and are easily transcended by the community as they are in 'The

Archers' on radio—it's as if 'Coronation Street' were a village in an urban setting.

We are still trying to work out what the implications of these images are for us as feminists and our theory still needs to be integrated into our empirical observations.

Our theoretical orientation is difficult to characterize, as we did not begin with any strongly partisan position in relation to contemporary debates. Our position has evolved in the course of our work and is still so doing. We shared the assumption that the general frame of reference which had most to offer was Marxism, especially the Marxist concept of ideology. We read and discussed recent developments in that area associated with the work of Louis Althusser and his followers, and we looked at the attempts to apply Althusserian and psychoanalytic concepts and theories to film. While recognizing that this work is still in its infancy and may yet produce a satisfactory approach to film, we yet found this work confused and confusing and at such a high level of abstraction as to be of little immediate relevance to our problems. In particular we could not accept the unremitting hostility of this approach to all forms of realism. This anti-realism too easily slides over into hostility to all or most popular forms and conventions. We wanted to study soap opera precisely because it *is* popular, it *is* for and about women, it *is not* prestigious and we wanted to discover why it gives pleasure to millions of people and to relate that to its ideological effects.

Our interest in soap opera and what it could become does not mean that we do not find it at present largely contemptible. Although it is for and about women it is dominated at the point of production by men and it gives us male definitions of women and how they relate to each other and to men. And in relation to the fundamental areas of reproduction (family) and production (work) soap opera's representations of women have to be uncompromisingly attacked. And yet it does have strengths and possibilities, as the Susi Hush episodes of 'Coronation Street' demonstrate. By its very nature it does have to validate positively what women are and achieve in the sphere of the world to which they are confined—that is, soap opera validates *relationships*; it is *not* about social structures, material realists, physical strength, dramas of career or struggles for power.

In looking at the ways in which representations of women are conceived within soap opera and the fictional limits of these representations we are conscious of the difficulty of ascertaining exactly how the audience 'reads' the ideology that emerges. We are certainly not suggesting a simple identification or distanciation. The multiplicity of feminine images is much greater, we would suggest, in television than in film or the other visual arts, and obviously reactions to these representations will vary according to class, age, place in the family, ideological formation and individual biography. But the need for women to see themselves mirrored in the society's representations is often much greater than for men due to women's marginality in the political, economic and power structures. As feminists we would support attempts to show women coping with their marginality not just in series like 'Helen, A Woman of Today' but also within the more conventionalized genres like the soap opera.

We have taken soap opera to mean a certain kind of serial drama on television. While it does not have the tight definition of a genre such as the Western or the sonnet, there are some overall similarities that bind the various programmes into a distinctive television kind.

They are set in small-scale interiors—the pub, the home, the rooms of the motel, the corner shop, the farmhouse. Sequences shot in exteriors or large public buildings are unusual or felt as exceptional, like the day in the country, or a character's uneasy encounter with officialdom. Even 'The Waltons', which is frequently shot out of doors, or 'Emmerdale Farm', manages to render the farm and the surrounding countryside mere extensions of the family nest. Camera style tends to be simple, not drawing attention to itself, and interaction between characters is stressed rather than interiority. Most soap operas are continuous, although not necessarily ('General Hospital', 'The Waltons'), and they either have a self-contained story in each episode or a multi-linear narrative with several plot strands interweaving ('Coronation Street', 'Crossroads'). They usually contain a range of equally important characters but Meg in 'Crossroads' and John Boy in 'The Waltons' are partial exceptions to this.

For this paper we have watched the following current soap operas: 'Coronation Street', 'Rooms', 'Emmerdale Farm', 'General Hospital', 'Cross-roads', 'The Waltons'. If we were to discuss them in detail then differences between them would obviously emerge which would require much more close analysis than we have yet had time for. We are concerned with soap operas as entertainment, as escapism, as pleasurable experience as well as where many people including children learn and see how fictional characters cope with personal relationships. We would like to suggest looking at this form of entertainment under the following headings—validation, reassurance and utopianism.

Validation

In *The Uses of Literacy*, Richard Hoggart writes:

> The overriding interest in the close detail of the human condition is the first pointer to an understanding of working class art. To begin with, working class art is essentially a 'showing' (rather than an 'exploration'), a presentation of what is known already. It starts from the assumption that human life is fascinating in itself.

And this is surely a description of soap opera—the pleasure it takes in the close detail of life, its sense of familiarity (one feels sorry when Elsie receives the letter from her husband about the divorce and cries) and even its predictability, the transparency of the characters. Hoggart's stress on art that 'presents' rather than 'explores' points to one of the prime ways in which soap opera is entertaining—namely that it validates everyday life as it is lived. This can have positive functions. Any way of life is richer for having a language (including images, stories, ways of speaking and interacting) in which to talk about itself.

Given that one of the major sources of such language in this society is television and given that the language of television is still largely expressive of bourgeois man, any programme that even half adequately offers a repository of images for women and the working class which doesn't just treat them as comic or victims is going to be pleasurable for those groups (although obviously since these programmes are not made by women or the working class then the pleasure is complex). Secondly, television grants such a language public recognition; it validates it beyond the immediate confines of the home and the local community. And thirdly, the humanistic emphasis of Hoggart's position, for all its current unfashionability, is not easily sneered at—the problem is that this validation procedure also involves several less admirable effects.

Hoggart has often been accused, rightly, of speaking of the working class in general and yet of describing in fact only a particular section of it—what is generally referred to as 'the respectable working class'—and predominantly through his view of the female culture of the class. Thus he omits for instance the experience of work, trade unions and other aspects of working-class life, including the more organized and politicized aspects and the more masculine aspects. Our concern here is not primarily with working-class culture (though 'The Uses of Literacy' at times reads like a description of 'Coronation Street') but with female culture, but the same general point can be made. That is, just as Hoggart took part of the working class for the whole, so soap opera takes part of women's lives for the whole of them.

The second weakness of Hoggart's approach is the unproblematic use of notions such as 'human life', 'the everyday', as if how we live our daily lives was not itself structured by both material realities and the patterns of ideology. This too is the problem with soap opera, for in its loving recreation of 'the close detail of the human condition', it takes how life is for humans now as the way things always have been and always will be. (Nor is it very hard for soap opera to do this, since the myth of motherhood and life-giver—the person who attends to men's very basic physiological needs —depends upon thinking of women as being outside of history, neither determined by the historically specific structures of a given society, nor having a hand in the transformation of that society as of now). In other words, while it is possible to validate and recognize the achievements of people—women—in 'their' sphere of the world, it is less so to mask the fact that this is nonetheless culturally and historically specific. Women's lives are changing and changing dramatically—in their intimate day-to-day existence as well as in relation to wider structures such as work and trade unions or the state and these changes are also affecting the way men relate to these aspects; and the danger for soap opera is that it too easily slips back into nostalgia for the old ways. ('The Waltons' specifically recreates this supposed post of the extended family where work and the home were still one and men and women's roles still predetermined.)

Reassurance

Where entertainment-as-validation is concerned above all to celebrate the achievements of the way people live now, reassurance is more concerned with exploring the problems people face and providing resolutions fictionally. To have one's problems recognized publicly and then resolved during the experience of the drama is reassuring. Soap opera is endlessly founded on this simple narrative structure and the drawbacks are obvious. Problems in life are frequently intractable for psychological, and social and other reasons and this kind of reassurance, that everything will turn out for the best etc., is false. On the other hand it might be possible to use reassurance in more interesting and stimulating ways—resolving problems more collectively perhaps.

Related to this is one of the fundamental problems for most soap operas. The reassurance pattern depends upon narrative closure—when the drama ends, the problem must end too. But soap opera does not end; their whole point is their ongoing open-endedness. Although in practice the writing adheres to the demand for narrative closure, one can always feel when one plot strand has come to the end—nonetheless the open-endedness of the form can present difficulties for the reassurance mode, problems that could be utilized effectively to suggest the real nature of the society in which people live.

Utopianism

By utopianism we are not so much thinking of the representation of ideal worlds—though this can be the case—as of the presentation of ideal *feeling*. Entertainment embodies the feelings that would be characteristic of an ideal world; it makes you experience utopia even if it does not show you either how utopia would be organized or how to get there.

The various utopian feelings that entertainment most typically embodies can be categorized as abundance, energy, intensity, transparency and community. Of these it is the last three that most characterize soap opera's utopianism. By intensity is meant the whole-hearted, unambiguous, all-out experience of feeling, taking one's emotions to their fullest pitch, without holding back, and laying oneself on the line emotionally. In soap opera it is above all women who bear this quality, and soap opera has taken over from show business in general the strong women types embodied by such as Meg in 'Crossroads', Elsie Tanner in 'Coronation Street'. By transparency, we refer to the way that relationships between people in soap opera are free from manipulation (except of a fairly obvious kind)—and plots may often be about the reassuring discovery of falsehood which effectively renders a relationship transparent, ambivalent, game-playing. People know where they are with each other. Community is fairly obvious in its meaning—a close, warm sense of togetherness, a network of relationships which depend on assumed trust rather than intellectual or other forms of communication. As noted before, community is central to the very definition of soap opera; even non-communities—families in 'The Waltons' and 'The Cedar Tree', workplaces in 'General Hospital' and 'Emmerdale Farm'—are rendered as communities, caring, rallying round, supportive.

It may seem strange that we have emphasized the radical possibilities of soap opera and yet our theoretical work suggests good reasons for this.

Marxist theory draws a central distinction between the use-value and exchange-value of commodities. Capitalist commodity production is the production of exchange-value in order to accumulate capital. It is the accumulation of capital which is the dynamic of capitalism, not production of socially useful objects. As such the capitalist is indifferent to use-value, and useful qualities of the articles produced.

Nevertheless a capitalist system of production has certain requirements for its continuation of viability. These requirements we shall refer to as the conditions of existence of capitalism. One aspect of this is the dominance of bourgeois ideology—that is to say, an ideology favourable in its effects to the reproduction of capitalist social relations. We accept that popular forms are rooted in the dominant ideology. But capitalism has no automatic means of ensuring that the media produce bourgeois ideological effects. Ideological production is always hazardous, uncertain and contradictory and we cannot know for certain what will be uncovered in any given product of the media from an ideological point of view. Ideological production always escapes full surveillance and this is especially true where ideological production is penetrated by capital.

Media women and men are not as such producing ideology. They are producing films, television programmes, books, etc. These are all bearers of ideology but they are each different and cannot be reduced to mere ideology. Viewers and spectators do not watch soap operas to consume bourgeois ideology but to be entertained. The producers of ideology are therefore in the first place constrained by the need to entertain—to produce a use-value that is wanted by the consumer, rather than the use-value (ideology) which is needed by capitalism. These two things may, but need not, overlap. They may and probably will come into contradiction with each other at times. Characteristically it may be precisely when capital and the accumulation of capital become the dynamic principle of cultural production (as with commercial TV and radio) that the ideological functions secured by that production escape social control and become problematic. There is, by this argument, good reason to hope for more possibilities within the despised area of commercial television than from the more state-controlled BBC sector.

5

Orientalism

Edward Said

From his *Orientalism* (Routledge and Kegan Paul, 1978; Penguin, 1985).

On a visit to Beirut during the terrible civil war of 1975–1976 a French journalist wrote regretfully of the gutted downtown area that 'it had once seemed to belong to . . . the Orient of Chateaubriand and Nerval'. He was right about the place, of course, especially so far as a European was concerned. The Orient was almost a European invention, and had been since antiquity a place of romance, exotic beings, haunting memories and landscapes, remarkable experiences. Now it was disappearing; in a sense it had happened, its time was over. Perhaps it seemed irrelevant that Orientals themselves had something at stake in the process, that even in the time of Chateaubriand and Nerval Orientals had lived there, and that now it was they who were suffering; the main thing for the European visitor was a European representation of the Orient and its contemporary fate, both of which had a privileged communal significance for the journalist and his French readers.

Americans will not feel quite the same about the Orient, which for them is much more likely to be associated very differently with the Far East (China and Japan, mainly). Unlike the Americans, the French and the British—less so the Germans, Russians, Spanish, Portuguese, Italians, and Swiss—have had a long tradition of what I shall be calling *Orientalism*, a way of coming to terms with the Orient that is based on the Orient's special place in European Western experience. The Orient is not only adjacent to Europe; it is also the place of Europe's greatest and richest and oldest colonies, the source of its civilizations and languages, its cultural contestant, and one of its deepest and most recurring images of the Other. In addition, the Orient has helped to define Europe (or the West) as its contrasting image, idea, personality, experience. Yet none of this Orient is merely imaginative. The Orient is an integral part of European *material* civilization and culture. Orientalism expresses and represents that part culturally and even ideologically as a mode of discourse with supporting institutions, vocabulary, scholarship, imagery, doctrines, even colonial bureaucracies and colonial styles. In contrast, the American understanding of the Orient will seem considerably less dense, although our recent Japanese, Korean, and Indochinese adventures ought now to be creating a more sober, more realistic 'Oriental' awareness. Moreover, the vastly expanded American political and economic role in the Near East (the Middle East) makes great claims on our understanding of that Orient.

It will be clear to the reader (and will become clearer still throughout the many pages that follow) that by Orientalism I mean several things, all of them, in my opinion, interdependent. The most readily accepted designation for Orientalism is an academic one, and indeed the label still serves in a number of academic institutions. Anyone who teaches, writes about, or researches the Orient—and this applies whether the person is an anthropologist, sociologist, historian, or philologist—either in its specific or its general aspects, is an Orientalist, and what he or she does is Orientalism. Compared with *Oriental studies* or *area studies*, it is true that the term *Orientalism* is less preferred by specialists today, both because it is too vague and general and because it connotes the high-handed executive attitude of nineteenth-century and early-twentieth-century European colonialism. Nevertheless books are written and congresses held with 'the Orient' as their main focus, with the Orientalist in his new or old guise as their main authority. The point is that even if it does not survive as it once did, Orientalism lives on academically through its doctrines and theses about the Orient and the Oriental.

Related to this academic tradition, whose fortunes, transmigrations, specializations, and transmissions are in part the subject of this study, is a more general meaning for Orientalism. Orientalism is a style of thought based upon an ontological and epistemological distinction made between 'the Orient' and (most of the time) 'the Occident'. Thus a very large mass of writers, among whom are poets, novelists, philosophers, political theorists, economists, and imperial administrators, have accepted the basic distinction between East and West as the starting point for elaborate theories, epics, novels, social descriptions, and political accounts concerning the Orient, its people, customs, 'mind', destiny, and so on. This Orientalism can accommodate Aeschylus, say, and Victor Hugo, Dante and Karl Marx. A little later in this introduction I shall deal with the methodological problems one encounters in so broadly construed a 'field' as this.

The interchange between the academic and the more or less imaginative meanings of Orientalism is a constant one, and since the late eighteenth century there has been a considerable, quite disciplined—perhaps even regulated—traffic between the two. Here I come to the third meaning of Orientalism, which is something more historically and materially defined than either of the other two. Taking the late eighteenth century as a very roughly defined starting point Orientalism can be discussed and analyzed as the corporate institution for dealing with the Orient—dealing with it by making statements about it, authorizing views of it, describing it, by teaching it, settling it, ruling over it: in short, Orientalism as a Western style for dominating, restructuring, and having authority over the Orient. I have found it useful here to employ Michel Foucault's notion of a discourse, as described by him in *The Archaeology of Knowledge* and in *Discipline and Punish*, to identify Orientalism. My contention is that without examining Orientalism as a discourse one cannot possibly understand the enormously systematic discipline by which European culture was able to manage—and even produce—the Orient politically, sociologically, militarily, ideologically, scientifically, and imaginatively during the post-Enlightenment period. Moreover, so authoritative a position did Orientalism have that I believe no one writing, thinking, or acting on the Orient could do so without taking account of the limitations on thought and action imposed by Orientalism. In brief, because of Orientalism the Orient was not (and is not) a free subject of thought or action. This is not to say that Orientalism unilaterally determines what can be said about the Orient, but that it is the whole network of interests inevitably brought to bear on (and therefore always involved in) any occasion when that peculiar entity, 'the Orient', is in question. How this happens is what this book tries to demonstrate. It also tries to show that European culture gained in strength and identity by selling itself off against the Orient as a sort of surrogate and even underground self.

Historically and culturally there is a quantitative as well as a qualitative difference between the Franco-British involvement in the Orient and—until the period of American ascendancy after World War II—the involvement of every other European and Atlantic power. To speak of Orientalism therefore is to speak mainly, although not exclusively, of a British and French cultural enterprise, a project whose dimensions take in such disparate realms as the imagination itself, the whole of India and the Levant, the Biblical texts and the Biblical lands, the spice trade, colonial armies and a long tradition of colonial administrators, a formidable scholarly corpus, innumerable Oriental 'experts' and 'hands', an Oriental professorate, a complex array of 'Oriental' ideas (Oriental despotism, Oriental splendour, cruelty, sensuality), many Eastern sects, philosophies, and wisdoms domesticated for local European use—the list can be extended more or less indefinitely. My point is that Orientalism derives from a particular closeness experienced between Britain and France and the Orient, which until the early nineteenth century had really meant only India and the Bible lands. From the beginning of the nineteenth century until the end of World War II France and Britain dominated the Orient and Orientalism; since World War II America has dominated the Orient, and approaches it as France and Britain once did. Out of that closeness, whose dynamic is enormously productive even if it always demonstrates the comparatively greater strength of the Occident (British, French, or American), comes the large body of texts I call Orientalist. [. . .]

I have begun with the assumption that the Orient is not an inert fact of nature. It is not merely *there*, just as the Occident itself is not just *there* either. We must take seriously Vico's great observation that men make their own history, that what they can know is what they have made, and extend it to geography: as both geographical and cultural entities—to say nothing of historical entities—such locales, regions, geographical sectors as 'Orient' and 'Occident' are man-made. Therefore as much as the West itself, the Orient is an idea that has a history and a tradition of thought, imagery, and vocabulary that have given it reality and presence in and for the West. The two geographical entities thus support and to an extent reflect each other.

Having said that, one must go on to state a number of reasonable qualifications. In the first place, it would be wrong to conclude that the Orient was *essentially* an idea, or a creation with no corresponding reality. When Disraeli said in his novel *Tancred* that the East was a career, he meant that to be interested in the East was something bright young Westerners would find to be an all-consuming passion; he should not be interpreted as saying that the East was *only* a career for Westerners. There were—and are—cultures and nations whose location is in the East, and their lives, histories, and customs have a brute reality obviously greater than anything that could be said about them in the West. About that fact this study of Orientalism has very little to contribute, except to acknowledge it tacitly. But the phenomenon of Orientalism as I study it here deals principally, not with a correspondence between Orientalism and Orient, but with the internal consistency of Orientalism and its ideas about the Orient (the East as career) despite or beyond any correspondence, or lack thereof, with a 'real' Orient. My point is that Disraeli's statement about the East refers mainly to that created consistency, that regular constellation of ideas as the pre-eminent thing about the Orient, and not to its mere being, as Wallace Stevens's phrase has it.

A second qualification is that ideas, cultures, and histories cannot seriously be understood or studied without their force, or more precisely their configurations of power, also being studied. To believe that the Orient was created—or, as I call it, 'Orientalized'—and to believe that such things happen simply as a necessity of the imagination, is to be disingenuous. The relationship between Occident and Orient is a relationship of power, of domination, of varying degrees of a complex hegemony, and is quite accurately indicated in the title of K.M. Panikkar's classic *Asia and Western Dominance*. The Orient was Orientalized not only because it was discovered to be 'Oriental' in all those ways considered commonplace by an average nineteenth-century European, but also because it *could be*—that is, submitted to being—*made* Oriental. There is very little consent to be found, for example, in the fact that Flaubert's encounter with an Egyptian courtesan produced a widely influential model of the Oriental woman; she never spoke of herself, she never represented her emotions, presence, or history. *He* spoke for and represented her. He was foreign, comparatively wealthy, male, and these were historical facts of domination that allowed him not only to possess Kuchuk Hanem physically but to speak for her and tell his readers in what way she was 'typically Oriental'. My argument is that Flaubert's situation of strength in relation to Kuchuk Hanem was not an isolated instance. It fairly stands for the pattern of relative strength between East and West, and the discourse about the Orient that it enabled.

This brings us to a third qualification. One ought never to assume that the structure of Orientalism is nothing more than a structure of lies or of myths which, were the truth about them to be told, would simply blow away. I myself believe that Orientalism is more particularly valuable as a sign of European-Atlantic power over the Orient than it is as a veridic discourse about the Orient (which is what, in its academic or scholarly form, it claims to be). Nevertheless, what we must respect and try to grasp is the sheer knitted-together strength of Orientalist discourse, its very close ties to the enabling socio-economic and political institutions, and its redoubtable durability. After all, any system of ideas that can remain unchanged as teachable wisdom (in academies, books, congresses, universities, foreign-service institutes) from the period of Ernest Renan in the late 1840s until the present in the United States must be something more formidable than a mere collection of lies. Orientalism, therefore, is not an airy European fantasy about the Orient, but a created body of theory and practice in which, for many generations, there has been a considerable material investment. Continued investment made Orientalism, as a system of knowledge about the Orient, an accepted grid for filtering through the Orient into Western consciousness, just as that same investment multiplied—indeed, made truly productive—the statements proliferating out from Orientalism into the general culture.

Gramsci has made the useful analytic distinction between civil and political society in which the former is made up of voluntary (or at least rational and non-coercive) affiliations like schools, families, and unions, the latter of state institutions (the army, the police, the central bureaucracy) whose role in the polity is direct domination. Culture, of course, is to be found operating within civil society, where the influence of ideas, of institutions, and of other persons works not through domination but by what Gramsci calls consent. In any society not totalitarian, then, certain cultural forms predominate over others, just as certain ideas are more influential than others; the form of this cultural leadership is what Gramsci has identified as *hegemony*, an indispensable concept for any understanding of cultural life in the industrial West. It is hegemony, or rather the result of cultural hegemony at work, that gives Orientalism the durability and the strength I have been speaking about so far. Orientalism is never far from what Denys Hay has called the idea of Europe, a collective notion identifying 'us' Europeans as against all 'those' non-Europeans, and indeed it can be argued that the major component in European culture is precisely what made that culture hegemonic both in and outside Europe: the idea of European identity as a superior one in comparison with all the non-European peoples and cultures. There is in addition the hegemony of European ideas about the Orient, themselves reiterating European superiority over Oriental backwardness, usually overriding the possibility that a more independent, or more sceptical thinker, might have had different views on the matter.

In a quite constant way Orientalism depends for its strategy on this flexible *positional* superiority which puts the Westerner in a whole series of possible relationships with the Orient without ever losing him the relative upper hand. And why should it have been otherwise, especially during the period of extraordinary European ascendancy from the late Renaissance to the present? The scientist, the scholar, the missionary, the trader, or the soldier was in, or thought about, the Orient because he *could be there*, or could think about it, with very little resistance on the Orient's part. Under the general heading of knowledge of the Orient, and within the umbrella of Western hegemony over the Orient during the period from the end of the eighteenth century, there emerged a complex Orient suitable for study in the academy, for display in the museum, for reconstruction in the colonial office, for theoretical illustration in anthropological, biological, linguistic, racial, and historical theses about mankind and the universe, for instances of economic and sociological theories of development, revolution, cultural personality, national or religious character. Additionally, the imaginative examination of things Oriental was based more or less exclusively upon a sovereign Western consciousness out of whose unchallenged centrality an Oriental world emerged, first according to general ideas about who or what was an Oriental, then according to a detailed logic governed not simply by empirical reality but by a battery of desires, repressions, investments, and projections. [. . .]

And yet, one must repeatedly ask oneself whether what matters in Orientalism is the general group of ideas overriding the mass of material—about which who could deny that they were shot through with doctrines of European superiority, various kinds of racism, imperialism, and the like, dogmatic views of 'the Oriental' as a kind of ideal and unchanging abstraction?—or the much more varied work produced by almost uncountable individual writers, whom one would take up as individual instances of authors dealing with the Orient. In a sense the two alternatives, general and particular, are really two perspectives on the same material: in both instances one would have to deal with pioneers in the field like William Jones, with great artists like Nerval or Flaubert. And why would it not be possible to employ both perspectives together, or one after the other? Isn't there an obvious danger of distortion (of precisely the kind that academic Orientalism has always been prone to) if either too general or too specific a level of description is maintained systematically?

My two fears are distortion and inaccuracy, or rather the kind of inaccuracy produced by too dogmatic a generality and too positivistic a localized focus. In trying to deal with these problems I have tried to deal with three main aspects of my own contemporary reality that seem to me to point the way out of the methodological or perspectival difficulties I have been discussing, difficulties that might force one, in the first instance, into writing a coarse polemic on so unacceptably general a level of description as not to be worth the effort, or in the second instance, into writing so detailed and atomistic a series of analyses as to lose all track of the general lines of force informing the field, giving it its special cogency. How then to recognize individuality and to reconcile it with its intelligent, and by no means passive or merely dictatorial, general and hegemonic context?

I mentioned three aspects of my contemporary reality: I must explain and briefly discuss them now, so that it can be seen how I was led to a particular course of research and writing.

1. *The distinction between pure and political knowledge.* It is very easy to argue that knowledge about Shakespeare or Wordsworth is not political whereas knowledge about contemporary China or the Soviet Union is. My own formal and professional designation is that of 'humanist', a title which indicates the humanities as my field and therefore the unlikely eventuality that there might be anything political about what I do in that field. Of course, all these labels and terms are quite unnuanced as I use them here, but the general truth of what I am pointing to is, I

think, widely held. One reason for saying that a humanist who writes about Wordsworth, or an editor whose specialty is Keats, is not involved in anything political is that what he does seems to have no direct political effect upon reality in the everyday sense. A scholar whose field is Soviet economics works in a highly charged area where there is much government interest, and what he might produce in the way of studies or proposals will be taken up by policymakers, government officials, institutional economists, intelligence experts. The distinction between 'humanists' and persons whose work has policy implications, or political significance, can be broadened further by saying that the former's ideological colour is a matter of incidental importance to politics (although possibly of great moment to his colleagues in the field, who may object to his Stalinism or fascism or too easy liberalism), whereas the ideology of the latter is woven directly into his material—indeed, economics, politics, and sociology in the modern academy are ideological sciences—and therefore taken for granted as being 'political'.

Nevertheless the determining impingement on most knowledge produced in the contemporary West (and here I speak mainly about the United States) is that it be nonpolitical, that is, scholarly, academic, impartial, above partisan or small-minded doctrinal belief. One can have no quarrel with such an ambition in theory, perhaps, but in practice the reality is much more problematic. No one has ever devised a method of detaching the scholar from the circumstances of life, from the fact of his involvement (conscious or unconscious) with a class, a set of beliefs, a social position, or from the mere activity of being a member of a society. These continue to bear on what he does professionally, even though naturally enough his research and its fruits do attempt to reach a level of relative freedom from the inhibitions and the restrictions of brute, everyday reality. For there is such a thing as knowledge that is less, rather than more, partial than the individual (with his entangling and distracting life circumstances) who produces it. Yet this knowledge is not therefore automatically nonpolitical. [. . .]

. . . Orientalism is not a mere political subject matter or field that is reflected passively by culture, scholarship, or institutions; nor is it a large and diffuse collection of texts about the Orient; nor is it representative and expressive of some nefarious 'Western' imperialist plot to hold down the 'Oriental' world. It is rather a *distribution* of geopolitical awareness into aesthetic, scholarly, economic, sociological, historical, and philological texts; it is an *elaboration* not only of a basic geographical distinction (the world is made up of two unequal halves, Orient and Occident) but also of a whole series of 'interests' which, by such means as scholarly discovery, philological reconstruction, psychological analysis, landscape and sociological description, it not only creates but also maintains; it *is*, rather than expresses, a certain *will* or *intention* to understand, in some cases to control, manipulate, even to incorporate, what is a manifestly different (or alternative and novel) world; it is, above all, a discourse that is by no means in direct, corresponding relationship with political power in the raw, but rather is produced and exists in an uneven exchange with various kinds of power, shaped to a degree by the exchange with power political (as with a colonial or imperial establishment), power intellectual (as with reigning sciences like comparative linguistics or anatomy, or any of the modern policy sciences), power cultural (as with orthodoxies and canons of taste, texts, values), power moral (as with ideas about what 'we' do and what 'they' cannot do or understand as 'we' do). Indeed, my real argument is that Orientalism is—and does not simply represent—a considerable dimension of modern political-intellectual culture, and as such has less to do with the Orient than it does with 'our' world.

The kind of political questions raised by Orientalism, then, are as follows: What other sorts of intellectual, aesthetic, scholarly, and cultural energies went into the making of an imperialist tradition like the Orientalist one? How did philology, lexicography, history, biology, political and economic theory, novel-writing, and lyric poetry come to the service of Orientalism's broadly imperialist view of the world? What changes, modulations, refinements, even revolutions take place within Orientalism? What is the meaning of originality, of continuity, of individuality, in this context? How does Orientalism transmit or reproduce itself from one epoch to another? In fine, how can we treat the cultural, historical phenomenon of Orientalism as a kind of *willed human work*—not of mere unconditioned ratiocination—in all its historical complexity, detail, and worth without at the same time losing sight of the alliance between cultural work, political tendencies, the state, and the specific realities of domination? Governed by such concerns a humanistic study can responsibly address itself to politics *and* culture. But this is not to say that such a study establishes a hard-and-fast rule about the relationship between knowledge and politics. My argument is that each humanistic investigation must formulate the nature of that connection in the specific context of the study, the subject matter, and its historical circumstances.

2. *The methodological question.* In a previous book* I gave a good deal of thought and analysis to the methodological importance for work in the human sciences of finding and formulating a first step, a point of departure, a beginning principle. A major lesson I learned and tried to present was that there is no such thing as a merely given, or simply available, starting point: beginnings have to be made for each project in such a way as to *enable* what follows from them. Nowhere in my experience has the difficulty of this lesson been more consciously lived (with what success—or failure—I cannot really say) than in this study of Orientalism. The idea of beginning, indeed the act of beginning, necessarily involves an act of delimitation by which something is cut out of a great mass of material, separated from the mass, and made to stand for, as well as be, a starting point, a beginning; for the student of texts one such notion of inaugural delimitation is Louis Althusser's idea of the *problematic*, a specific determinate unity of a text, or group of texts, which is something given rise to by analysis. Yet in the case of Orientalism (as opposed to the case of Marx's texts, which is what Althusser studies) there is not simply the problem of finding a point of departure, or problematic, but also the question of designating which texts, authors, and periods are the ones best suited for study. [. . .]

* *In My Beginnings: Intention and Method* (1975).

. . . What German Orientalism had in common with Anglo-French and later American Orientalism was a kind of intellectual *authority* over the Orient within Western culture. This authority must in large part be the subject of any description of Orientalism, and it is so in this study. Even the name *Orientalism* suggests a serious, perhaps ponderous style of expertise; when I apply it to modern American social scientists (since they do not call themselves Orientalists, my use of the word is anomalous), it is to draw attention to the way Middle East experts can still draw on the vestiges of Orientalism's intellectual position in nineteenth-century Europe.

There is nothing mysterious or natural about authority. It is formed, irradiated, disseminated; it is instrumental, it is persuasive; it has status, it establishes canons of taste and value; it is virtually indistinguishable from certain ideas it dignifies as true, and from traditions, perceptions, and judgements it forms, transmits, reproduces. Above all, authority can, indeed must, be analyzed. All these attributes of authority apply to Orientalism, and much of what I do in this study is to describe both the historical authority in and the personal authorities of Orientalism.

My principal methodological devices for studying authority here are what can be called *strategic location*, which is a way of describing the author's position in a text with regard to the Oriental material he writes about, and *strategic formation*, which is a way of analyzing the relationship between texts and the way in which groups of texts, types of texts, even textual genres, acquire mass, density, and referential power among themselves and thereafter in the culture at large. I use the notion of strategy simply to identify the problem every writer on the Orient has faced: how to get hold of it, how to approach it, how not to be defeated or overwhelmed by its sublimity, its scope, its awful dimensions. Everyone who writes about the Orient must locate himself vis-à-vis the Orient; translated into his text, this location includes the kind of narrative voice he adopts, the type of structure he builds, the kinds of images, themes, motifs that circulate in his text—all of which add up to deliberate ways of addressing the reader, containing the Orient, and finally, representing it or speaking on its behalf. None of this takes place in the abstract, however. Every writer on the Orient (and this is true even of Homer) assumes some Oriental precedent, some previous knowledge of the Orient, to which he refers and on which he relies. Additionally, each work on the Orient *affiliates* itself with other works, with audiences, with institutions, with the Orient itself. The ensemble of relationships between works, audiences, and some particular aspects of the Orient therefore constitutes an analyzable formation—for example, that of philological studies, of anthologies of extracts from Oriental literature, of travel books, of Oriental fantasies—whose presence in time, in discourse, in institutions (schools, libraries, foreign services) gives it strength and authority. [. . .]

. . . I believe it needs to be made clear about cultural discourse and exchange within a culture that what is commonly circulated by it is not 'truth' but representations. It hardly needs to be demonstrated again that language itself is a highly organized and encoded system, which employs many devices to express, indicate, exchange messages and information, represent, and so forth. In any instance of at least written language, there is no such thing as a delivered presence, but a *re-presence*, or a representation. The value, efficacy, strength, apparent veracity of a written statement about the Orient therefore relies very little, and cannot instrumentally depend, on the Orient as such. On the contrary, the written statement is a presence to the reader by virtue of its having excluded, displaced, made supererogatory any such *real thing* as 'the Orient'. Thus all of Orientalism stands forth and away from the Orient: that Orientalism makes sense at all depends more on the West than on the Orient, and this sense is directly indebted to various Western techniques of representation that make the Orient visible, clear, 'there' in discourse about it. And these representations rely upon institutions, traditions, conventions, agreed-upon codes of understanding for their effects, not upon a distant and amorphous Orient. [. . .]

3. *The personal dimension.* In the *Prison Notebooks* Gramsci says: 'The starting-point of critical elaboration is the consciousness of what one really is, and is "knowing thyself" as a product of the historical process to date, which has deposited in you an infinity of traces, without leaving an inventory.' The only available English translation inexplicably leaves Gramsci's comment at that, whereas in fact Gramsci's Italian text concludes by adding, 'therefore it is imperative at the outset to compile such an inventory'.

Much of the personal investment in this study derives from my awareness of being an 'Oriental' as a child growing up in two British colonies. All of my education, in those colonies (Palestine and Egypt) and in the United States, has been Western, and yet that deep early awareness has persisted. In many ways my study of Orientalism has been an attempt to inventory the traces upon me, the Oriental subject, of the culture whose domination has been so powerful a factor in the life of all Orientals. This is why for me the Islamic Orient has had to be the centre of attention. Whether what I have achieved is the inventory prescribed by Gramsci is not for me to judge, although I have felt it important to be conscious of trying to produce one. Along the way, as severely and as rationally as I have been able, I have tried to maintain a critical consciousness, as well as employing those instruments of historical, humanistic, and cultural research of which my education has made me the fortunate beneficiary. In none of that, however, have I ever lost hold of the cultural reality of, the personal involvement in having been constituted as, 'an Oriental'.

The historical circumstances making such a study possible are fairly complex, and I can only list them schematically here. Anyone resident in the West since the 1950s, particularly in the United States, will have lived through an era of extraordinary turbulence in the relations of East and West. No one will have failed to note how 'East' has always signified danger and threat during this period, even as it has meant the traditional Orient as well as Russia. In the universities a growing establishment of area-studies programmes and institutes has made the scholarly study of the Orient a branch of national policy. Public affairs in this country include a healthy interest in the Orient, as much for its strategic and economic importance as for its traditional exoticism. If the world has become immediately accessible to a Western citizen living in the electronic age, the Orient too has drawn nearer to him, and is now less a myth perhaps than a place crisscrossed by Western, especially American, interests.

One aspect of the electronic, postmodern world is that there has been a reinforcement of the stereotypes by which the Orient is viewed. Television, the films, and all the media's resources have forced information into more and more standardized moulds. So far as the Orient is concerned, standardization and cultural stereotyping have intensified the hold of the nineteenth-century academic and imaginative demonology of 'the mysterious Orient'. This is nowhere more true than in the ways by which the Near East is grasped. Three things have contributed to making even the simplest perception of the Arabs and Islam into a highly politicized, almost raucous matter: one, the history of popular anti-Arab and anti-Islamic prejudice in the West, which is immediately reflected in the history of Orientalism; two, the struggle between the Arabs and Israeli Zionism, and its effects upon American Jews as well as upon both the liberal culture and the population at large; three, the almost total absence of any cultural position making it possible either to identify with or dispassionately to discuss the Arabs or Islam. Furthermore, it hardly needs saying that because the Middle East is now so identified with Great Power politics, oil economics, and the simple-minded dichotomy of freedom-loving, democratic Israel and evil, totalitarian, and terroristic Arabs, the chances of anything like a clear view of what one talks about in talking about the Near East are depressingly small.

My own experiences of these matters are in part what made me write this book. The life of an Arab Palestinian in the West, particularly in America, is disheartening. There exists here an almost unanimous consensus that politically he does not exist, and when it is allowed that he does, it is either as a nuisance or as an Oriental. The web of racism, cultural stereotypes, political imperialism, dehumanizing ideology holding in the Arab or the Muslim is very strong indeed, and it is this web which every Palestinian has come to feel as his uniquely punishing destiny. It has made matters worse for him to remark that no person academically involved with the Near East—no Orientalist, that is—has ever in the United States culturally and politically identified himself wholeheartedly with the Arabs; certainly there have been identifications on some level, but they have never taken an 'acceptable' form as has liberal American identification with Zionism, and all too frequently they have been radically flawed by their association either with discredited political and economic interests (oil-company and State Department Arabists, for example) or with religion.

The nexus of knowledge and power creating 'the Oriental' and in a sense obliterating him as a human being is therefore not for me an exclusively academic matter. Yet it is an *intellectual* matter of some very obvious importance. I have been able to put to use my humanistic and political concerns for the analysis and description of a very worldly matter, the rise, development, and consolidation of Orientalism. Too often literature and culture are presumed to be politically, even historically innocent; it has regularly seemed otherwise to me, and certainly my study of Orientalism has convinced me (and I hope will convince my literary colleagues) that society and literary culture can only be understood and studied together.

In addition, and by an almost inescapable logic, I have found myself writing the history of a strange, secret sharer of Western anti-Semitism. That anti-Semitism and, as I have discussed it in its Islamic branch, Orientalism resemble each other very closely is a historical, cultural, and political truth that needs only to be mentioned to an Arab Palestinian for its irony to be perfectly understood. But what I should like also to have contributed here is a better understanding of the way cultural domination has operated. If this stimulates a new kind of dealing with the Orient, indeed if it eliminates the 'Orient' and 'Occident' altogether, then we shall have advanced a little in the process of what Raymond Williams has called the 'unlearning' of 'the inherent dominative mode'.*

Note: In this extract, specialist and mainly historical references to 'the Orient' have been removed.

* *Culture and Society* (1958), p. 376.

6

Concepts of culture—public policy and the cultural industries

Nicholas Garnham

Originally published as a discussion paper by the Greater London Council in 1983; reprinted in the GLC's *The State of the Art or the Art of the State?* (1985) and in *Cultural Studies*, vol. 1, no. 1 (1987).

To mobilize the concept of the cultural industries as central to an analysis of cultural activity and of public cultural policy is to take a stand against a whole tradition of idealist cultural analysis. This tradition, well delineated in the British form, for instance, by Raymond Williams in *Culture and Society*, defines culture as a realm separate from, and often actively opposed to, the realm of material production and economic activity.

This is important for our present purposes because, in general, public cultural policies have evolved from within that tradition. Public intervention, in the form of subsidy, is justified on the grounds (1) that culture possesses inherent values, of life enhancement or whatever, which are fundamentally opposed to and in danger of damage by commercial forces; (2) that the need for these values is universal, uncontaminated by questions of class, gender and ethnic origin; and (3) that the market cannot satisfy this need.

A further crucial component of this ideology is the special and central status attributed to the 'creative artist' whose aspirations and values, seen as stemming from some unfathomable and unquestionable source of genius, inspiration or talent, are the source of cultural value. The result of placing artists at the centre of the cultural universe has not been to shower them with gold, for artistic poverty is itself an ideologically potent element in this view of culture, but to define the policy problem as one of finding audiences for their work, rather than vice versa. When audiences cannot be found, at least at a price and in a quantity which will support the creative activity, the market is blamed and the gap is filled by subsidy.

It is important to note that most of those on the left who have challenged this dominant view of culture as élitist have themselves tacitly if not explicitly accepted the remaining assumptions of the tradition they were rejecting. Indeed, in my view this in part accounts for their limited success in shifting the terms of the policy debate and the effortless ease with which they have been incorporated.

One result of this cultural policy-making tradition has been to marginalize public intervention in the cultural sphere and to make it purely reactive to processes which it cannot grasp or attempt to control. For, while this tradition has been rejecting the market, most people's cultural needs and aspirations are being, for better or worse, supplied by the market as goods and services. If one turns one's back on an analysis of that dominant cultural process, one cannot understand either the culture of our time or the challenges and opportunities which that dominant culture offers to public policy makers.

We can get some idea of the relative orders of magnitude between public-sector expenditure on cultural activity and private, market expenditure if we compare the £673.8 million of public expenditure on libraries, museums and galleries and other cultural activities in the United Kingdom in 1981–2 with the £15,538 million of 1982 consumer expenditure on recreation, enter-tainment and education, and with the total media advertising expenditure in 1982 of £3,216 million. [. . .]

An analysis of culture structured around the concept of the cultural industries, on the other hand, directs our attention precisely at the domi-nant private market sector. It sees culture, defined as the production and circulation of symbolic meaning, as a material process of production and exchange, part of, and in significant ways determined by, the wider eco-nomic processes of society with which it shares many common features.

Thus, as a descriptive term, 'cultural industries' refers to those institu-tions in our society which employ the characteristic modes of production and organization of industrial corporations to produce and disseminate symbols in the form of cultural goods and services, generally, although not exclusively, as commodities. These include newspapers, periodical and book publishing, record companies, music publishers, commercial sports organizations, etc. In all these cultural processes, we characteristically find at some point the use of capital-intensive, technological means of mass production and/or distribution, highly developed divisions of labour and hierarchical modes of managerial organization. [. . .]

Consumption time

For most people, cultural consumption is confined to a so-called free time, the extension of which is limited by the material necessities of work and sleep. If we assume a working week (including travel) of 45 hours and sleep time of 48 hours per week, that leaves 75 hours per week in which all other activities have to be fitted. On average, 20 hours per week are taken up by TV viewing.

Cultural consumption is particularly time-consuming in the sense that the most common and popular form of culture, namely narrative and its musical equivalent, are based upon manipulation of time itself, and thus they offer deep resistances to attempts to raise the productivity of consumption time. This scarcity of consumption time explains:

1) the acute competition for audiences in the cultural sector;
2) the tendency to concentrate cultural consumption in the home, thus cutting out travel time;
3) as recent Swedish studies have shown, a sharp rise in the unit cost

of each minute of consumption time, in particular as investment on domestic hardware increases while the time for using such hardware does not. Thus in Sweden between 1970 and 1979 time spent listening to music rose by 20 per cent while the cost rose by 86 per cent, with each hour of listening costing 55 per cent more.

The labour market

The various cultural industries compete in the same market for labour. Individual film-makers, writers, musicians or electricians may move in their work from film, to television, to live theatre. The electronic engineer may work in manufacturing or broadcasting. The journalist may work in newspapers, periodicals, radio or television.

This unified labour market is reflected in trade-union organizations. The Association of Cinematograph, Television and Allied Technicians (ACTT) organizes across film, television and radio, the National Union of Journalists (NUJ) across newspapers, books, magazines, radio and television. The Musicians' Union members work in film, radio, television and records as well as live performances, and so on.

As a result of these levels of integration within the cultural sector, a shift in one place affects the structure of the whole sector. The introduction of a new television channel, such as Channel 4, restructures the broadcasting, film and advertising market in specific ways. Even more, of course, will this be the case with cable and satellite services. The introduction of a new colour supplement has repercussions upon the finances of other publications, but may well also have cross-effects on broadcasting revenue. The same holds true for public intervention. One needs to be aware that one may be playing a zero-sum game, and that all options are not simultaneously open.

A classic example of this interaction and of the ways in which the dynamics of the private sector impact on the public sector is the relation between ITV and BBC. Because ITV holds a monopoly of television advertising, and because there has in general been a high demand for this commodity, extra broadcasting hours mean, for ITV, extra revenue, more efficient utilization of plant and thus higher profit. There has therefore been steady pressure from ITV, in common with commercial broadcasting systems throughout the world, to expand the hours of broadcasting—pressure which has been successful. For the BBC, on the other hand, expansion of hours leads to increases in costs with no increase in revenue. They have, however, been forced to respond to ITV because of the need to compete for audiences, thus increasing the pressure to spend more public money on broadcasting if the balance between public and private sectors is to be maintained.

The structure and dynamics of the cultural industries

The particular economic nature of the cultural industries can be explained in terms of the general tendencies of commodity production within the capitalist mode of production as modified by the special characteristics of the cultural commodity. Thus we find competition driving the search for profits via increased productivity, but it takes specific forms.

There is a contradiction at the heart of the cultural commodity. On the one hand, there is a very marked drive towards expanding the market share or the form this takes in the cultural sector, audiences. This is explained by the fact that in general, because one of the use-values of culture is novelty or difference, there is a constant need to create new products which are all in a sense prototypes. That is to say, the cultural commodity resists that homogenization process which is one of the material results of the abstract equivalence of exchange to which the commodity form aspires. This drive for novelty within cultural production means that in general the costs of reproduction are marginal in relation to the costs of production (the cost of each record pressing is infinitesimal compared to the cost of recording, for instance). Thus the marginal returns from each extra sale tend to grow, leading in turn to a powerful thrust towards audience maximization as the preferred profit maximization strategy.

On the other hand, the cultural commodity is not destroyed in the process of consumption. My reading of a book or watching of a film does not make it any less available to you. Moreover, the products of the past live on and can be relatively easy and cheaply reproduced anew. Thus it has been difficult to establish the scarcity on which price is based. And thus cultural goods (and some services, such as broadcasting, for technical reasons) tend towards the condition of a public good. Indeed, one can observe a marked tendency, where they are not *de jure* so treated, for consumers to so treat them *de facto* through high levels of piracy, as is now the case with records, video cassettes and books. (It should be noted that this in its turn relates to another contradiction in the cultural sphere, on which I shall comment shortly, between the producers of cultural hardware and software. It is the development of a market in cheap reproduction technology that makes piracy so difficult to control.) In contradiction, then, to the drive to maximize audiences, a number of strategies have had to be developed for artificially limiting access in order to create scarcity.

The drive to audience maximization leads to the observed tendency towards a high level of concentration, internationalization and cross-media ownership in the cultural industries. The strategies to limit access have taken a variety of forms:

1) Monopoly or oligopolistic controls over distribution channels, sometimes, as in broadcasting, linked to the state. One often finds here a close relationship between commercial interests and those of state control.
2) An attempt to concentrate the accumulation process on the provision of cultural hardware—e.g. radio and television receivers, hi-fi, VCRs, etc. —with the programmes, as in the early days of British broadcasting, as necessary loss-leaders. The rationale for the introduction of cable in the UK is an example of this.
3) The creation of the audience as a commodity for sale to advertisers, where the cultural software merely acts as a free lunch. This has proved itself the most successful solution; both the increased proportion

of advertising to sales revenue in the press and periodicals market, culminating in the growth of free newspapers and magazines, and the steady expansion of wholly advertising-financed broadcasting services, are indications of this.

4) The creation of commodities, of which news is the classic example, which require constant reconsumption.

Audiences, cultural repertoire and distribution

The third key characteristic of the cultural commodity lies in the nature of its use-values. These have proved difficult if not impossible to pin down in any precise terms, and demand for them appears to be similarly volatile. As I have already remarked, culture is above all the sphere for the expression of difference. Indeed, some analysts would claim that cultural goods are pure positional goods, their use-value being as markers of social and individual difference. While this aspect of culture merits much deeper and more extended analysis, it is only necessary here to draw one key conclusion, namely that demand for any single cultural product is impossible to predict. Thus the cultural industries, if they are to establish a stable market, are forced to create a relationship with an audience or public to whom they offer not a simple cultural good, but a cultural repertoire across which the risks can be spread. For instance, in the record industry only 1 in 9 singles and 1 in 16 LPs makes a profit, and 3 per cent of the output can account for up to 50 per cent of turnover. Similarly, in films the top ten films out of 119 in the UK market in 1979 took 32 per cent of the box-office receipts and the top 40 took 80 per cent.

Thus the drive to audience maximization, the need to create artificial scarcity by controlling access and the need for a repertoire bring us to the central point in this analysis. *It is cultural distribution, not cultural production, that is the key locus of power and profit*. It is access to distribution which is the key to cultural plurality. The cultural process is as much, if not more, about creating audiences or publics as it is about producing cultural artefacts and performances. Indeed, that is why that stress upon the cultural producers that I noted earlier is so damaging.

We need to recognize the importance, within the cultural industries and within the cultural process in general, of the function which I shall call, for want of a better word, editorial: the function not just of creating a cultural repertoire matched to a given audience or audiences but at the same time of matching the cost of production of that repertoire to the spending powers of that audience. These functions may be filled by somebody or some institution referred to variously as a publisher, a television channel controller, a film distributor, etc. It is a vital function totally ignored by many cultural analysts, a function as creative as writing a novel or directing a film. It is a function, moreover, which will exist centrally within the cultural process of any geographically dispersed society with complex division of labour.

Taking these various factors into account, we are now in a position to understand why our dominant cultural processes and their modes of organization are the way they are. The newspaper and the television and radio schedule are montages of elements to appeal to as wide a range of readers, viewers and listeners as possible. The high levels of concentration in the international film, record and publishing industries are responses to the problem of repertoire. The dominance of broadcast television stems from its huge efficiency as a distribution medium, with its associated economies of scale.

For this reason, the notion that the new technologies of cable and VCR are fragmenting the market rather than shifting the locus of oligopolistic power needs to be treated with caution, since there are strict limits to how far such fragmentation can go economically.

The hierarchy of cultural industries

As I have noted, power in the cultural sector clusters around distribution, the channel of access to audiences. It is here that we typically find the highest levels of capital intensity, ownership concentration and multinationalization, the operation of classic industrial labour processes and relations of production with related forms of trade-union organization. These characteristics are exhibited to their highest degree in the manufacture of the hardware of cultural distribution, especially domestic hardware. This is a sub-sector increasingly dominated by a few Japanese corporations such as Matsushita, Sony, Sanyo, Toshiba and Hitachi, together with Eastman Kodak, Philips and RCA. The major UK firm of this type is Thorn-EMI.

Then there are the major controllers of channels of software distribution, often closely linked to specific modes of reproduction, such as record pressing or newspaper printing. In non-print media there is again a high level of concentration and internationalization, and US firms dominate, owing to the large size of the domestic US market. Here we find some of the same firms as in hardware, e.g. RCA, Thorn-EMI and Philips joined by firms such as Warner, CBS, Time-Life, Gulf-Western and MCA. The multinationalization of print media has been limited by barriers of language. None the less, apart from the high levels of concentration in the national UK market, with three groups controlling 74 per cent of daily newspaper circulation, two of these groups—News International and Reed International—have extensive foreign interests.

The increasing tendency in this field, as an extension of the principle of repertoire, is the formation of multi-media conglomerates. Examples are Pearson-Longman and Thorn-EMI in the UK, who own interests across a number of media, thus enabling them both to exploit the same product, be it a film, a book or a piece of music, across several media, and also to expand the principles of risk-spreading not only across a range of consumer choice in one medium, but also across consumers' entire range of cultural choice. The development of such centres of cultural powers also, of course, raises barriers to entry.

Around these centres of power cluster groups of satellites. These satellites can be either small companies, for instance independent production companies in relation to Channel 4, or individual cultural workers such as freelance journalists, writers, actors and film directors. In these satellite sectors we find high levels of insecurity, low levels of profitability, low levels of unionization and, where they exist, weak trade-union organizations. Often labour is not waged at all, but labour power is rented out for a royalty.

The existence of this dependent satellite sector fulfils a very important function for the cultural industries because it enables them to shift much of the cost and risk of cultural research and development off their own shoulders and on to this exploited sector, some of which is then indeed supported from the public purse. It also enables them to maintain a consistently high turnover of creative cultural labour without running the risk of labour unrest, or bearing the cost of redundancy or pension payments. Their cup brimmeth over when, as is often the case, the workers themselves willingly don this yoke in the name of freedom.

The market and culture

[. . .] [O]ne last general analytical question must be raised: what should be our attitude to the relation between the market and the cultural process? There is that general tradition, to which I alluded at the beginning of this paper, which regards culture and the market as inherently inimical. This view is powerfully reinforced within the socialist tradition by opposition to the capitalist mode of production.

I think it is crucial, however, to separate the concept of the market from the concept of the capitalist mode of production, that is to say from a given structure of ownership and from the special features derived from labour as a market commodity. In terms of this relationship between consumers, distributors and producers of cultural goods and services, the market has much to recommend it, provided that consumers enter that market with equal endowments and that concentration of ownership power is reduced, controlled or removed. However, we must be clear that removal of the power vested in private or unaccountable public ownership will not remove the need for the function I have described as editorial, whether such a function is exercised individually or collectively. It also has to be stressed that even within the capitalist mode of production the market has, at crucial historical junctures, acted as a liberating cultural force. One thinks of the creation of both the novel and the newspaper by the rising bourgeoisie in the eighteenth century and of working men's clubs and the working-class seaside holiday in the late nineteenth century.

Indeed, the cultural market, as it has developed in the last 150 years in the UK as a substitute for patronage in all its forms, cannot be read either as a destruction of high culture by vulgar commercialism or as a suppression of authentic working-class culture, but should be read as a complex hegemonic dialectic of liberation and control—which makes an analysis, for instance, of the role of broadcasting and of the BBC public-service tradition so difficult.

What analysis of the cultural industries does bring home to us is the need to take the question of the scarcity and thus of the allocation of cultural resources seriously, together with the question of audiences—who they are, how they are formed and how they can best be served. For it needs to be said that the only alternative to the market which we have constructed, with the partial exception of broadcasting, has tended either simply to subsidize the existing tastes and habits of the better-off or to create a new form of public culture which has no popular audience; cultural workers create for the only audience they know, namely the cultural bureaucrats who pay the bill and upon whom they become psychologically dependent even while reviling them. [. . .]

7

Reading *Reading the Romance*

Janice Radway

Introduction to the English edition of her *Reading the Romance* (Verso, 1987); the book was originally published in the USA by University of North Carolina Press in 1984.

It seems especially fitting that a book about the *particular* nature of the relationship between audiences and texts, which was itself initially conceived for and addressed to a specific community of readers, should require a new introduction precisely at the moment that it is to be offered to a new and different set of readers situated in another social context. Indeed, in reading *Reading the Romance* for the first time since the manuscript was completed, in preparation for offering it to a British audience, I have been struck by how much the book's argument is a product of my own intellectual history and that of the community I intended and hoped to address. As a consequence, these new remarks will constitute something of an apologia for the book's limitations and an effort to secure a particular reading in the British context.[1] I want to situate and explain the polemic of *Reading the Romance* because I suspect that the book's early theoretical claim to be doing something new will seem odd to a British audience, which will also particularly note the absence of certain references and concepts. Despite those absences, however, *Reading the Romance* does take up specific questions that have preoccupied British feminists and cultural studies scholars for some time. Thus I would like to highlight those questions, consider how and why they were posed as they were in *Reading the Romance*, and explore their similarity to and differences from the questions posed by British scholars working on subcultures and the culture of women and girls. Finally, I would like to say something about the political implications of *Reading the Romance* as I now understand them, because they have been articulated more clearly for me by my continuing engagement with the work of British feminists and cultural studies scholars.

British readers of *Reading the Romance* will note immediately that the book's theoretical argument is directed generally to American Studies scholars working in the United States (although this latter qualification is not stated specifically) and more particularly to those who take literature as their primary object of concern. The resulting preoccupation with the question of what a literary text can be taken as evidence for may seem a peculiar and oblique focus for a book that has largely been read as a contribution to feminist scholarship or as a contribution to discussions within communications theory about the status of the reader and the nature of mass cultural consumption.[2] This latter fact simply demonstrates, however, that whatever her intentions no writer can foresee or prescribe the way her book will develop, be taken up, or read. Neither can she predict how it will transform her, I might add, a subject to which I will return. Still, I think it will be helpful to know something about the immediate personal and intellectual situation which served as the polemical ground and orienting context for the writing of *Reading the Romance* because I think it goes a long way toward explaining why the book was eventually hijacked by its own theory and subject and, en route to its intended destination, gradually found itself directed to another.

As much as the theoretical argument of chapter one is the product of an intellectual quarrel, so too is it the product of an institutional and political one as well. It was born of the fact that I had been hired in 1977 by the American Civilization Department at the University of Pennsylvania, which has been known within the American Studies community in the United States for its particular challenge to an earlier American Studies orthodoxy. That orthodoxy, formed in the late 1940s and early 1950s, developed as part of the reaction to the hegemony of New Criticism in American English Departments. Disturbed by the extreme preoccupation with formalist criticism in an historical context that seemed to cry out for a consideration once again of what constituted 'the American', certain students of the national literature began to reassert the validity of an enterprise that would reunite the classic American literary texts with the historical context within which they were conceived. Resulting largely in an alliance between literary scholars and intellectual historians, the impulse led to the creation of American Studies programmes and departments which, whatever their differences with more traditional English Departments, at least still assumed that the most reliable and complex record of the American past could be found in the country's 'greatest' works of art.[3]

In opposition to such claims, however, the American Civilization Department at Pennsylvania began to elaborate a critique of the assumption that works selected on the basis of their aesthetic achievement would necessarily be representative of the large sections of the population that had never read such books. Writing within the framework prescribed by the social sciences and preoccupied therefore with questions of evidentiary validity and statistical representivity, my future colleagues (who were not, for the most part, literary critics) argued that while 'elite' literature might be taken as evidence for the beliefs of a particular section of the American population, assertions based upon it could not easily be extrapolated to wholly different classes or ethnic groups. They argued that if accurate statements were to be made about more 'ordinary' Americans, the popular literature produced for and consumed by large numbers ought to become the primary focus of culturally-oriented scholarship.[4]

I was hired, then, because much of my graduate work had been preoccupied with popular literature of one sort or another. That work had been directed by Russel Nye, one of the first serious scholars of American popular culture in the United States.[5] Although Nye was himself trained as an historian, he worked within the English Department at Michigan State University. Therefore, under his tutelage, its American Studies programme articulated the need for the study of popular culture even though it remained theoretically more traditional than that at Pennsylvania. The methods of analysis it taught were still primarily those of formal analysis and textual exegesis. Thus I went to Pennsylvania as a student of popular culture but also as a literary critic. *Reading the Romance* clearly demonstrates that provenance in the conversations it chooses to join.

By the time I arrived in the department my colleagues had turned away somewhat from statistical models for the study of society and behaviour and had elaborated instead a complex rationale for the use of ethnographic methods in the effort to make sense of American culture. Drawing on anthropology rather than sociology, they argued that cultural investigation must always take account of spatial and temporal specificity. Thus they moved from what Stuart Hall and others have called the 'literary-moral' definition of culture to an anthropological one, defining it as the whole way of life of a historically and temporally situated people.[6] The department's essential graduate seminars were structured as ethnographies of particular communities which were studied synchronically and in depth. Interestingly enough, these were initiated at almost the same time as investigators at the Birmingham Centre for Contemporary Cultural Studies, prompted by arguments made by Raymond Williams, E.P. Thompson, Hall, and others, were turning to ethnographic methods in their effort to study the necessary 'struggle, tension, and conflict' between subcultures or different ways of life.[7] Because this latter move originated within the well-developed Marxist tradition in Britain, even the earliest work at the Centre made an effort to consider the nature of the relationship between ethnographic investigation of behaviour and cultural meaning and ideological analysis of the structures of determination.[8] Although the turn to ethnography in American Studies was prompted by a concern with the relationship (if not the struggle) between subgroups within a complex society and by an interest in the relationship between behaviour and 'belief systems', the relative weakness of the Marxist tradition in the USA meant that most of the early work did not explicitly engage debates over ideology or the place of specifically cultural production in securing the domination of one group over another.

In any case, the ethnographic turn began to have relevance for me when I simultaneously began to engage with the theoretical work developing within the literary critical community on the reader and semiotic conceptions of the literary text. I grappled with this work as a result of discussions carried on within the Penn Semiotics Seminar which was heavily influenced by Dell Hymes, Erving Goffman, and Barbara Herrnstein Smith, among others. Thus, even as I was attempting to respond to my departmental colleagues' questions about what a literary text could be taken as evidence for, I was being gradually convinced by the theoretical arguments about the social and hence variable nature of semiotic processes. If one could talk of the necessity for ethnographies of speaking, I saw no reason why one shouldn't also assume that as speech varied across space and over time so, too, reading must as well. If this was true and one could discover how actual communities actually read particular texts, I thought I saw a way to answer my colleagues' questions about the evidentiary status of literature. If reading varied spatially and temporally and one did wish to use literature in an effort to reconstruct culture, it would be necessary to connect particular texts with the communities that produced and consumed them and to make some effort to specify how the individuals involved actually constructed those texts as meaningful semiotic structures. Hence my conclusion that what American Studies needed were ethnographies of reading.

Reading the Romance was therefore conceived in response to a set of theoretical questions about literary texts. As a consequence, it was designed initially to see whether it was possible to investigate reading empirically so as to make 'accurate' statements about the historical and cultural meaning of literary production and consumption. The decision to move beyond the various concepts of the inscribed, ideal, or model reader and to work with actual subjects in history was thus a product of the difficult questions that had been put to me by colleagues trained in the social science tradition and in culture theory. The resulting empiricism of *Reading the Romance*, embodied most obviously in its claim that empirically-based ethnographies of reading should replace *all* intuitively conducted interpretation in cultural study, precisely because such empiricism would guarantee a more *accurate* description of what a book meant to a given audience, was thus a function of my situation within the American Studies intellectual community as it carried on the familiar debate about the relative merits of 'scientific' as opposed to 'literary' methods in cultural study.[9]

The book that resulted did not ultimately sustain its initial project, however, because the activity of actually 'doing ethnography' produced many surprises, not the least of which was the realization that even ethnographic description of the 'native's' point of view must be an interpretation or, in words adapted from Clifford Geertz, my own construction of my informants' construction of what they were up to in reading romances. This, of course, will not be news to anyone familiar with anthropological method or with the ethnographic work of the CCCS, but it was something I only really discovered in the course of attempting to write the ethnography. I tried to acknowledge this point in the introduction to the American edition which, like so many others, was substantially revised after all the other chapters were completed. I attempted to do this by proclaiming openly my feminism and by acknowledging that it had affected the way I evaluated or reacted to my subject's self-understanding. However, I now think that my initial preoccupation with the empiricist claims of social science prevented me from recognizing fully that even what I took to be simple descriptions of my interviewee's self-understandings were produced through an internal organization of data and thus mediated by my own conceptual constructs and ways of seeing the world.[10]

I would therefore now want to agree with Angela McRobbie when she states flatly that 'representations are interpretations'.[11] As she goes on to say, they can never be pure mirror images of some objective reality but exist always as the result of 'a whole set of selective devices, such as highlighting, editing, cutting, transcribing and inflecting'. Consequently,

I no longer feel that ethnographies of reading should *replace* textual inter-pretation completely because of their greater adequacy to the task of revealing an objective cultural reality. Rather, I think they should become an essential and necessary component of a multiply-focussed approach that attempts to do justice to the ways historical subjects understand and partially control their own behaviour while recognizing at the same time that such behaviour and self-understanding are limited if not in crucial ways complexly determined by the social formation within which those subjects find themselves.

In practice, if not perhaps in theory, I think *Reading the Romance* actually does make an effort to do this in large part because my attempts to deal with literary production and consumption as complex social processes were affected by my first serious engagement with Marxist literary theory. That engagement had been prompted initially by Jerry Palmer's suggestion that I might want to read Terry Eagleton's *Criticism and Ideology*.[12] This initiated the pursuit of a trail of bibliographic references through the Marxist literature on ideology, an intellectual move that was reinforced by my ongoing reading in feminist literature as I began to grapple with the social situations of the women who were sharing their perceptions with me. The question of determination was thus posed for me by my attention to the material and social context within which romance reading generally occurs.

I had first taken up the subject of romances in graduate school as part of my dissertation on the differences between 'popular' and 'elite' literature.[13] Searching for a way to trace the variable use of generic conventions across these evaluative categories, I chose the gothic romance because my participation in a feminist consciousness-raising group had made me curious about feminist scholarly writing and I saw the study of the romance as a way to engage with this literature. Thus I hoped to bring together my feminist 'personal' life with my supposedly non-gendered academic work which, until that point, had not focussed on women. This decision set in motion a slow, imperfect, often painful process of transformation which only really gathered impetus in the actual writing of *Reading the Romance* some six to seven years later, when the difficulties of accounting for the complexities of actual romance reading produced a more intense and personal engagement with feminist theory and its analysis of women's situation. That engagement was fostered by the romance readers' eloquence about their own lives. Even as I began to see myself in their accounts of themselves and thus to admit my identification with them, feminist writers helped me to analyze women's situation and to begin to trace its various determinants. Thus, another of the major surprises produced by doing ethnographic work was my own growing politicization. This politicization had not proceeded very far, however, at the time I began writing, and that fact, along with my preoccupation with the methodological questions about how to conduct the cultural study of literature, caused me to misread earlier feminist work on the romance resulting in a blindness to the continuity between my own arguments and those of scholars such as Tania Modleski and Ann Barr Snitow.[14]

As a consequence, the way the study was formulated and carried out was largely a function of my first theoretical concerns, concerns that I formulated at the outset within the terms of literary critical debates. Since I was assuming from the start with reader theorist Stanley Fish that textual interpretations are constructed by interpretive communities using specific interpretive strategies, I sought to contrast the then-current interpretation of romances produced by trained literary critics with that produced by fans of the genre.[15] Thus, in going into the field, I still conceived of reading in a limited fashion *as interpretation* and saw the project largely as one focussing on the differential interpretation of texts. It was only when the Smithton women repeatedly answered my questions about the meaning of romances by talking about the meaning of romance *reading* as a social event in a familial context that the study began to intersect with work being carried on in Britain.

What is so striking to me now is the way in which the romance readers themselves and their articulation of their concerns pushed me into a consideration of many of the same issues then preoccupying Paul Willis, David Morley, Charlotte Brunsdon, Angela McRobbie, Dorothy Hobson and many others.[16] Indeed, it was the women readers' construction of the act of romance reading as a 'declaration of independence' that surprised me into the realization that the meaning of their media-use was multiply determined and internally contradictory and that to get at its complexity it would be helpful to distinguish analytically between the significance of the *event* of reading and the meaning of the *text* constructed as its consequence. Although I did not then formulate it in so many words, this notion of the event of reading directed me towards a series of questions about the uses 'to which a particular text is put, its function within a particular conjuncture, in particular institutional spaces, and in relation to particular audiences'.[17] What the book gradually became, then, was less an account of the way romances as texts were interpreted than of the way romance reading as a form of behaviour operated as a complex intervention in the ongoing social life of actual social subjects, women who saw themselves first as wives and mothers.

As a consequence, *Reading the Romance* bears striking similarities to Dorothy Hobson's *Crossroads*, to the work on the TV programme 'Nationwide' by David Morley and Charlotte Brunsdon, and to Angela McRobbie's work on the culture of working-class girls. Although the central problematic of the book is not formulated in the languages they employ, nor is their work cited specifically, *Reading the Romance* shares their preoccupation with questions about the degree of freedom audiences demonstrated in their interaction with media messages and their interest in the way such cultural forms are embedded in the social life of their users. The theoretical position taken up in the book is quite close to Dorothy Hobson's conclusion that 'there is no overall intrinsic message or meaning in the work', and that 'it comes alive and communicates when the viewers add their own interpretation and understanding to the programme'.[18] Indeed, because I agreed at the outset with Stanley Fish's claim that textual features are not an essential structure upon which an interpretation is hung but rather produced *through* the interpretive process, I think the theoretical position of *Reading the Romance* is also close to Hobson's additional observation that 'there can be as many interpretations of a programme [or text] as the individual viewers bring to it'.[19] However, the book argues additionally that whatever the theoretical possibility of an infinite number of readings, in fact, there are patterns or regularities to what viewers and readers bring to texts and media messages in large part because they acquire specific cultural competencies as a consequence of their particular social location. Similar readings are produced, I argue, because similarly located readers learn a similar set of reading strategies and interpretive codes which they bring to bear upon the texts they encounter.

Reading the Romance turns to Fish's notion of 'interpretive communities' to theorize these regularities and then attempts to determine whether the Smithton women operate on romances as an interpretive community that is somehow different from the community of trained literary scholars. However, because Fish developed the notion of the interpretive community only to account for varying modes of literary criticism within the academy, that is, to account for the differing interpretations produced by Freudian, Jungian, mythic, or Marxist critics, the concept is insufficiently theorized to deal with the complexities of social groups or to explain how, when, and why they are constituted precisely *as* interpretive communities. Thus it cannot do justice to the nature of the connection between social location and the complex process of interpretation. It is inadequate finally to the task of explaining determination.

The question of determination and regularities became immediately relevant to the research, however, because the group I examined was relatively homogeneous. Not only did the women give remarkably similar answers to my questions about romances, but they referred constantly and *voluntarily* to the connection between their reading and their daily social situation as wives and mothers. I thus theorized the correlation between their patterned answers and their similar social location by resorting to the explanatory constructs of feminist theory, to the notion of 'patriarchal marriage' in particular. Not only have I used the concept to account for the social situation within which their reading occurs and thus employed it to make sense of their reading as an intervention within that situation, but I have also projected it back in time as a social form and, with the help of the psychoanalytic theories of Nancy Chodorow, used it to explain the construction of desire responsible for their location and their partial dissatisfaction with it, which itself leads ultimately to repetitive romance reading.

While I now feel this reification of patriarchal marriage was helpful in generating detailed knowledge about the ways in which romances engage these women, I also think it permitted me to avoid certain crucial theoretical questions about the precise mechanisms of determination. Had I designed the study comparatively, perhaps some of the issues David Morley has raised in his critical postscript to *The 'Nationwide' Audience* might have come more prominently to the fore.[20] He points there in particular to the inadequacies he sees in his own earlier discussion of the determinations upon meaning produced by the effectivity of the traditional sociological/structural variables—age, sex, race and class. Many of the problems Morley identifies in his work with respect to this problem are also present in mine. Whereas he notes his excessive concentration on the single variable of class and the rather simple way in which the concept itself was constructed, so I might point in my own study to the exclusive preoccupation with gender and to the use of a rather rigid notion of patriarchy. Indeed I would now want to organize an ethnography of romance reading comparatively in order to make some effort to ascertain how other sociological variables like age, class, location, education and race intersect with gender to produce varying, even conflicting engagements with the romance form. It might also be interesting to study similarly situated women who are non-romance readers in an effort to locate the absence (or perhaps the addition) of certain discursive competencies which render the romance incomprehensible, uninteresting, or irrelevant.

Whatever the sociological weaknesses of *Reading the Romance*, I continue to feel that the particular method (or aggregate of methods) employed there to map the complexities of the romance's 'purchase' on this small group of women can serve as a starting point for further discussion and perhaps for future analysis. I think this true, in part, because the understanding of reading that is worked out in the course of the discussion is close to the very useful generic or discursive model Morley has recommended in place of the earlier encoding–decoding formulation. I don't mean simply to imply here that *Reading the Romance* does what Morley calls for, although there are some striking similarities between what he recommends and the set of procedures the Smithton women's observations eventually pushed me toward. Rather, I want to suggest that his thoughful comments in the postscript can usefully be employed to identify some of the other insufficiently theorized steps in my own analysis and thus might be used to extend and improve it.

Having identified what he takes to be the principal sociological problems with his earlier work on the 'Nationwide' audience, Morley suggests that audience research might be more successful if it turned to a genre-based theory of interpretation and interaction instead of to a simple encoding–decoding model. Such a theory, he observes, might more adequately theorize the process of reading as a complex and interrelated series of actions which involves questions of relevance/irrelevance and comprehension/incomprehension in addition to that of ideological agreement. A theory in which genre is conceived as a set of rules for the production of meaning, operable both through writing and reading, might therefore be able to explain why certain sets of texts are especially interesting to particular groups of people (and not to others) because it would direct one's attention to the question of how and where a given set of generic rules had been created, learned, and used. This genre framework would focus attention on interdiscursive formations, that is, on questions about the kinds of cultural competencies that are learned as a consequence of certain social formations and how those are activated and perpetuated within and through multiple, related genres or discourses. Thus, just as one might want to ask what sorts of social grammars prepare working-class kids to understand Kung-fu movies and to find them interesting, so one might also want to ask what competencies prepare certain women to recognize romances as relevant to their experience and as potential routes to pleasure.

Although *Reading the Romance* does not use Morley's terms, it does work toward a kind of genre theory as he conceives it. To begin with, it attempts to understand how the Smithton women's social and material situation prepares them to find the act of reading attractive and even necessary. Secondly, through detailed questioning of the women about their own definition of romance and their criteria for distinguishing between ideal and failed versions of the genre, the study attempts to characterize the structure of the particular narrative the women have chosen to engage because they find it especially enjoyable. Finally, through its use of psychoanalytic theory, the book attempts to explain how and why such a structured 'story' might be experienced as pleasurable by those women as a consequence of their socialization within a particular family unit. I would like to elaborate briefly on each of these moments in *Reading the Romance* in order to prepare the reader for what she or he will find in the subsequent pages and point to issues which would repay further exploration.

Most of the first half of *Reading the Romance* is devoted to a discussion of the social and material situation within which romance reading occurs. Thus I initially survey the collection of social forces resulting in the mass production of romances in the 1970s and '80s, which are marketed in ways particularly appropriate to women, that is, through mail order and at commercial outlets largely frequented by them.[21] Although the move is analogous to Dorothy Hobson's detailed effort to explore the production of *Crossroads*, I have not gone so far as to investigate the professional ideologies informing the writing and editing of romances as she has done with the soap opera. The text does, however, recognize the importance of the romance writing community even to readers, because the Smithton women made it absolutely clear that they understood themselves to be reading particular and individual authors, whose special marks of style they could recount in detail, rather than identical, factory-produced commodities. Despite the mediations of the publishing industry, romance reading was seen by the women as a way of participating in a large, exclusively female community. Were I conducting this study today, I would want to compare the meaning and significance of the romance as it is inserted in the day-to-day existence of both writers and readers, for such a move might demonstrate the problems inherent in a simple reading off of cultural meaning or ideology from a single text.[22]

Turning from the particular processes impinging on production which create the conditions of possibility for regular romance purchases, *Reading the Romance* then attempts a parallel look at the conditions organizing women's private lives which likewise contribute to the possibility of regular romance reading. It is in this context that I distinguish analytically between the event of reading and the text encountered through the process. I found it necessary to do so, the reader will discover, because the Smithton women so insistently and articulately explained that their reading was a way of temporarily refusing the demands associated with their social role as wives and mothers. As they observed, it functioned as a 'declaration of independence', as a way of securing privacy while at the same time providing companionship and conversation. In effect, what chapters two and three try to do as a result is to unpack the significance of the phrase 'escape' by taking it somewhat more literally than have most analysts of the media in order to specify the origin and character of the distance the women find it necessary to maintain between their 'ordinary' lives and their fantasies.[23] I have therefore tried to take seriously the dual implications of the word escape, that is, its reference to conditions left behind and its intentional projection of a utopian future.

It is this move, I think, that specifically relates *Reading the Romance* to Hobson's 'Crossroads' work, to her work on housewives, and to McRobbie's work on the culture of working-class girls. Indeed there are remarkable similarities to the way all of the women who contributed to these studies use traditionally female forms to resist their situation *as women* by enabling them to cope with the features of the situation that oppress them. Thus, just as the adolescent girls studied by McRobbie manipulate the culture of femininity to 'combat the class-based and oppressive features of the school' and the housewives in Hobson's study rely on radio and TV to address their extreme loneliness, so the romance readers of Smithton use their books to erect a barrier between themselves and their families in order to declare themselves temporarily off-limits to those who would mine them for emotional support and material care. What the reader will find in chapter three, then, is an effort to explore the myriad ways in which the simple act of taking up a book addresses the personal costs hidden within the social role of wife and mother. I try to make a case for seeing romance reading as a form of individual resistance to a situation predicated on the assumption that it is women alone who are responsible for the care and emotional nurturance of others. Romance reading buys time and privacy for women even as it addresses the corollary consequence of their situation, the physical exhaustion and emotional depletion brought about by the fact that no one within the patriarchal family is charged with *their* care. Given the Smithton women's highly specific reference to such costs, I found it impossible to ignore their equally fervent insistence that romance reading creates a feeling of hope, provides emotional sustenance and produces a fully visceral sense of well-being.

It was the effort to account for the ability of romance reading to address the women's longing for emotional replenishment that subsequently direc-ted my attention to the cultural conditions that had prepared the women to choose romances from among all the other books available to them. Thus I found myself wondering how, given the particular 'needs' the event of reading seemed to address for the Smithton women, the romance story itself figured in this conjuncture. I began to wonder what it was about the romance heroine's experience that fostered the readers' ability to see her story as interesting and accounted for their willingness to seek their own pleasure through hers precisely at the moment when they were most directly confronting their dissatisfaction with traditionally struc-tured heterosexual relationships. What contribution did the narration of a romance make to their experience of pleasure? Why didn't the Smithton women choose to read detective stories, Westerns or bestsellers in their precious private moments?

In thus searching for a way to link a specific desire with a particularly chosen route to the fulfilment of that desire, I turned to psychoanalytic theory in general and to Nancy Chodorow's feminist revision of Freud in particular. Her work seemed relevant in this context because it insistently focussed on the precise manner in which the social fact of parenting by women constitutes a female child with an ongoing need for the style of care associated originally with her primary parent, that is, with her mother. What I was trying to explain was the fact that the Smithton women apparently felt an intense need to be nurtured and cared for and that despite their universal claim to being happily married (a claim I did not doubt), that need was not being met adequately in their day-to-day existence. Romance reading, it appeared, addressed needs, desires, and wishes that a male partner could not. Chodorow's work looked useful precisely because it theorized an asymmetrical engendering process constituting women and men in profoundly mismatched ways. That work appeared additionally relevant when an investigation of the romances the Smithton women like best revealed that the heroines they most appreciated were virtually always provided with the kind of attention and care the Smithton women claimed to desire and further that the hero's ministrations were nearly always linked metaphorically with maternal concern and nurturance. Thus I found Chodorow's theories attractive because they could account for the ongoing search for the *mother* that I detected in the Smithton women's discussion of the act of romance reading and in their preferences for particular examples of the genre.

Chodorow's revision of the psychoanalytic account of the family romance was interesting to me, in other words, because it postulated in women an ongoing, unfulfilled longing for the mother even after the oedipal turn to the father and heterosexuality had been negotiated. Although Chodorow's principal argument was that the tripartite internal object configuration with which women are therefore endowed is addressed by a woman's subsequent turn to mothering and to her child (an argument that might be taken to imply that the constructed desire for the preoedipal mother may be met through particular social arrangements), it seemed to me that what the Smithton readers were saying about romance reading indicated that in fact not even the activity of mothering could satisfy that lack or desire for the women, at least for some women.[24] I thought this might be true because so much of what the women consciously said and unconsciously revealed through their evaluative procedures pointed to the centrality of the fact that in ideal romances the hero is constructed androgynously. Although the women were clearly taken with his spectacularly masculine phallic power, in their voluntary comments and in their revealed preferences they emphasized equally that his capacity for tenderness and attentive concern was essential as well. Chodorow's theories seemed helpful because of their capacity to explain what I thought of as the twin objects of desire underlying romance reading, that is, the desire for the nurturance represented and promised by the preoedipal mother and for the power and autonomy associated with the oedipal father. Romance reading, it seemed to me, permitted the ritual retelling of the psychic process by which traditional heterosexuality was constructed for women, but it also seemed to exist as a protest against the fundamental inability of heterosexuality to satisfy the very desires with which it engendered women.[25]

Reading the Romance turns to Chodorow's revision of psychoanalytic theory in order to explain the construction of the particular desires that seem to be met by the *act* of romance reading. However, it additionally uses that theory to explore the psychological resonance of the romantic *narrative* itself for readers so constructed and engendered, a narrative which is itself precisely about the process by which female subjectivity is brought into being within the patriarchal family. Psychoanalysis is thus used also to explain why the story hails these readers, why they believe it possible to pursue their own pleasure by serving as witness to the romantic heroine's achievement of hers. What the psychoanalytically based interpretation reveals is the deep irony hidden in the fact that women who are experiencing the consequences of patriarchal marriage's failure to address their needs turn to a story which ritually recites the history of the process by which those needs are constituted. They do so, it appears, because the fantasy resolution of the tale ensures the heroine's achievement of the very pleasure the readers endlessly long for. In thus reading the story of a woman who is granted adult autonomy, a secure social position, and the completion produced by maternal nurturance, all in the person of the romantic hero, the Smithton women are repetitively asserting to be true what their still-unfulfilled desire demonstrates to be false, that is, that heterosexuality can create a fully coherent, fully satisfied, female subjectivity.[26]

In the end, *Reading the Romance* argues that romance reading is a profoundly conflicted activity centred upon a profoundly conflicted form. Thus the view of the romance developed here is similar to Valerie Walkerdine's account of girls' comics as a practice that channels psychic conflicts and contradictions in particular ways. It is also close to the view developed by Valerie Hey[27] as well as to that of Alison Light, who argues in her conclusion to her analysis of Daphne du Maurier's *Rebecca* that women's romance reading is 'as much a measure of their deep dissatisfaction with heterosexual options as of any desire to be fully identified with the submissive versions of femininity the texts endorse. Romance imagines peace, security and ease precisely because there is dissension, insecurity and difficulty.'[28] Light herself points to the crucial question raised by these fundamental ambiguities surrounding and infusing the act of romance reading, that is, to the crucial question of the ultimate effects the fantasy resolution has on the women who seek it out again and again. Does the romance's endless rediscovery of the virtues of a passive female sexuality merely stitch the reader ever more resolutely into the fabric of patriarchal culture? Or, alternatively, does the satisfaction a reader derives from the act of reading itself, an act she chooses, often in explicit defiance of others' opposition, lead to a new sense of strength and independence? *Reading the Romance* ends without managing to resolve these questions, asserting that an adequate answer will come only with time and with careful investigation of the developmental trajectory of the lives of adult romance readers. However much I would like to resolve the issue here, once and forever, I continue to believe that such a resolution is theoretically impossible simply because the practices of reading and writing romance continue and their effects, even now, are not fully realized.

Recent critical work on the romance that focusses both on developments within the genre and within the changing profession of romance writing itself suggests that the recontainment of protest and the channelling of desire staged by the form have not been perfect enough to thwart all change. Indeed, Ann Jones has shown in an analysis of recent Mills & Boon romances that the genre has found it increasingly necessary to engage specifically with feminism.[29] She demonstrates that the contradictions within the genre have been intensified by a tendency to consolidate certain feminist agendas for women in the character of a working, independent heroine even while disparaging the women's movement itself, usually through the speeches of the hero. This 'conflict between feminism as emergent ideology and romance as a residual genre,' contends Jones, produces three kinds of contradiction, including narrative discontinuity, irreconcilable settings, and inconsistency in realist dialogue.

I have found similar contradictions in recent American romances and have been struck by the urgency, indeed, by the near hysteria, with which romance authors assert that the newly active, more insistent female sexuality displayed in the genre is still most adequately fulfilled in an intimate, monogamous relationship characterized by love and permanence. Endless assertions of this claim are necessary because many of the more sexually explicit romances in lines such as Candlelight Ecstasy, Silhouette Desire, and Harlequin Temptation come very close to validating female desire and even to locating its origins within the woman herself. Many of the books in these lines, in fact, contain explicit depictions of premarital sexual relationships between hero and heroine and acknowledge that the heroine desires the hero as much as he does her and that she derives pleasure from the encounter. Yet in every case, these romances refuse finally to unravel the connection between female sexual desire and monogamous marriage. The stories therefore close off the vista they open up by virtue of their greater willingness to foreground the sexual fantasy at the heart of the genre. The editorial guidelines concerning the treatment of sex in Harlequin Temptations are illuminating in this context:

> Because this series mirrors the lives of contemporary women, realistic descriptions of love scenes should be included, provided they are tastefully handled. Each book should sustain a high level of sexual tension throughout, balanced by a strong story line. Sensuous encounters should concentrate on passion and the emotional sensations aroused by kisses and caresses rather than the mechanics of sex. Of course, the couple have to be obviously in love, with emphasis put on all that being in love entails. They should definitely consummate their relationship before the end of the story, at whatever point fits naturally into the plot. The love scenes may be frequent, but not overwhelming, and should never be gratuitously included.

It seems clear that while the sexually explicit romance of the '80s may begin positively to valourize female sexuality and thus to question the equation of femininity with virtue and virginity, it must nevertheless continue to motivate sexual activity through love. It does so by retaining the notion of passion as the natural and inevitable expression of a prior *emotional* attachment, itself dependent on a natural, biologically based sexual difference. Thus, as Jones has suggested, 'critiques of the double standard are now admissible; the notion that sexuality is socially constructed, variable, re-inventable rather than instinctive is not.'[30] Consequently, even the most progressive of recent romances continue to bind female desire to a heterosexuality constructed as the only natural sexual alliance, and thus continue to prescribe patriarchal marriage as the ultimate route to the realization of a mature female subjectivity.

The recuperation is clearly important, but again I feel that we must not allow it to blind us to the fact that the romance *is* being changed and struggled over by the women who write it. Indeed it is essential to note that in response to the creation of these sexually explicit romances, publishers have found it necessary to retain the more traditional 'sweet' romance and to create other new forms such as the 'evangelical', or 'inspirational' romance as it is called, for women who still cannot incorporate a more explicit sexuality into the ideology of love. Thus while some romance writers are perfectly willing to identify themselves as feminists, as Catherine Kirkland has found in her study of a local chapter of the Romance Writers of America, others vociferously assert that the romance is in fact the proper response to the havoc wrought by feminism on gender relations.[31] Furthermore, it cannot be said with any certainty whether the writers who are trying to incorporate feminist demands into the genre have been moved to do so by their recognition of the contradictions within the form itself or by the pressures exerted by developments in the larger culture. What does seem clear, however, is that the struggle over the romance is itself part of the larger struggle for the right to define and to control female sexuality. Thus, it matters enormously what the cumulative effects of the act of romance reading are on actual readers. Unfortunately, those effects are extraordinarily difficult to trace.

That the problem might be even more complicated than we think is suggested by Kirkland's discovery that most of the women in the group of romance writers she studied had been avid readers *before* they tried their hand at romance writing. Some of those women suggested that they turned to writing in order to intensify the fantasy experience they associated with the act of romance reading. Others, however, did so out of newfound confidence, which they attributed to romance reading, and which led to a desire to provide pleasure for other women. Romance reading, it would seem, profoundly changes at least some women by moving them to act and to speak in a public forum. Prompted to purchase their own word processor, to convert the former sewing-room into a study, and to demand time, not now for pleasure but for their own work, such women clearly begin to challenge in a fundamental way the balance of power in the traditional family. Of course this does not happen to all romance readers, but we should not discount it as an insignificant phenomenon since the crossover rate from consumer to producer seems to be unusually high within this genre. Indeed the romance boom could not continue to the extent it has were not thousands of women producing their own manuscripts and mailing them off regularly to Harlequin, Silhouette and Candlelight. Whether the satisfaction they derive from this activity ever prompts them to demand changes outside the privatized family environment is impossible to say but I am not willing to rule out the possibility. Indeed positive political strategies might be developed from the recognition that the practices of romance writing and reading continue, that they are fluid and actively being changed by both writers and readers, and that their final effects can neither be foreseen nor guaranteed in advance.

Such open-endedness, of course, immediately raises questions about specific modes of intervention, about how romance writers and readers, as well as feminist intellectuals, might contribute to the rewriting of the romance in an effort to articulate its founding fantasy to a more relevant politics. However, as many feminist theorists have acknowledged, to call for such a project from within the privileged space of the academy is highly problematic, since that call is almost inevitably grounded on a residual elitism which assumes that feminist intellectuals alone know what is best for all women. In this context, Angela McRobbie's admonition that academic feminists tend to 'underestimate the resources and capacities of "ordinary" women and girls . . . to participate in their own struggles as women but quite autonomously' is well taken.[32] What is needed, I have come to feel, is a recognition that romance writers and readers are themselves struggling with gender definitions and sexual politics *on their own terms* and that what they may need most from those of us struggling in other arenas is our support rather than our criticism or direction. To find a way to provide such support, however, or alternatively to learn from romance writers and readers is not easy for we lack the space and channels for integrating our practices with theirs. Our segregation by class, occupation, and race, once again, works against us.

I am drawn finally to McRobbie's brilliant suggestion that it might be our traditional restriction to the arena of personal relations and our resultant penchant for talk about them that will enable us to come together as women and to explore both our common cause and our divergent agendas.[33] What we perhaps need most, then, is a place and a vocabulary with which to carry on a conversation about the meaning of such personal relations and the seemingly endless renewal of their primacy through the genre of romance. If we could begin to talk to each other from within our culture's 'pink ghetto', we might indeed learn how 'to make talk walk'.[34] We might learn how to activate the critical power that even now lies buried in the romance as one of the few widely shared womanly commentaries on the contradictions and costs of patriarchy.

Notes

1 Although I am still somewhat uncomfortable with the voice I have adopted here, in part because I fear this sort of discussion can be read as simple personal display, I have finally decided to use it because I agree with Angela McRobbie's argument in 'The Politics of Feminist Research,' *Feminist Review* 12 (1982) that we must begin to acknowledge the ways in which our private, professional and intellectual lives intersect. Thus what I have tried to do is to indicate the ways in which my personal situation and insertion into already existing social institutions and theoretical conversations both served

as the conditions of possibility for *Reading the Romance* and structured its limitations.

2 See, for instance, Sandra Gilbert's review in the *New York Times Book Review* 30 December (1984).

3 For a comprehensive history of these debates, see Gene Wise, 'Paradigm dramas,' *American Quarterly* 31 (1979), pp. 293–337.

4 See, for instance, Murray Murphey, 'American civilization at Pennsylvania,' *American Quarterly* 22 (Summer, 1970), pp. 489–502.

5 See, for instance, *The Unembarrassed Muse: The Popular Arts in America*, New York: The Dial Press, 1970.

6 Stuart Hall, 'Cultural studies and the centre: some problematics and problems,' in *Culture, Media, Language: Working Papers in Cultural Studies, 1972–79*, London: Hutchinson, p. 19. See also his 'Cultural studies: two paradigms,' *Media, Culture and Society* 2 (1980), pp. 52–72.

7 Apparently, no one in my department knew at that time of the work carried out at the Birmingham Centre. I also remained unaware of this research until after I had completed *Reading the Romance*. I cannot now recall exactly how I learned of British ethnographic studies of media use but I would like to express my great gratitude to Patrick Hagopian and Elaine Collins who directed my attention to many references, xeroxed chapters and articles in their possession not easily available in Philadelphia, and discussed all of it with me. Thanks also to Larry Grossberg for his more recent bibliographic help, criticism, and support.

8 I am thinking here of Paul Willis's early work, including his 'Notes on method' in *Culture, Media, Language* and his *Profane Culture* as well as of the work by the Women's Studies Group at Birmingham collected in *Women Take Issue: Aspects of Women's Subordination*, London: Hutchinson, 1978.

9 For a perceptive discussion of the dangers inherent in conceptualizing empirical work as objectively scientific and interpretive work as subjectively humanist and therefore as categorical opposites, see Lawrence Grossberg, 'Critical theory and the politics of research,' *Mass Communication Yearbook* 6 (Forthcoming).

10 Paul Willis, 'Notes on method,' p. 90.

11 Angela McRobbie, 'The politics of feminist research,' p. 51.

12 See Palmer's *Thrillers: Genesis and Structure of a Popular Genre*, London: Edward Arnold, 1978; Terry Eagleton, *Criticism and Ideology: A Study in Marxist Literary Theory*, London: NLB, 1976.

13 *A Phenomenological Theory of Popular and Elite Literature*, Ph.D. Dissertation, Michigan State University, 1977.

14 See, for instance, my comments throughout the introduction to the American edition. However, I should not minimize the fact that significant differences in method and political perspective, particularly with respect to the audience for mass culture, continue to separate my approach and that taken by Modleski. See, for instance, her introduction to the recent *Studies in Entertainment: Critical Approaches to Mass Culture*, Bloomington: University of Indiana, 1986, pp. ix–xix, where she specifically takes issue with the work of the 'Birmingham School' and related approaches to the study of mass culture and charges that work with being celebratory rather than critical.

15 See his *Is There a Text in This Class?: The Authority of Interpretive Communities*, Cambridge, Mass.: Harvard University Press, 1980.

16 See the aforementioned titles by Willis and David Morley and Charlotte Brundson, *Everyday Television: 'Nationwide'*, London: British Film Institute (1978), David Morley, *The 'Nationwide' Audience*, London: British Film Institute (1980), Angela McRobbie, 'Working class girls and the culture of femininity,' in

Women Take Issue, 96–108; 'Settling accounts with subcultures: a feminist Critique,' *Screen* 34 (Spring, 1980), 39–49; and '*Jackie*: an ideology of adolescent femininity,' in *Popular Culture Past and Present*, ed. Bernard Waites *et al.*, London (1982), 263–83; Dorothy Hobson, 'Housewives: isolation as oppression,' in *Women Take Issue*, pp. 79–95; and '*Crossroads': The Drama of a Soap Opera*, London: Methuen (1982).

17 David Morley, *The 'Nationwide' Audience*, p. 18.

18 Dorothy Hobson, *Crossroads*, p. 170.

19 *Ibid*.

20 David Morley, 'The "Nationwide" Audience—A Critical Postscript,' *Screen Education* 39 (Summer, 1981), 3–14.

21 I should perhaps note here that this boom was initiated in the USA by the Canadian firm of Harlequin Enterprises, which began its rise to prominence in mass market publishing by reprinting the romances of Mills & Boon in the 1950s and 1960s. The genre took off in the USA when Harlequin began to issue romance written by American women and when other firms simultaneously introduced explicit sex into the genre. The Smithton women did not confine themselves to a single kind of romance but read widely in the genre and appreciated many different variations.

22 On this point, see Grossberg's discussion in 'Critical theory and the politics of research,' *Mass Communications Yearbook* 6 (Forthcoming, 1987).

23 The tendency to deplore the 'escapist' nature of popular fantasy seems much less pronounced in British work than in American. See, for instance, Valerie Walkerdine's sensitive discussion of the nature of fantasy escape for girls in 'Some day my prince will come: young girls and the preparation for adolescent sexuality,' in Angela McRobbie and Mica Nava (eds.), *Gender and Generation*, London: Macmillan (1984), pp. 162–84.

24 The British reader will no doubt note that this did not lead me to reconsider Chodorow's work and its relation to object-relations theory. Walkerdine's comments in 'Some Day My Prince Will Come' (pp. 178–81) have since suggested to me that the revision romance reading caused me to propose in Chodorow's theory may be of more significance than I had thought. It may not be the case that mothering fails to work only for some (aberrant) women, but in fact that the struggle over gender identity is never resolved as she suggests, following Freud, Lacan, and Rose.

25 For a somewhat different use of Chodorow that also connects romance reading to the search for pre-oedipal merging, see Angela Mile's fascinating unpublished article, 'Confessions of a Harlequin reader: romance and the fantasy of male mothering.'

26 Cora Kaplan has recently advanced an argument which suggests that readers do not identify only with the romantic heroine but in fact identify in multiple and wandering fashion with the seducer, the seduced and the process of seduction itself. See '*The Thorn Birds*: Fiction, Fantasy, Femininity,' in *Sea Changes: Feminism and Culture* (London: Verso, 1986), pp. 117–46. Although I found little evidence of this kind of multiple identification in the group I interviewed (at least at a conscious level), I have been told by many romance writers that the act of writing a romance is especially enjoyable because it gives them the opportunity to imagine themselves as the hero. It is also interesting to note that several American publishers of romances have recently permitted writers to experiment with the writing of a romance entirely from the hero's point of view. Thus, it might be possible that this sort of multiple identification actually varies from reader to reader and therefore can be increased by cultural or personal changes.

27 Valerie Hey, 'The necessity of romance,' University of Kent at Canterbury, Women's Studies Occasional Papers, no. 3, 1983.

28 Alison Light, ' "*Returning to Manderley*"—romance fiction, female sexuality and class,' *Feminist Review* 16 (April, 1984), pp. 7–25.

29 Ann Rosalind Jones, 'Mills & Boon Meets Feminism,' in Jean Radford (ed.), *The Progress of Romance: The Politics of Popular Fiction*, London: Routledge & Kegan Paul (1986), pp. 195–220.

30 Ann Jones, 'Mills & Boon Meets Feminism,' p. 210.

31 Catherine Kirkland, *For the Love of It: Women Writers and the Popular Romance*, Ph.D. diss., University of Pennsylvania, 1984.

32 Angela McRobbie, 'The Politics of Feminist Research,' p. 53.

33 Angela McRobbie, 'The Politics of Research,' p. 57.

34 The phrases are Catherine Kirkland's and Angela McRobbie's respectively.

8

Cultural studies at the crossroads

Graham Murdock

From *Australian Journal of Communication*, no. 16 (December 1989).

Abstract

This paper argues that if cultural studies is to maintain its intellectual vitality and its relevance to contemporary conditions and political debates, it needs to broaden its core concerns and establish new points of connection with work at the cutting edge of the social sciences.

Conceptual and methodological issues addressed include problems with ethnographic methodology; the commercial populism of the New Conservatism; the rejection of the 'dominant ideology' thesis and the development of 'critical pluralism'; the 'condition of England question' and the shifting relation between national, sub-national, and supranational cultural formations in the 1990s; and the need to integrate a critical political economy approach with the academic analyses of discourse.

Introduction

It is a truism, but nonetheless true, that what you see depends on where you stand and which direction you look in. My own view of the present state of cultural studies and its prospects is inevitably coloured by my experience of ten years of Thatcherism and of the ways in which it has reshaped the intellectual and political agenda in Britain. [. . .]

A set of broadly shared question marks is now beginning to form over the future of cultural studies, prompted by a general recognition that a crossroads has been reached and that it's time to take a long hard look at our central projects and preoccupations, at our dominant conceptualizations and preferred methodologies, and at the interventions we wish to make.

You don't have to subscribe to the more apocalyptic visions of postmodern theory to accept that the 1990s will be a decade of substantial realignment and change at the economic, political, and cultural levels both within nation states and within the world system as a whole. If cultural studies is going to have something distinctive and worthwhile to say about these shifts we will need to examine the intellectual baggage that we carry around with us and decide what to keep and what to throw away. To do this, we have to backtrack a little, and re-examine the projects, procedures, and politics which have shaped our practice up until now. I shall confine my remarks to work in Britain, not because I believe it is in any way privileged or paradigmatic, but because it highlights the conceptual and methodological issues we have to address particularly clearly.

British cultural studies' three projects

Cultural Studies in Britain developed in reaction to the dominant definition of 'culture' bequeathed by the conservative tradition of cultural criticism, and challenged it at two basic levels.

In opposition to the identification of 'culture' with a particular selection of canonized texts and legitimized practices, it reasserted the anthropological conception of culture as all the ways in which people make sense of their situation and express these understandings. It was therefore as interested in the 'lived texts' of social rituals and social institutions as in artefacts. Where cultural criticism saw only an absence of 'culture' within the working class, cultural studies set out to uncover the variety and vitality of situated practices and beliefs, and to demonstrate their authentic roots in popular experience.

At the same time, it was clear that resources for meaning construction were not generated entirely within particular situations. Key elements were provided by the products promoted by the commercial cultural industries, by the discourses of state agencies and political parties, and by the paternalistic rhetorics of the public institutions such as schools, museums, and public broadcasting, which actively promoted the 'selective tradition'. Consequently, Cultural Studies' second major project was to show how these top-down initiatives worked ideologically to mobilize popular understanding and practice in the service of the asymmetric power relations between producers and consumers, government and citizens, and intellectuals and publics.

These two projects converged to produce a third, which was expressly concerned with the interplay between situated cultures and ideological formations, and particularly with the ways in which the first provides resources for negotiating, refusing, and resisting the second.

There are a range of problems with each of these strands, but in the space available here I want to concentrate on the issues that seem to me to be the most pressing as we enter the 1990s.

Everyday culture and popular creativity

Cultural Studies' concerns with the active audience for commercially provided culture and the dialectical relations between concrete experience and mediated meaning have been elaborated in a wide range of studies, from

Richard Hoggart's portrait of working-class culture between the Wars, through the successive waves of research on youth subcultures, popular decodings of televisual texts and women's pleasure, to the current vogue for studies of domestic consumption. Each of these literatures deserves detailed discussion, but for the moment I want to underline some basic problems with this whole tradition of work. The first has to do with the methods of inquiry employed.

Although Central Studies has taken over cultural anthropology's central focus on the making and taking of meaning in everyday life, it has not used properly ethnographic methods. There are some exceptions, most notably Paul Willis, but, by and large, empirical evidence has been gathered through casual observation, one-off interviews, and single group discussions. This produces 'thin' rather than 'thick' descriptions (Geertz, 1973), and means that interpretations are insufficiently contextualized.

This problem is particularly acute in instances such as Dick Hebdige's (1979) reading of youth subcultural styles, where the interpretations on offer are detached almost completely from the situational dynamics being analysed and from the self-understandings of participants. As a reading of 'lived texts' it has great elegance and panache, but as an account of how working-class youth subcultures actually developed and what they meant to their supporters, it contains a number of errors and misunderstandings that better ethnography could have avoided (see Hobbs, 1989, Chapter 6).

Even where direct evidence is available, as in Dorothy Hobson's work on housewives watching soap operas or David Morley's research on decoding, insufficient knowledge about the life situation and beliefs of the subjects often forces the analyses to explain particular readings by resorting to the general structural categories of class, gender, and ethnicity. To avoid this and generate more complex accounts of the social bases of everyday cultural activity we need not only better ethnographies but also bridging concepts that can link situations and formations, practices, and structures. [. . .] As I have argued elsewhere (Murdock, 1989a), Pierre Bourdieu's work provides a more productive starting point for this enterprise than de Certeau's currently fashionable writings. Whereas de Certeau focusses on the ways in which the 'procedures and ruses of consumers compose the network of an antidiscipline' (de Certeau, 1988, p. xv), Bourdieu underscores the inertia exerted by the prevailing structures of economic and symbolic capital and the ways they penetrate and organize everyday practice by regulating access to the competencies required for particular forms of consumption (Bourdieu, 1977, 1984).

From romanticism to populism

De Certeau's voluntaristic formulation reinforces the romanticism that has underpinned a good deal of work in Cultural Studies up until now. This stance has fuelled a continual search for signs of popular resistance against the regularities, routines, and ideologies of industrial capitalism. John Fiske, for example, is in no doubt at all that 'The culture of everyday life is best described through metaphors of struggle or antagonism: strategies opposed to tactics, the bourgeoisie by the proletariat; hegemony met by resistance, ideology countered or evaded; top-town power opposed by bottom-up power, social discipline faced with disorder' (Fiske, 1989, p. 47). There are several problems with this preference for refusal. Firstly, as Stanley Cohen has noted in relation to studies of youth subcultures, 'the constant impulse to decode only in terms of opposition and resistance means that instances are sometimes missed' when interpretations and practices are 'taken over intact from dominant commercial culture' (Cohen, 1980, p. xii). Secondly, and more importantly, the romantic celebration of consumer activity can easily support a stance which colludes (however unwittingly) with the commercial populism of the New Conservatism.

This is the case with John Fiske's view that because successful pro- grammes like 'Dallas' have to connect with the lives and values of a variety of social groups to retain a mass audience, there is no need to press for a production system committed to defending and extending programme diversity. Indeed, in his view, 'diversity of readings may best be stimulated by a greater homogeneity of programming' (Fiske, 1987, p. 319). This argument is fundamentally mistaken. Whilst it is self-evidently the case that prime-time programming has to provide multiple points of pleasure for a socially differentiated audience, the formats it employs clearly operate to regulate the range of discourses and presentations called into play in important ways, preferring some whilst marginalizing or excluding others. As a consequence there are identities, experiences, and forms of knowledge which are consistently pushed to or off the edge of the schedules. To argue otherwise is to accept commercial television's claim that it gives people what they want and need, and to undermine the case for new forms of public broadcasting that can address the full range of contemporary cultures. If John Fiske had been sitting in 10 Downing Street when the relevant legislation was going through Parliament, Britain would never have launched Channel 4 with its statutory obligation to extend programme diversity, and the country would have missed the most significant attempt to engage with cultural plurality to date.

The view of audience members as first and foremost active consumers also helps to reinforce the new conservatives' promotion of the market- place as the fundamental sphere of liberty and of the freedom to choose between competing products as the core of individual rights. This con- ception operates to displace the alternative view of audience members as citizens with other entitlements, including rights of access to the full range of information, argument, and interpretation they need in order to understand their situation and to intervene to change it if they so choose. (See Murdock and Golding, 1989.) The question of citizenship—its nature and future—is set to become one of the key issues of the 1990s. If Cultural Studies is to make an effective intervention in this debate, it needs to recover its commitment to 'a more dense and participatory culture (and) not merely endorse the goals of greater individual freedom to choose' between cultural commodities and to develop counter interpretations and uses (Rustin, 1989, p. 68).

This involves a move away from the expressive individualism of some recent work on audiences back towards a more thorough engagement with the ways that meanings and identities are negotiated socially, and with the way that these grounded processes are structured by wider economic and ideological formations.

Critical pluralism and the contest of discourse

Recent work on ideology has been marked by a decisive and irreversible rejection of the 'dominant ideology' thesis in all its forms, and the development of what we can call 'critical pluralism'. This new perspective views the cultural field as the site of a continual struggle between competing discourses, each offering a particular way of looking at or speaking about the social world (or particular segments of it), and engaged in a contest for visibility and legitimacy across a range of social institutions. Whilst it accepts the pluralist stress on competition, it retains critical theory's insistence on the unequal nature of discursive struggles arising from the fact that some discourses are backed by greater material resources and have preferential access to the major means of publicity and policy-making. Consequently, to talk about the cultural field is 'to speak of a field of relations structured by power and difference' in which some discourses are more central and dominant than others, but where these 'positions are never permanently fixed' (Hall, 1989, p. 51). In a number of late capitalist societies, the commercial speech of the consumer system and the discourses of neo-conservatism enjoy a number of advantages. However, their command of popular consciousness cannot be guaranteed simply by their present ubiquity and centrality; it has to be constantly worked and struggled for.

Their success will largely depend on their ability to 'articulate' common sense, in the double sense of linking its separate and contradictory elements together in a functioning whole (in the same way that an articulated lorry is made up of a cab and a trailer that can be uncoupled), and of finding forms of rhetoric and signification that anchor this discursive formation convincingly in everyday experience (Grossberg, 1986, p. 53). Since the rise of Thatcherism provides a particularly rich instance of this process of 'articulation' in action, it has, not surprisingly, become a major focus of debate in Britain, and one in which Stuart Hall has played a leading role (see Hall and Jacques, 1983; Hall, 1988; Gamble, 1988). Underlying this discussion is an essentially simple question: how has Mrs Thatcher managed to get away with it?

Stuart Hall's work illustrates the strengths and weaknesses of approaching this question from within a cultural studies framework. The strengths are in the analysis of Thatcherism as a new discursive formation which combines the 'liberal discourses of the "free market" and economic man and the organic conservative themes of tradition, family, and nation, respectability, patriarchalism and order' (Hall, 1988, p. 2). The problems lie in the evaluation of its popular impact and Hall's relative lack of interest in the available evidence. Despite Thatcherism's acute orchestration of key themes in common-sense thinking, there is a good deal of evidence to suggest that it has been rather less successful in achieving hegemony in Hall's sense of the term (see Hall, 1988, p. 7) than his analysis would predict. Not only are Mrs Thatcher's electoral successes more plausibly explained as the outcome of pragmatic choices and the absence of a credible alternative government rather than as indications of popular support for Thatcherism (Hirst, 1989, Chapter 1), but recent research indicates that collectivist values have more than held their ground during the Thatcher years (Rentoul, 1989).

The rights and wrongs of these arguments, and their implications for political strategy, are mainly of interest to those of us living in Britain and hoping to see a change of government at the next General Election. But Hall's work on Thatcherism also points to another, deeper, problem with Cultural Studies as it is currently constituted. This has to do with its continuing fixation with the state of the nation.

Cultural studies and the condition of England

The British tradition of cultural criticism was always strongly linked to what came to be known as 'the condition of England question'. The question was this: how was it possible to construct a common culture in a situation where the uneven growth of industrial capitalism was creating deep class divisions and where organized religion was losing its always slim hold over the popular imagination. The conservative response was to embark on a general 'invention of tradition' (Hobsbawn and Ranger, 1983) designed to provide new symbols and rituals of nationhood that would bind the country together in an imagined community, strong enough to displace the solidarities of class, region, and locality. The construction of a selective cultural tradition which embodied the essential qualities of 'Englishness' in their 'highest' form was an integral part of this project (Dodd, 1986).

Although Cultural Studies expressly set out to deconstruct this formation of nation and people, it has inevitably ended up working within its general framework. Indeed, a good deal of work in British cultural studies can be read as a series of meditations on 'the condition of England' devoted to interrogating national ideologies and exploring the counter formations of class, and to a lesser extent region. As a consequence it has had little to say about the explosive growth of transnational culture. However, there is little doubt that questions about the shifting relation between national, sub-national, and supranational cultural formations will play a much more prominent role in the 1990s.

Coming to terms with the multinationals and multiculturalism

Interest in the transnational circulation of representations has grown over the last decade as a result of three main factors. Firstly, the spread of new communications technologies, particularly video cassette recorders and satellite television, has enabled the Hollywood studios, the major advertising agencies, and the multinational entrepreneurs of the moving image to get around many of the regulations governing national broadcasting and cinema systems and open up new markets for their products. Secondly, this process has been given an added boost in many countries by the enthusiasm for privatization policies (Murdock, 1989b). Thirdly, there is now considerable interest in exploring the cultural implications of groupings such as the European Community and the Pacific Rim.

The dynamics of globalization are of course more complex than the cruder characterizations of 'cultural imperialism' allow for. To argue that they impose alien cultures on indigenous peoples simply revives the 'dominant ideology' thesis. It is more productive to see them as changing the terms of existing struggles by introducing new discursive formations and new points of identity and pleasure and by facilitating new kinds of cultural practice. Understanding how these dynamics are worked through at the level of everyday life and how they impinge on the ideological strategies employed in nation building is one of the central tasks for cultural studies in the coming decade.

This does not mean abandoning studies of particular local conditions. On the contrary, if we are to avoid facile generalizations and comparisons we need the widest possible range of research on specific situations. At the same time, in an era when every country is locked into an emerging world cultural system, knowledge of how that system works provides an indispensable context for interpreting and explaining situated activity. We must learn how to think globally while acting locally, and put some energy into developing concepts and forms of writing which will explicate the links between knowable communities and larger systems (see Marcus and Fischer, 1986, Chapter 4).

One powerful experiential connection between national conditions and the world system operates through exile, migration, and resettlement. These movements have assumed particular significance in the post-colonial era and have made multiculturalism a key issue for a growing number of societies, including Britain.

Within cultural studies writings Britain's black population has frequently been celebrated as a source of white style or empathized with as victims of racism, but until comparatively recently their own cultural strategies remained mostly uncharted. Consequently, black students coming to the area often experienced its analyses of the national condition as a 'morbid celebration of England and Englishness from which blacks (were) systematically excluded' (Gilroy, 1987, p. 12). This situation has now changed as a new generation of black British intellectuals has begun to speak from within black British experience and to interrogate the cultural legacy of empire from the other end of the colonial chain. Even so, the issues posed by Britain's transition to a multicultural society remain inadequately theorized and only partially integrated into cultural studies' core projects. Nor is this simply a British problem.

Although it expressly sets out to challenge the prevailing belief in 'a monolithic Australian culture' by revealing the 'richness and diversity' of the country's lived cultures, Fiske, Hodge and Turner's recent book, *Myths of Oz* (1987), offers no sustained analysis of the new ethnic communities and their complex relations to white Australia. Yet here, as elsewhere in the post-colonial world, questions of national culture and identity can no longer be adequately posed, let alone answered, without taking the dynamics of a multicultural formation fully into account.

Coming to terms with political economy

The other major problem with contemporary cultural studies is its continuing refusal to incorporate a critical political economy of culture. True, there have been some recent moves in this direction, but as recent writings on postmodernism show all too clearly, there is still some way to go before a theoretical synthesis is achieved. At the moment, work on the post modern condition falls into two broad categories. There is a burgeoning literature on the emergence of postmodernist forms of representation and aesthetics. There is also a growing volume of commentary on the transition from a Fordist economic regime to one organized around flexible accumulation, in which information and communication systems come to play a central role as factors of production. As yet, however, there have been few attempts to theorize the possible linkages between these two movements, and most of these have come from social scientists, rather than from cultural studies (e.g. Lash and Urry, 1987; Harvey, 1989).

The need for cultural studies to take the insights of critical political economy seriously is clearly signalled by the popularity of the notion of 'cultural industries' which is now to be found peppering the speeches and reports of politicians and policy-makers as well as academics. Its currency points to a growing awareness that the cultural industries are both similar to and different from other industries. On the one hand, they are clearly organized industrially in specifiable ways and are part of the general productive system. On the other hand, the goods they manufacture—the movies, ads, and TV shows—are unlike the products of other industries in that they play a pivotal role in organizing the images and discourses through which we make sense of the world. They do not simply make commodities; they make available the repertoire of meanings through which the social world, including the world of commodities, is understood and acted on. It is not enough simply to acknowledge this duality (see Fiske 1989, Chapter 2), we need to conceptualize the relations between the material and discursive organization of culture without reducing one to the other.

It is precisely this focus on the *interplay* between the symbolic and the economic which distinguishes a political economy approach from one ground solely in academic economics. Where economists are primarily interested in how the cultural industries work as part of the bounded domain of 'the economy', political economy is concerned to show how different ways of financing and organizing cultural production (and production in general) have traceable consequences for the range of discourses and representations in the public domain and their accessibility to audiences. Neo-conservatives see markets as the best guarantor of diverse production and consumer choice. Those like myself, in the critical camp, point to the distorting effects of inequalities in the distribution of wealth and income and argue for positive public intervention to underwrite plurality and public access.

In principle, many of those working in cultural studies accept the need for a critical political economy, but stop short of integrating its insights into their own analytical practice. Stuart Hall, for example, has recently argued that, although the structure of ownership and control is not 'a sufficient explanation of the way the ideological universe is structured, it is a *necessary starting point*' (Hall, 1986, p. 11). (My italics.) Yet in another recent piece, he castigates critical political economists for having 'no conception of the struggle for meaning' and dismisses their analyses as crude and reductionist (Hall, 1989, p. 50). This may be true of some variants (e.g. Herman and Chomsky, 1988, Chapter 1), but it is not a necessary consequence of pursuing critical political economy's core project. The sticking point is the vexed question of 'determination'.

Instead of persisting with Marx's original proposition that the economic determines 'in the last instance', with its implication that there is always a direct link between economic organization and cultural activity (however attenuated), we can adopt Stuart Hall's own very useful suggestion to think of the economic as determining in the 'first instance' (Hall, 1983). This immediately opens up the possibility of combining recent work in critical political economy with advances in the analyses of discourse. In my own recent work, for example, I have sought to argue firstly, that the changing economics of cultural production promotes certain cultural forms and practices at the expense of others (e.g. Murdock, 1989c), and secondly, that once in play, these cultural forms play a key role in organizing the contest of discourse on their own account by granting or withholding visibility and legitimacy (e.g. Schlesinger, Murdock and Elliott, 1983). A parallel argument that can be made for cultural consumption (see Murdock, 1989a).

Into the 1990s

I have argued that if cultural studies is to maintain its intellectual vitality and its relevance to contemporary conditions and political debates, it needs to broaden its core concerns and establish new points of connection with work at the cutting edge of the social sciences. There are a number of areas where social scientists are developing ideas which are directly relevant to cultural studies' main projects. Instances include sociological work on how the contest of discourses around key issues is organized (e.g. Hilgartner and Bosk, 1988; Gamson and Modigliani, 1989), and research in social psychology on the role of discourse and texts in the social constitution of identity (e.g. Shotter and Gergen, 1989). Cultural studies' relative isolation from these initiatives is one of the penalties of its emergence as a self-sustaining area of academic study with its own selective tradition of canonized texts. To counter this we need to recover the original interdisciplinary impetus and be more adventurous in crossing intellectual check-points.

We also need to restore cultural studies' commitment to making practical as well as academic interventions. This certainly involves arguing with policy makers and contributing to debates on the funding and organization of cultural activity, but it also means renewing and developing the dialogue with the subjects of our inquiries, through adult and continuing education, public speeches, journalism, and programme making. The barriers to this enterprise arise not only from the crisis of intellectual practice. [. . .] but also from the institutional crisis of the public sphere. If cultural studies is to contribute in a central way to the debates of the 1990s we will need to fight long and hard to defend and extend the spaces and resources that allow intellectual work and political debate to proceed independently of commercial pressures and the encroachments of state and government. If a decade of Thatcherism has taught us in Britain anything, it is this.

References

Bourdieu, P. (1977) *Outline of a Theory of Practice*, Cambridge: Cambridge University Press.

Bourdieu, P. (1984) *Distinction: A Social Critique of the Judgement of Taste*, London: Routledge & Kegan Paul.

Cohen, S. (1980) *Folk Devils and Moral Panics: The Creation of the Mods and Rockers*, Oxford: Martin Robertson.

de Certeau, M. (1988) *The Practice of Everyday Life*, Berkeley: University of California Press.

Dodd, P. (1986) 'Englishness and national culture' in R. Colls and P. Dodd (eds.), *Englishness: Politics and Culture 1880–1920*, Beckenham: Croom Helm Ltd.

Fiske, J. (1987) *Television Culture*, London: Methuen.

Fiske, J. (1989) *Understanding Popular Culture*, London: Unwin Hyman Ltd.

Fiske, J., Hodge, B. and Turner, G. (1987) *Myths of Oz: Reading Australian Popular Culture*, Sydney: Allen & Unwin.

Gamble, A. (1988) *The Free Economy and the Strong State: The Politics of Thatcherism*, London: Macmillan.

Gamson, V.A. and Modigliani, A. (1989) 'Media discourse and public opinion on nuclear power: a constructionist approach', *American Journal of Sociology*, vol. 95, no. 1, pp. 1–37.

Geertz, C. (1973) *The Interpretation of Cultures*, New York: Basic Books Inc.

Gilroy, P. (1987) *There Ain't No Black in the Union Jack: The Cultural Politics of Race and Nation*, London: Hutchinson.

Grossberg, L. (1986) 'On postmodernism and articulation: an interview with Stuart Hall', *Journal of Communication Inquiry*, vol. 10, no. 2, pp. 45–60.

Hall, S. (1983) 'The problem of ideology: Marxism without guarantees' in B. Matthews (ed.), *Marx: A Hundred Years On*, London: Lawrence & Wishart, pp. 57–85.

Hall, S. (1986) 'Media power and class power' in J. Curran et al. (eds.), *Bending Reality: The State of the Media*, London: Pluto Press, pp. 5–14.

Hall, S. (1988) *The Hard Road to Renewal: Thatcherism and the Crisis of the Left*, London: Verso.

Hall, S. (1989) 'Ideology and communication theory' in B. Dervin *et al.* (eds.), *Rethinking Communication, Volume One: Paradigm Issues*, London: Sage Publications, pp. 40–52.

Hall, S. and Jacques, K. (eds.), (1983) *The Politics of Thatcherism*, London: Lawrence & Wishart.

Harvey, D. (1989) *The Condition of Postmodernity*, Oxford: Basil Blackwell.

Hebdige, D. (1979) *Subculture: The Meaning of Style*, London: Methuen.

Herman, E. and Chomsky, N. (1988) *Manufacturing Consent: The Political Economy of the Mass Media*, New York: Pantheon.

Hilgartner, S. and Bosk, C.L. (1988) 'The rise and fall of social problems: a public arenas model', *American Journal of Sociology*, vol. 94, no. 1, pp. 53–78.

Hirst, P. (1989) *After Thatcher*, London: Collins.

Hobbs, D. (1988) *Doing the Business: Entrepreneurship, the Working Class, and Detectives in the East End of London*, Oxford: Oxford University Press.

Hobsbawn, E. and Ranger, T. (eds.), (1983) *The Invention of Tradition*, Cambridge: Cambridge University Press.

Lash, S. and Urry, J. (1987) *The End of Organised Capitalism*, Cambridge: Polity Press.

Marcus, G.E. and Fischer, M. (1986) *Anthropology as Cultural Critique: An Experimental Movement in the Human Sciences*, Chicago: University of Chicago Press.

Murdock, G. (1989a) 'Critical inquiry and activity', in B. Dervin *et al.* (eds.), *Rethinking Communication, Volume Two: Paradigm Exemplars*, London: Sage Publications, pp. 226–49.

Murdock, G. (1989b) 'Redrawing the map of the communications industries: Concentration and ownership in the era of privatisation' in M. Ferguson, *Public Communication: The New Imperatives*, London: Sage Publications (in press).

Murdock, G. (1989c) 'Televisual tourism: national image-making and international markets' in C.W. Thomsen (ed.), *Cultural Transfer or Electronic Imperialism?*, Heidelberg: Carl Winter Universitatsverlag, pp. 171–84.

Murdock, G. and Golding, P. (1989) 'Information poverty and political inequality: citizenship in the age of privatised communication', *Journal of Communication* (in press).

Rentoul, J. (1989) *Me and Mine: The Triumph of the New Individualism?*, London: Unwin Hyman.

Rustin, M. (1989) 'The politics of post-Fordism: or, the trouble with new times', *New Left Review*, no. 175, pp. 54–77.

Schlesinger, P., Murdock, G. and Elliott, P. (1983) *Televising 'Terrorism': Political Violence in Popular Culture*, London: Comedia.

Shotter, J. and Gergen, K.J. (1989) *The Texts of Identity*, London: Sage Publications.

Section II

Difference and identity

This section includes works which in a variety of ways explore questions of difference and identity, with a certain emphasis on lived culture, and begins significantly with **Phil Cohen**'s seminal study which marked out one of the major trajectories of British cultural studies, that of youth culture and consumption. Rooted concretely in the East End of London, Cohen's piece discusses the consequences of economic planning of the mid-sixties for its inhabitants in terms of fragmentation and breakdown of the extended family and kinship networks, isolation and lack of communal space; a socio-ecology in which Commonwealth immigrants were scapegoated by a disorganized working class. [See Cohen 1988 for his analysis of the complexities of class, race and youth (Baines and Cohen 1988).] Turning specifically to young white working-class males, Cohen argues that youth subcultures, in their various forms, were responses to an experienced tension between the conflicting ideologies of the period; those of spectacular consumption and production, or work ethic. Substantively and theoretically this was the precursor of much important work by Cohen himself (Robins and Cohen 1978; Cohen 1985 and 1990) but also that which is more readily identified with the Centre for Contemporary Cultural Studies (CCCS) at Birmingham (Jefferson et al. 1975; Willis 1977; Hebdige 1979), rather than Cohen's subsequent work. (See also Schwartz 1990 for a contemporary analysis of London's East End Docklands.)

If the early work of CCCS was preoccupied with the 'magical resolution' function of male youth subcultures, this formed the subject of strong feminist critique exemplified by the CCCS Women's Studies Group collection *Women Take Issue* published in 1978, but more specifically tackled by Angela McRobbie in 'Settling accounts with subcultures', in which she challenges the inherent masculinity of the studies of youth subculture then dominating the field, and by her concrete analysis of working-class girls and femininity (McRobbie 1978). (See also McRobbie 1980 and 1991.) The feminist intervention in cultural studies has led to some of the most interesting and productive work in the field (Stacey et al. 1991).

Erica Carter's interesting argument around young women and their relationship to consumerism and the market more generally owes much to that early feminist critique. She insists that the 'image industries' are acutely aware of gender difference which operates as a 'dominant variable for the construction of consumer groups', and takes the youth subcultural theorists to task for not recognizing this. She chooses to focus her study on the female consumer culture in post-war (West) Germany, and places youth studies in a broader, historical and national context.

The third piece indicates the second major challenge to British cultural studies in the 1980s; questions of 'race'. Here **Paul Gilroy** recovers the hidden history of African Caribbean music in the dance halls of Britain, and in particular shows how, through a series of exchanges and interactions, the politics of race have been lived out and transcended through popular musical forms, in the name of youth. (See also Centre for Contemporary Cultural Studies, 1982; Baines and Cohen 1988.)

Theoretically informed by the post-structuralist challenges to the unified subject and developments within psychoanalysis, questions of identity have become quite central in recent cultural studies work, and **Stuart Hall**'s second piece included here exemplifies the twin focus of this trajectory: a politics of difference and a politics of reflexivity. Hall insists, however, that 'Who I am—the "real" me'—was formed in relation to a whole set of other narratives. Identity for him is formed where subjectivity meets 'the narratives of history, of a culture'.

The 'Rushdie Affair' has, since 1989, brought a number of issues to the surface whilst provoking strange alliances amongst left, right and liberal intellectuals retaliating against the perceived unacceptable protests from the British Muslim community against the publication of *The Satanic Verses*. However, their most vociferous outrage was reserved for the *fatwa* of Ayatolla Khomeni, declared in 1989. Here **Bhikhu Parekh** looks closely at *The Satanic Verses* and seeks to understand both the authorial standpoint and the complexities of its reception within the fraught race relations of post-colonial Britain (Akhtar 1989; Apignanesi and Maitland 1989; Kabbani 1989; Webster 1990).

Small-scale qualitative research projects have remained an important feature of cultural studies, particularly British, but see also Lull 1990 and 1991. **Marie Gillespie**'s 'ethnographic' study focusses on young British Asians and their parents and grandparents in Southall, West London, and on their relationship to a newer form of technology, the video cassette recorder. It reveals the complex use to which such technologies can be put and, surprisingly perhaps, in her example, shows how it maintains and reinforces the older cultural traditions of a community as well as the generational differences within it.

The final piece in this section by **Kobena Mercer** raises questions of the politics of representation, particularly in relation to pornography and race. Mercer takes issue with 'white' feminist anti-pornography polemics which on the one hand use the phenomenon of racial hatred as analogous with male violence and on the other can readily be taken up by the New Right in an allied call for censorship. Through his own changing readings of the controversial and challenging homoerotic images of black male nudes produced by the gay male photographer, Robert Mapplethorpe, Mercer draws our attention to his strategies of transgression across the boundaries of 'high' and 'low' or popular culture, fine art and pornography and calls for complexities of reading which resist fixity and simple accusations of 'racism'. Finally, Mercer places Mapplethorpe's subversive aesthetics within the deadly political climate of the AIDS crisis where new and fertile ground has appeared for the legitimacy of political homophobia and the spread of popular/authoritarian tendencies across the left/right spectrum.

References and further reading

Akhtar, S. (1989) *Be Careful With Muhammad! The Salman Rushdie Affair*, London: Bellew.

Apignanesi, L. and Maitland, S. (1989) *The Rushdie File*, London: Fourth Estate.

Bains, H. and Cohen, P. (1988) *Multi-racist Britain*, London: Macmillan.

Bennet, T., Martin, G., Mercer, C. and Woollacott, J. (eds.) (1981) *Culture, Ideology and Social Process*, London: Batsford.

Campbell, B. (1984) *Wigan Pier Revisited: Poverty and Politics in the Eighties*, London: Virago.

Centre for Contemporary Cultural Studies (CCCS) University of Birmingham (1982) *The Empire Strikes Back: Race and Racism in 70s Britain*, London: Hutchinson.

Cohen, P. (1985) *Rethinking the Fourth Question*, Working Papers, Post Sixteen Education Centre, University of London, Institute of Education.

Cohen, P. (1988) 'The perversions of inheritance—studies in the making of multi-racist Britain' in Cohen, P. and Bains, H. (eds.) op cit.

Cohen, P. (1990) *Really Useful Knowledge*, Photography and Cultural Studies in pre-vocational education. London: Trentham Books.

Coward, R. (1984) *Female Desire: Women's Sexuality Today*, London: Paladin.

Corner, J. and Harvey, S. (1991) *Enterprise and Heritage: Cross-currents of National Culture*, London/New York: Routledge.

Franklin, S., Lury, C. and Stacey, J. (1991) *Off-Centre: Feminism and Cultural Studies*, London: Harper Collins.

Gray, A. (1992) *Video Playtime: The Gendering of a Leisure Technology*, London: Routledge.

Hall, S. (1988) 'New ethnicities' in *Black Film British Cinema*, Institute of Contemporary Arts Document 7. London: ICA.

Hebdige, D. (1979) *Subculture: The Meaning of Style*, London: Methuen.

Hebdige, D. (1988) *Hiding in the Light: On Images and Things*, London: Routledge.

Jefferson, T. (ed.) (1975) *Resistance through Rituals*, Birmingham CCCS; republished by Hutchinson, London (1976).

Kabbani, R. (1989) *A Letter to Christendom*, London: Virago.

Lull, J. (1990) *Inside Family Viewing*, London: Virago.

Lull, J. (1991) *China Turned On*, London: Routledge.

McRobbie, A. (1980) 'Settling accounts with subcultures' in *Screen Education* 34; reprinted in Bennett *et al.* (1981).

McRobbie, A. (1991) *Feminism and Youth Culture: From Jackie to Just Seventeen*, London: Macmillan.

McRobbie, A. and McCabe, T. (eds.) (1981) *Feminism for Girls: An Adventure*, London: Routledge & Kegan Paul.

Robins, D. and Cohen, P. (1978) *Knuckle Sandwich—Growing Up in the Working-Class City*, London: Penguin.
Walkerdine, V. (1990) *Schoolgirl Fictions*, London: Verso.
Webster, R. (1990) *A Brief History of Blasphemy—Liberalism, Censorship and 'The Satanic Verses'*, Southwold: Orwell Press.
Winship, J. (1987) *Inside Women's Magazines*, London: Pandora Press.

9

Subcultural conflict and working-class community

Phil Cohen

From *Working Papers in Cultural Studies 2* (Centre for Contemporary Cultural Studies, University of Birmingham, Spring 1972)

[. . .] The fifties saw the development of new towns and large estates on the outskirts of East London, Dagenham, Greenleigh etc., and a large number of families from the worst slums of the East End were rehoused in this way. The East End, one of the highest density areas in London, underwent a gradual depopulation. But as it did so, certain areas underwent a re-population, as they were rapidly colonized by a large influx of West Indians and Pakistanis. One of the reasons why these communities were attracted (in the weak sense of the word) to such areas is often called 'planning blight'. This concept has been used to describe what happens in the take-off phase of comprehensive redevelopment in the inner residential zones of large urban centres. The typical pattern is that as redevelopment begins, land values inevitably rise, and rental values fall; the most dynamic elements in local industry, who are usually the largest employers of labour, tend to move out, alongside the migrating families, and are often offered economic incentives to do so; much of the existing dilapidated property in the area is bought up cheaply by property speculators and the Rachman-type landlords, who are only interested in the maximum exploitation of their assets—the largest profits in the shortest time; as a result the property is often not maintained and becomes even further dilapidated. Immigrant families, with low incomes, and excluded from council housing, naturally gravitate to these areas, and their own trades and service industries begin to penetrate the local economy. This in turn accelerates the migration of the indigenous community to the new towns and estates. The only apparent exception to planning blight, in fact, proves the rule. For those few areas which are linked to invisible assets—such as possessing houses of 'character', i.e. late Georgian or early Victorian, or amenities such as parks—are actually bought up and improved, renovated for the new middle class, students, young professionals, who require easy access to the commercial and cultural centre of the city. The end result on the local community is the same; whether the neighbourhood is upgraded or downgraded, long-resident working-class families move out.

As the worst effects of the first phase, both on those who moved, and on those who stayed behind, became apparent, the planning authorities decided to reverse their policy. Everything was now concentrated on building new estates on slum sites within the East End. But far from counteracting the social disorganization of the area, this merely accelerated the process. In analysing the impact of redevelopment on the community, these two phases can be treated as one. No one is denying that redevelopment brought an improvement in material conditions for those fortunate enough to be rehoused (there are still thousands on the housing list). But while this removed the tangible evidence of poverty, it did nothing to improve the real economic situation of many families, and those with low incomes may, despite rent rebate schemes, be worse off. But to this was added a new poverty—the impoverishment of working-class culture. Redevelopment meant the destruction of the neighbourhood, the breakdown of the extended kinship network, which as we've seen combined to exert a powerful force for social cohesion in the community. [. . .]

The first effect of the high density, high rise schemes, was to destroy the function of the street, the local pub, the corner shop, as articulations of communal space. Instead there was only the privatized space of the family unit, stacked one on top of each other, in total isolation, juxtaposed with the totally public space which surrounded it, and which lacked any of the informal social controls generated by the neighbourhood. The streets which serviced the new estates became thoroughfares, their users 'pedestrians', and by analogy so many bits of human traffic, and this irrespective of whether or not they were separated from motorized traffic. It's indicative of how far the planners failed to understand the human ecology of the working-class neighbourhood that they could actually talk about building 'vertical streets'! The people who had to live in them weren't fooled. As one put it—they might have running hot water and central heating, but to him they were still prisons in the sky. Inevitably the physical isolation, the lack of human scale and sheer impersonality of the new environment was felt worst by people living in the new tower blocks which have gradually come to dominate the East End landscape.

The second effect of redevelopment was to destroy what we have called 'matrilocal residence'. Not only was the new housing designed on the model on the nuclear family with little provision for large, low income families (usually designated as problem families!) and none at all for groups of young single people, but the actual pattern of distribution of the new housing tended to disperse the kinship network; families of marriage were separated from their families of origin, especially during the first phase of the redevelopment. The isolated family unit could no longer call on the resources of wider kinship network, or of the neighbourhood, and the family itself became the sole focus of solidarity. This meant that any problems were bottled up within the immediate interpersonal context which produced them; and at the same time family relationships were invested with a new intensity, to compensate for the diversity of relationships previously generated through neighbours and wider kin. The trouble was that although the traditional kinship system which corresponded to it, has broken down, the traditional patterns of socialization (of communication and control) continued to reproduce themselves in the interior of the family. The working-class family was thus not only isolated from the outside, but undermined from within. There is no better example of what we are talking about than the plight of the so called 'housebound mother'. The street or turning was no longer available as a safe playspace, under neighbourly supervision. Mum, or Auntie, was no longer just round the corner to look after the kids for the odd morning. Instead the task of keeping an eye on the kids fell exclusively to the young wife, and the only safe playspace was the 'safety of the home'. Feeling herself cooped up with the kids, and cut off from the outside world, it wouldn't be surprising if she occasionally took out her frustration on those nearest and dearest! Only market research and advertising executives imagine that the housebound mother sublimates everything in her G-plan furniture, her washing machine or non-stick frying pans.

Underlying all this, however, there was a more basic process of change going on in the community, a change in the whole economic infrastructure of the East End.

In the late fifties, the British economy began to recover from the effect of the war, and to apply the advanced technology developed during this period to the more backward sectors of the economy. Craft industries and small-scale production in general were the first to suffer; automated techniques replaced the traditional hand skills and their simple division of labour. Similarly the economies of scale provided for by the concentration of capital resources meant that the small-scale family business was no longer a viable unit. Despite a long rearguard action many of the traditional industries, tailoring, furniture making, many of the service and distributive trades linked to the docks, rapidly declined, or were bought out. Symbolic of this was the disappearance of the corner shop; where these were not demolished by redevelopment, they were replaced by the larger supermarkets often owned by large combines. Even where corner shops were offered places in the redevelopment area often they could not afford the high rents. There was a gradual polarization in the structure of the labour force: on the one side the highly specialized, skilled and well-paid jobs associated with the new technology, and the high growth sectors that employed them; on the other the routine, dead end, low paid and unskilled jobs associated with the labour intensive sectors, especially the service industries. As might be expected, it was the young people, just out of school, who got the worst of the deal. Lacking openings in their fathers' trades, and lacking the qualifications for the new industries, they were relegated to jobs as vanboys, office boys, packers, warehousemen, etc., and long spells out of work. More and more people, young and old, had to travel out of the community to their jobs, and some eventually moved out to live elsewhere, where suitable work was to be found. The local economy as a whole contracted, became less diverse. The only section of the community which was unaffected by this was dockland, which retained its position in the labour market, and with it, its traditions of militancy. It did not, though, remain unaffected by the breakdown of the pattern of integration in the East End as a whole, vis-à-vis its sub-community structure. Perhaps this goes some way to explain the paradoxical fact that within the space of twelve months, the dockers could march in support of Enoch Powell, and take direct action for community control in the Isle of Dogs!

If someone should ask why the plan to 'modernize' the pattern of East End life should have been such a disaster, perhaps the only honest answer is that, given the macro-social forces acting on it, given the political, ideological, and economic framework within which it operated, the result was inevitable. For example many local people wonder why the new environment should be the way it is. The reasons are complex; they are political in so far as the system does not allow for any effective participation by local working-class community in the decision-making process at any stage or level of planning. The clients of the planners are simply the local authority or commercial developer who employs them. They are ideological in so far as the plans are unconsciously modelled on the structure of the middle-class environment, which is based on the concept of *property*, and *private ownership*, on individual differences of status, wealth, etc.; whereas the structure of the working-class environment is based on the concept of community, or collective identity, common lack of ownership, wealth, etc. Similarly needs were assessed on the norms of the middle-class nuclear family, rather than the extended working-class family, etc. But underpinning both these sets of reasons lie the basic economic factors involved in comprehensive redevelopment. Quite simply—faced with the task of financing a large housing programme, the local authorities were forced to borrow large amounts of capital, and also to design schemes which would attract capital investment to the area. This means that they have to borrow at the going interest rates, which in this country are very high, and that to subsidize housing, certain of the best sites have to be earmarked for commercial developers. A further and perhaps decisive factor is the cost of land, since very little of it is publicly owned and land values rise as the area develops.

All this means that planners have to reduce the cost of production to a minimum, through the use of capital intensive techniques—prefabricated and standardized components, allowing for semi-automated processes in construction. The attraction of high rise developments (tower blocks outside the trade) is not only that they meet these requirements, but they allow for certain economies of scale, such as the input costs of essential services, which can be grouped around a central core. As to 'non-essential' services, i.e. ones that don't pay, such as playspace, community centres, youth clubs and recreational facilities, these often have to be sacrificed to the needs of commercial developers, who of course have quite different priorities. Perhaps the best example of this happening is the notorious St Catherine's Dock scheme. This major contribution towards solving the East End's housing problem includes a yachting marina, a luxury hotel, luxury apartment blocks, and various cultural amenities for their occupants plus—a small section of low income accommodation, presumably to house the families of the low paid staff who will service the luxury amenities. And lest anyone becomes too sentimental about the existing site, Telford's warehouses etc., it should be mentioned that the original development was by the East India Company in the early nineteenth century, involved the destruction of the homes of thousands of poor families in the area, and met with such stiff opposition from them that it eventually required an Act of Parliament to get the scheme approved!

The situation facing East Enders at present, then, is not new. When the first tenements went up in the nineteenth century they raised the same objections from local people, and for the same very good reasons as their modern counterparts—the tower blocks. What *is* new is that in the nineteenth century the voice of the community was vigorous and articulate on these issues, whereas today, just when it needs it most, the community is faced with a crisis of indigenous leadership.

The reasons for this are already implicit in the analysis above. The labour aristocracy, traditional source of leadership, has virtually disappeared along with the artisan mode of production. At the same time there has been a split in consciousness between the spheres of production and consumption. More and more East Enders are forced to work outside the area; young people especially are less likely to follow family traditions in this respect. As a result the issues of the workplace are no longer experienced as directly linked to community issues. Of course there has always been a 'brain drain' of the most articulate, due to social mobility. But not only has this been intensified as a result of the introduction of comprehensive schools, but the recruitment of fresh talent from the strata below—i.e. from the ranks of the respectable working class—has also dried up. For this strata, traditionally the social cement of the community, is also in a state of crisis.

The economic changes, which we have already described, also affected their position and as it were *de-stabilized it*. The 'respectables' found themselves caught and pulled apart by two opposed pressures of social mobility —downwards, into the ranks of the new suburban working-class elite. And more than any other section of the working class were caught in the middle of the two dominant but contradictory ideologies of the day: the ideology of spectacular consumption, promoted by the mass media, and the traditional ideology of production, the so-called work ethic which centred on the idea that a man's dignity, his manhood, even, was measured by the quantity of quality of his effort in production. If this strata began to split apart it was because their existing position had become untenable. Their bargaining power in the labour market was threatened by the introduction of new automated techniques, which eliminated many middle-range, semi-skilled jobs. Their economic position excluded them from entering the artificial paradise of the new consumer society; at the same time changes in the production process itself have made the traditional work ethic, the pride in the job, impossible to uphold. They had the worst of all possible worlds.

Once again this predicament was registered most deeply in and on the young. But here an additional complicating factor intervenes. We have already described the peculiar strains imposed on the 'nucleated' working-class family. And their most critical impact was in the area of parent/child relationships. What had previously been a source of support and security for both, now became something of a battleground, a major focus of all the anxieties created by the disintegration of community structures around them. One result of this was to produce an increase in early marriage. For one way of escaping the claustrophobic tensions of family life was to start a family of your own! And given the total lack of accommodation for young single people in the new developments, as well as the conversion of cheap rented accommodation into middle-class owner-occupied housing, the only practicable way to leave home was to get married. The second outcome of generational conflict (which may appear to go against the trend of early marriage, but in fact reinforced it) was the emergence of specific youth subcultures in opposition to the parent culture. And one effect of this was to weaken the links of historical and cultural continuity, mediated through the family, which had been such a strong force for solidarity in the working-class community. It is perhaps not surprising that the parent culture of the respectable working class, already in crisis, was the most 'productive' vis-à-vis subcultures; the internal conflicts of the parent culture came to be worked out in terms of generational conflict. What I think seems to happen is that one of the functions of generational conflict is to decant the kinds of tensions which appear face to face in the family and replace them by a generational specific symbolic system so that the tension is taken out of the interpersonal context and placed in a collective context, and mediated through various stereotypes which have the function of defusing the anxiety that interpersonal tension generates.

It seems to me that the latent function of subculture is this—to express and resolve, albeit 'magically', the contradictions which remain hidden or unresolved in the parent culture. The succession of subcultures which this parent culture generated can thus all be considered as so many variations on a central theme—the contradiction, at an ideological level, between traditional working-class puritanism, and the new hedonism of consumption; at an economic level between a future as part of the socially mobile elite, or as part of the new lumpen. Mods, parkers, skinheads, crombies, all represent, in their different ways, an attempt to retrieve some of the socially cohesive elements destroyed in their parent culture, and to combine these with elements selected from other class fractions, symbolizing one or other of the options confronting it.

It is easy enough to see this working in practice if we remember that subcultures are symbolic structures, and must not be confused with the actual kids who are their bearers and supports. Secondly a given lifestyle is actually made up of a number of symbolic subsystems, and it is the way these are articulated in the total lifestyle which constitutes its distinctiveness. There are basically four subsystems—and these can be divided into the relatively 'plastic' forms—dress and music, which are not directly produced by the subculture, but which are selected and invested with subcultural value in so far as they express its underlying thematic; and then the more 'infrastructural' forms—argot, and ritual, which are more resistant to innovation but of course reflect changes in the more plastic forms. I'm suggesting here that mods, parkers, skinheads, crombies are a succession of subcultures which all correspond to the same parent culture and which attempt to work out through a system of transformations, the basic problematic or contradiction which is inserted in the subculture by the parent culture. So you can distinguish three levels in the analysis of subcultures: one is historical analysis which isolates the specific problematic of a particular class fraction, in this case, the respectable working class; and secondly a structural or semiotic analysis of the subsystems and the way they are articulated and the actual transformations which those subsystems undergo from one subcultural moment to another; and thirdly the phenomenological analysis of the way the subculture is actually lived out by those who are the bearers and supports of the subculture. No real analysis of subculture is complete without all those levels being in place.

To go back to the diachronic string we are discussing, the original mod lifestyle could be interpreted as an attempt to real-ize, *but in an imaginary relation*, the conditions of existence of the socially mobile white-collar worker. While their argot and ritual forms stressed many of the traditional values of their parent culture, their dress and music reflected the hedonistic image of the affluent consumer. The lifestyle crystallized in opposition to the rockers (viz. the famous riots in the early sixties) and it seems to be a law of subcultural evolution that its dynamic comes not only from the relations to its own parent culture, but from the relation to subcultures belonging to *other class fractions*, in this case the manual working class.

The next member of our string—the parkers or scooter boys—were in some senses a transitional form between the mods and skinheads. The alien elements introduced into music and dress by the mods were progressively de-stressed and the indigenous components of argot and ritual re-asserted as the matrix of subcultural identity. The skinheads themselves carried the process to completion. Their lifestyle in fact rep-resents a systematic inversion of the mods—whereas the mods explored the upwardly mobile option, the skinheads explored the lumpen. Music and dress again became the central focus of the lifestyle; the introduction of reggae (the protest music of the West Indian poor) and the 'uniform' (of which more in a moment) signified a reaction against the contamina-tion of the parent culture by middle-class values, and a re-assertion of the integral values of working-class culture—through its most recessive traits—its puritanism and chauvinism. This double movement gave rise to a phenomenon sometimes called 'machismo'—the unconscious dynamics of the work ethic translated into the out of work situation; the most dramatic example of this was the epidemic of 'queer bashing' across the country in '69/70. The skinhead uniform itself could be interpreted as a kind of caricature of the model worker—the self image of the working class as distorted through middle-class perceptions; a metastatement about the whole process of social mobility. Finally the skinhead lifestyle crystallized in opposition both to the greasers (successors to the rockers) and the hippies—both subcultures representing a species of hedonism which the skinheads rejected.

Following the skinheads there emerged another transitional form vari-ously known as crombies, casuals, suedes, etc. (the proliferation of names being a mark of transitional phases). They represent a movement back towards the original mod position, although this time it's a question of incorporating certain elements drawn from a middle-class *subculture*—the hippies, which the skinheads had previously ignored. But even though the crombies, etc. have adopted some of the external mannerisms of the hippy lifestyle, viz. dress, soft drug use, they still conserve many of the distinctive features of earlier versions of the subculture.

If the whole process as we've described it seems to be circular, forming a closed system, then this is because subculture, by definition, cannot break out of the contradiction derived from the parent culture, it merely transcribes its terms at a microsocial level, and inscribes them in an imaginary set of relations.

But there is another reason. Apart from its particular, thematic, contradiction, every subculture shares a general contradiction, which is inherent in its very conditions of existence. Subculture invests the weak points in the chain of socialization, between the family/school nexus, and integration into the work process which marks the resumption of the patterns of the parent culture for the next generation. But subculture is also a compromise solution, between two contradictory needs: the need to create and express *autonomy and difference* from parents, and by extension, their culture; and the need to maintain the security of existing ego defences, and the *parental identifications* which support them. For the initiate subculture provides a means of 'rebirth' without having to undergo the pain of symbolic death. The autonomy it offers is thus both real, but partial, and illusory, as a total 'way of liberation'. And far from constituting an improvised *rite de passage* into adult society, as some anthropologists have claimed, it is a collective and highly ritualized defence against just such a transition. And because defensive functions predominate, ego boundaries become cemented to subcultural boundaries. In a real sense subcultural conflict (i.e. greasers versus skinheads, mods versus rockers) serves as a displacement of generational conflict, both at a cultural level, and at an interpersonal level within the family. One consequence of this is to artificially foreclose the natural trajectory of adolescent revolt. For the kids who are caught up in the internal contradictions of a subculture, what began as a break in the continuum of social control can easily become a permanent hiatus in their lives. Although there is a certain amount of subcultural mobility, i.e. kids evolving from mods to parkers, or even switching subcultural affiliations, greasers 'becoming' skinheads, there are no career prospects as such! There are two possible solutions; one leads out of subculture into early marriage, and as we've said for working-class kids this is the normal solution. Alternatively subcultural affiliation can provide a way in to membership of one of the deviant subgroups, which exist in the margins of subculture, often adopt its protective colouration, but which nevertheless are not structurally dependent on it; such groups as pushers, petty criminals, junkies, even homosexuals.

This leads us into another contradiction inherent in subculture. Although as a symbolic structure it *does* provide a diffuse sense of affinity in terms of a common lifestyle, it does not in itself prescribe any crystallized group structure. We believe that it is through the function of *territoriality* that subculture becomes anchored in the collective reality of the kids who are its bearers, and who in this way become not just its passive support, but its conscious agents. Territoriality is simply the process through which environmental boundaries (and foci) are used to signify group boundaries (and foci) and become invested with a subcultural value. This is the function of football teams for the skinheads, for example. Territoriality is thus not only a way in which kids live subculture as a collective behaviour, but the way in which the subcultural group becomes rooted in the situation of its community. In the context of the East End it is a way of retrieving the solidarities of the traditional neighbourhood, destroyed by redevelopment. The existence of communal space is reasserted as the common pledge of group unity—you belong to the Mile End mob in so far as the Mile End belongs to you. Territoriality appears as a magical way of expressing ownership; for the Mile End is not owned by the people but by the property developers. Territorial division therefore appears within the subculture, and in the East End mirror many of the traditional divisions of sub-communities: Bethnal Green—Hoxton—Mile End—Whitechapel—Balls Pond Road, etc. Thus in addition to conflict between subcultures, there also exists conflict within them, on a territorial basis. Both these forms of conflict can be seen as displacing or weakening the dynamics of generational conflict, which is in turn a displaced form of the traditional parameters of class conflict. [. . .]

10

Alice in the consumer wonderland

Erica Carter

From Angela McRobbie and Mica Nava (eds.), *Gender and Generation* (Macmillan, 1984).

Changing gear: a reappraisal of the politics of style

> People say . . . well, what don't they say about teenagers?! They start with the accusation that we have no manners or sense of good behaviour, and that we're hopelessly lacking in all religious belief. Then we are told off, either for dressing too sloppily, or looking too old for our age . . . 'Either', we are told, 'you run around like tramps in floppy jackets buttoned up at the back and drainpipe trousers which are far too tight—or else you slavishly follow the latest fashion trends.'
> We would like for once to give our point of view . . . We teenagers have our own style. And that's what makes many people see red.
> (Advertisement for 'Triumph' underwear, *Bravo* magazine, no. 42, 1958)

Since the beginning of the 1970s, theorists of youth subcultures in Britain have appropriated the notion of 'style' from marketers of teenage fashion commodities, and mobilized it for their studies of oppositional subcultures in the post-war period. Recalling a tradition of cultural studies which reaches back to Richard Hoggart's *Uses of Literacy* (Hoggart, 1958), early analysts of subcultural deviance and opposition* seem implicitly to share his distaste for the plastic glamour of commercialized youth culture; their gaze falls rather on visible subversions of dominant forms. The discordant notes sounded by Teds, rockers, mods, rastas or punks are seen to be pitched against the harmony of mass consumer culture; appropriating commodities from fashion, music and media industries, subcultural youths reassemble them into symbolic systems of their own which, if only at the moment of their birth, strike chords of disenchantment, rebellion and resistance. Like the phenomena which they examine, the analyses themselves are founded on a number of unspoken oppositions: conformity and resistance, harmony and rupture, passivity and activity, consumption

---

* The seminal work in this field was Phil Cohen's 1972 study of 'Subcultural Conflict and Working-class Community' (Birmingham, 1972). Other works to which both explicit and implicit reference will be made in the following pages include Hall and Jefferson (1976), Hebdige (1979), and Willis (1977).

and appropriation, femininity and masculinity.

In a discussion of sexism amongst the working-class lads of his 'Hammertown' study, Paul Willis finds himself slipping with ease into the discourse of consumerism.

> The male counter-school culture promotes its own sexism—even celebrates it as part of its overall confidence. Girls are pursued, sometimes roughly, for their sexual favours, often dropped and labelled 'loose' when they are given. Girls are asked to be sexy and inviting as well as pure and monogamous; to be consumed and not to be consumed. (Willis, 1977, p. 146)

In a study from which girls are largely absent, the moment of their appearance is profoundly significant. Girls, it seems, are written into youth cultural theory in the language of consumption; initially—though not, as we shall see, of necessity—as objects for consumption by men. Under the regime of Althusserian structuralism in British cultural theory, this led to the perception of girls at best as an absence, a silence, a lack which could perhaps only be filled in some separate world of autonomous female culture. Ideology was an 'instance', consumption a 'sphere', severed from its tangled roots in the social institutions with which structuralism was primarily concerned—the family, ideology and the repressive State. Feminist researchers then turned towards the family as the pivotal point around which the existence of teenage girls revolved.

> If women are marginal to the male cultures of work (middle and working class) it is because they are central and pivotal to a subordinate area, which mirrors, but in a complementary and subordinate way, the 'dominant' masculine arenas. They are 'marginal' to work because they are central to the subordinate, complementary sphere of the family. (McRobbie and Garber, 1976, p. 211)

Following working-class girls into the closed arena of the family allowed the researchers of female culture privileged insights into the possibilities of specifically female cultural forms. So-called 'bedroom culture' was analogous to male subcultures, in that here too dominant signs and symbols were appropriated, reassembled and reproduced in homology* with an already existing set of social relations. In male youth subcultures, these homologies existed between the lived culture of a subordinate *class* and the symbolic systems through which its members made that culture 'mean'. In bedroom culture, gender relations overlaid, overlapped and took precedence over relations of race and class.

Yet the search for autonomous female cultural forms in the bedroom hideaways of teenage girls has been consistently dogged by nagging doubts as to the creative, productive and potentially subversive power of this mode of femininity. The study of 'teeny bopper culture', for

---

* The term 'homology' is used in subcultural theory to describe the 'degree of fit' between the structure of group experience and the cultural forms through which that experience is expressed. Thus for example in Paul Willis's studies of hippy and bike-boy culture, the music of each group was seen to exist in a relationship of 'homology' with its lifestyle and values. 'The preferred music must have the potential, at least in its formal structure, to express meanings which resonate with other aspects of group life.' (Willis, 'The cultural meaning of drug use', in Hall and Jefferson, 1976, p. 106)

example, was recognized as a key which might unlock the potentialities of specifically female forms; on the other hand, teenage adulation of male pop idols remained a symbol of the 'future general subordination' of adolescent girls (McRobbie and Garber, 1976, p. 219). One problem with taking subculture theory as a starting point for studies of female culture was that the homologies which 'profane culture' moulded and shaped for itself were always preformed—and more readily reformed at the slightest hint of female autonomy—by an ever-watchful capitalist market.

The spectacle of working-class subcultures erupted into a yawning gap between class relations as they are lived by working-class youth, and the classless categories according to which capitalist markets are structured. Ever since Warner's classic study of social class in America (Warner, 1960) the marketing establishment has measured consumers against typological grids on which 'class' appears primarily as an attribute of personal status and income; working-class subcultures are, in part, a raucous rejection of a consumer culture which has continually repressed the seamier side of class subordination from view. Gender, on the other hand, operates as a dominant variable for the structuring of consumer groups. Thus not only have market researchers developed a vast apparatus of consumer surveillance which ensures the immediate recuperation and reassimilation of new—or hitherto unheeded—facets of femininity; the 'image industries' (fashion, cosmetics, the female mass media) have also consistently drawn on these marketing data to produce symbolic representations which fit skintight to female experiences. Hence the difference in mood, tone and resonance of masculine and feminine revolts into style. Male 'semiological guerillas' plunder the symbolic treasure chests of consumer culture, recreating their booty as signifiers of resistance whose signifier—the disaffection of subordinate class fractions—was until recently banished from the symbolic landscape of the teenage mass market. Conversely, even the unpleasures of femininity find continual, if oblique, reflection in commodities on the female market, from perfect cures for the imperfections of the female body (slimming pills, aerobic outfits, beauty aids), to more expensive, and correspondingly drastic remedies for the psychic ailments of the female condition—from nerve-tonics to psychoanalysis, with Babycham to add a touch of sparkle.

Deviance, resistance, autonomy, revolt: in the sociological tradition of the academic Left, these are located beyond the hostile walls of an impassive monolith—the Market. Analyses of subcultural style represented an attempt to freeze commodities-as-signifiers into fixed relations of subversive opposition; the (re)marketing of punk safety-pins and crazy-colour hairstyles was dubbed a 'recuperation'—silencing, defeat. The first punk safety-pin to spill off the end of the mass production line did indeed dislodge punk from its anchorage in the adolescent culture of the urban working classes; yet at the same time, it carried the meanings and values of punk into a wider field of teenage mass culture, where its progress has yet to be properly charted.

If subculture theory has traditionally remained standing somewhat suspiciously on the sidelines of commercial youth culture, the same has not always been true of research into girls' culture. Women researchers have had to plunge, head-on at times, into the seething morass of capital flows, emerging with a proliferation of critiques of the commodities which pattern the fabric of girls' lives: advertising images, fashionable clothes, mass magazines, popular fiction. In feminist theory too, the theoretical terrain for a re-engagement with market mechanisms has been prepared since the beginning of the break with Althusser and structuralism. The market is not an institution with rigidly defined (if consistently subverted) hierarchies, structures, orders and conventions; neither is it a tightly-knit subculture whose practices and rituals can be traced onto frozen 'maps of meaning'. It is instead a vast machine for the regulation of interconnecting circulatory flows: the flow of capital and labour through the production process, the flows of money, commodities, visual and textual signifiers through the circuits of consumption unlocked by capital.

Recognizing market practices as constant and unbroken flows demands a similarly supple set of categories for their analysis; the homologies and oppositions of structuralist symbolic deconstructions offer only one of many routes into the fragmented and splintered realities of female consumption. Shifting onto more fluid epistemological ground will not entail a feminist farewell to subcultures: charting the labyrinth of female market practices, we will be led to girls and women within *and* outside subcultures, all of whom participate in the regulation and organization of market processes. The machine itself, if vast and apparently all-embracing, is never intrinsically monstrous; it is both manipulative and manipulated, controlled and controlling. Girls and women surface on a multitude of levels as both objects and agents of market processes: so, for example, the eighties boom in the second-hand rag trade owes its greatest debt to the 'nouvelle entrepreneuse' of New Wave subculture (and signals, incidentally, a successful attempt to divert fashion's commodity flows from their source in monopoly capitalist production).

An 'archaeology' of female consumption

Across the landscape of post-war mass markets, female consumers, too, emerge both as 'objects' (of market research, advertising campaigns, sexual consumption by men) and as active agents in consumption processes. The work presented in the following pages—studies of specific instances of female 'consumer culture' in post-war West Germany—represents a first step towards a latter-day 'archaeology' of female consumption; an attempt to grasp and represent aspects of female consumerism in all their myriad complexities; and an appeal for the postponement of premature outrage at the 'co-option', 'recuperation', 'objectification' of women and girls in post-war consumer culture.

The nascent Federal Republic of Germany may seem an unlikely point of departure. Yet the very distance between areas of study (in this case, both geographical and conceptual in nature) forces the disruption of established modes of understanding, pointing the way towards potentially more fertile theoretical terrain. In the first instance, looking at German attempts to build a new democracy out of the shattered ruins of Germany's Nazi past can shed light on processes which, in Britain, took on less visible forms. Germany in 1945 lacked the cosy security of the cultural institutions in which British democratic values were founded—from fair play in English cricket, to resonances of Empire in the British cup of tea. Analogous cultural forms and practices in post-war Germany resounded still with echoes of Nazism; meanwhile, the allied Western powers demanded tangible evidence of a decisive break with the totalitarian past. The West German constitution of 1949, then, was offered as an anchorage point for the fragile floating remnants of Weimar democracy; it contained, importantly, explicit guarantees of the equality of women and men before the law. The first section of the following study traces some of the processes whereby these constitutional promises came to be realized in the course of the 1950s. In practice, the explicit inscription of women as equal subjects in legal discourse was negotiated through their installation as consumers in a 'social market economy'; citizenship for women thus came to be defined through consumption on a capitalist mass market.

This, then, is a study of the ways in which the post-war market colonized and rooted itself in political discourses and institutions. The caesura of 1945 in Germany; attempts to suffocate a Nazi past under the cushion of consumer democracy; these may throw into sharper relief analogous developments in the consumerism of post-war Britain. Here as in Germany the middle-class housewife enacted her political enfranchisement through the exercise of economic rationality; choosing to buy or not to buy, to spend or to save, to covet or to shun.

Certainly in 1950s West Germany, this was part of the 'political' future to which teenage girls were widely urged to aspire; at the same time, the expanding market in teenage leisure commodities transported adolescent consumption into a separate dimension of 'symbolic' and 'hedonistic' pleasures (Woods, 1960). [. . .] I look at some aspects of fifties' leisure consumption for girls; at the symbolic systems of teenage lifestyles; and at one specific instance of female mass consumption: artificial 'silk' stockings for teenage girls. Heavily laden though nylons may be with predetermined 'sexist' meanings, a cool appraisal of the actual mode of their consumptions reveals teenage girls engaged in the production of meanings and values more appropriate to their own needs. Nylon stockings, imported *en masse* from the USA, may appear simply as one of the more visible manifestations of American cultural hegemony. Yet a closer look at this one element in an emergent, and largely imported, teenage culture of consumption, points towards different questions to be asked of the process of consumption itself. Passive manipulation or active appropriation, escapist delusion or Utopian fantasy, consumerism can be all or none of these. [. . .]

Teenage girls in the consumer public

There are no simple connections to be made between women's position within relations of consumption for the fifties family, and the situation of adolescent girls as consumers on a mass teenage market. On the one hand, it was clearly the case that women taking up their new position of equality were seen to be lacking in the qualities necessary for democratic citizenship. Since women's assumed tendency to be over-emotional was said to hamper them in the exercise of rational consumer choice, it became the task of both state and private institutions (centrally, of course, the advertising establishment) to educate women into the required patterns of consumption.

There is, then, indeed a sense in which drives towards the end of the decade to initiate girls into new modes of consumption were simply preparing them for their entry into an adult female world. On the one hand, teenage consumption, revolving as it did around leisure commodities, was clearly distinct from that practised by housewives. Why, after all, should girls with a well-trained eye for fashionable colour combinations—the right shade of lipstick to set off matching gloves and shoes—necessarily be similarly adept at differentiating between an increasingly confusing variety of washing-powder brands?

Yet via the notion of the 'public', there are crucial links to be made. For the fifties housewives, one component of domestic labour—shopping—was lifted out of the enclaves of home and the local street, and transferred to the 'public' terrain of the supermarket and the neighbourhood or regional shopping centre. Abstract promises of a public identity for women as consumers took concrete form in the reorganization of public space around centralized loci of commodity exchange. Shops and stores gradually abandoned earlier styles of personal service, in favour of more up-to-date self-service methods. A number of stores introduced the so-called 'Kiebitz' system, displaying placards or badges which invited the customer to 'come in and look around', with no obligation to buy. Shop displays were reordered accordingly, with an emphasis on the commodity as image and spectacle; at the same time, posters and labels on or near individual articles drew the customers' attention to their particular advantages. Firms originally specializing in mail-order delivery expanded their department store chains; in urban centres in particular, specialist shops began to lose custom to larger department stores and supermarkets.

Developments in town planning further accelerated the centralization of the consumption process. West Berlin was particularly interesting in this respect; having sustained heavy bombing in the Second World War, the city centre was a blank page across which architects and town planners would write the forms of their social Utopias. In 1946 a town planning collective under the directorship of Hans Scharoun opened debates on the future of the city with an exhibition, 'Berlin plant' (Berlin plans). They proposed using the wide-open spaces left by bomb damage to break with previous traditions of high-density housing and closed communities in which living, sometimes also working-space, had been integrated with leisure facilities—the obligatory 'Eckkneipe' (local bar)—and other points of commodity exchange: the equally indispensable 'Tante-Emma-Laden' ('Aunt Emma's corner shop'). The post-war Berlin of Scharoun was to draw sharp boundaries between these diverse spheres of city life; strips of parkland and fast, wide roads were to divide off residential areas from commercial quarters, and from sites of work and leisure—including centralized shopping areas.

Through their integration into an expanding teenage market, adolescent girls were drawn in increasing numbers into this new public space. The new generation of young consumers were particularly attracted to self-service and department stores, where they were free to look, compare and admire at their leisure, with no immediate compulsion to buy. A 1957 Intermarket survey of West German consumer habits records the preference of teenagers for these more impersonal stores, as well as their predilection for the 'Americanized' off-the-peg fashions still regarded with suspicion by their older compatriots.

If girls are absent from subcultures, then, they become visible at the point of consumption. Working-class girls in particular have never been entirely absent from the street, the cinema or the dancehall; they have not lived a life of seclusion away from the eyes of predatory men. A favourite occupation of young female factory workers in 1950s West Germany was an evening stroll along main streets in search of excitement and the company of contemporaries. Again, it was shopping which drew them onto the street and into public life. In a series of sociological monographs published in 1958 (Wurzbacher and Jaide, 1958, pp. 169–70), Bärbel—fifteen-years-old at the time of the study, and employed since leaving school in a knitwear factory – relates how she is sent out every evening to fetch milk for the family (a duty she is only too happy to perform, since the dairy is a favourite meeting place for a large proportion of the local village youth).

> Here new films and the latest fashions are discussed. The boys at first set themselves a little apart, in order to be able to pass comment on the girls; later they make attempts to pick them up. This is a place for young people to talk together; this is the place where dates are made. There is always something going on at the dairy.

If the market offers itself to women and girls as a stage for the production of themselves as public beings, then it does so on particularly unfavourable terms. Bärbel's dairy was a meeting place for separate groups of boys and girls: the girls, whatever their own motives for assembling there, found themselves on display to boys angling for a date—or something more. It is this overwhelming power of men to position women as sexual prey that has made the feminist search for autonomous female subcultures so consistently difficult. Doubtless, though, the difficulty resides equally in the subculturalists' choice of object, cultural resistance being located chiefly in formal innovations by an adolescent avant-garde. If anything is to be learned about the lived realities of consumption, then we must shift the terms of the youth culture debate, looking first at the dominant forms of a supposedly conformist culture of consumerism (as well as its everyday subversions). One route into this project is the examination of teenage lifestyles: of their assemblage on the production line of commodities for the teenage market, and their deconstruction, appropriation, subversion and reassemblage by teenage girls themselves.

Girls in West Germany and the teenage dream

The word teenager first entered the German language in the 1950s, imported like chewing gum and Coca-Cola from the USA, and vibrant with connotations of crazy styles, zany humour, rock'n'roll parties, Elvis, James Dean, loud music and soft park-bench romance. Its partner, the 'Twen', arrived around the same time and is of somewhat more dubious origin. Signifying 'young people in their twenties', it relied on associations of Americanness ('false' ones, insofar as the 'Twen' does not exist outside Germany) to construct an image of the older, more responsible, but none-theless fun-loving party-going free-spending twenty-year-old. The average marital age in late 1950s Germany was twenty-six, and the relatively high disposable income of unmarried 'Twens' made them particularly attractive to producers of consumer goods in the upper price range of the leisure market. A survey carried out by the DIVO Market Research Institute in 1961 estimated the disposable income of twenty-one to twenty-four-year-olds by 1960 at DM192 per month for men (compared with DM91 for seventeen to twenty-year-olds), and DM180 per month for women (compared with DM100 for their seventeen- to twenty-year-old counterparts).

It was on the teenage market, then, that girls represented a particularly attractive target group for the leisure industries. During their late teens (from the age of fifteen onwards) girls in general drew a higher income than boys, but dropped back below their male contemporaries on reaching the age of twenty. In part, this resulted from their greater store of 'cultural capital' (Bourdieu, 1967); girls leaving school in their mid-teens were likely to be initially better qualified for jobs requiring school certificates (Volksschulabschlüsse), while boys tended to make up for their lack of academic qualifications by entering an initially lower-paid apprenticeship or trainee post. The most lucrative section of the female market, then, was the group of 'Angestellte' (clerical and secretarial workers); their disposable income amounted to three or four times that of their grammar school and college counterparts, or of working-class girls in unskilled factory work. Girls on the margins of the middle income bracket were, in a sense, the deviants of marketing discourse, and 'Angestellte' the norm against which teenage market potential was measured.

To the marketing establishment, it was clear that the golden egg of the female market had to be cracked with care. The male leisure market offered no adequate model for marketing to girls for whom leisure and pleasure were elastic and unstable terms. Female consumption constantly slipped between the grey world of work on the one hand and, on the other, the glittering but (above all sexually) dangerous domain of unbounded hedon-ism. The leisure commodities favoured by boys offered pathways to present and immediate pleasures; for girls, on the other hand, so-called 'leisure' commodities embodied their more sober demands for future security in a precarious world. Girls in the middle to higher income brackets spent a significant portion of their income as unmarried females on collecting objects for their bottom drawer. This traditional female institution, having gone into decline in the austerity years of the forties and early fifties, celebrated its comeback towards the end of the decade, when girls began once again to collect bedclothes, table linen, crockery, cutlery, glassware—the accoutrements of the bourgeois domestic idyll. Teenage boys and young men, meanwhile, were busily buying motor-bikes, cars, cameras, sports equipment and other consumer durables: the only piece of technical equipment more highly favoured by female consumers was the typewriter (Scharmann, 1965, pp. 33–8). Like the bottom drawer (which raised women's value on the marriage market) the typewriter represented an investment in a comfortable future, girls' production of themselves as desirable commodities on a competitive job market, and a key to the door of future financial security.

Private faces in public places

As girls and women entered the post-war market place, whole new areas of their lives began to become the 'public' property of marketing institutions. Modern surveillance systems were installed in shops and supermarkets for the observation and control of consumer behaviour: consumer panels were constituted as a source of information on attitudes to specific commodities and brands: 'in-depth' psychological testing came into vogue with the rise of motivation research. Investigations into consumer behaviour required a massive apparatus for the gathering and processing of data on consumer habits, preference, tastes and whims; hence the post-war boom in market research, when the five major West German institutes (DIVO, EMNID, GfM, IFD, INFRATEST) were founded in the space of as many years, between 1945 and 1950. The unifying principle of diverse market research techniques was the regulation of information flows, which were to proceed in one direction only: from the consumer upwards to the institutions of the image production industries. Here, data on consumers would be 'reprocessed', before being returned to them in the shape of commodity representations: product design, packaging, advertising, public relations. Until reaching the stage of its reproduction in these more palatable forms, knowledge of the consumer was channelled through scientific discourses within which she was placed only as object, never as subject of the consumption process. In commodity representations the situation was reversed. The same knowledge was used by the image industries to construct image commodities-as-symbols, from advertising images to fashionable clothes for a teenage mass market. First, however, it had to be 'translated' from the terms of social science into those of what may be called the 'commodity aesthetic' within which, importantly, consumers were replaced as subjects of consumption practices.

Since the second half of the nineteenth century, the proliferation and increasing differentiation of public images of and for women has been intimately bound up with their role as consumers. The effects of market research have been visible for almost a century in the newspaper industry; as early as the 1890s in America, newspapers began to extend society news and entertainment sections, after they discovered that women—the audience at whom these features were primarily aimed—carried the greatest potential as a future consumer market (Noelle, 1940, p. 92). Yet it was not until well into the 1950s that market research in Germany first turned its attention to the younger generation of female consumers. In 1959, the Gesellschaft für Marktforschung carried out a survey of 1500 male and female teenagers between the ages of fourteen and nineteen. The study was supplemented by further investigations in 1960, which aimed both 'to re-examine certain findings of the previous year' and 'to gain further basic insights into this important consumer group' (Scharmann, 1965, p. 17). While sociological and media research carried out earlier in the decade had confined itself to quantitative studies of adolescent leisure pursuits the GfM study was the first to focus specifically on the teenager as consumer and to attempt a broad sociometric analysis of teenage habits, preference and tastes.

In 1961, DIVO followed the GfM lead with a report commissioned by the advertising editors of *Bravo* magazine, a music, film, television, fashion and fiction teenage weekly which had been launched five years previously in 1956. By the early sixties, *Bravo* had already established itself as a leading light on the developing market for magazines aimed at a specifically teenage (male and female) readership. The 1961 survey aimed to spotlight the potential of the teenage market for the advertisers on whose revenue the magazine increasingly depended. *Bravo*, they argued, could operate as a bridge to span the gap between commodity producers, advertisers and consumers; its potential for success lay in its proven ability to capture and sustain a loyal readership amongst young people between the ages of twelve and twenty-four. In offering advertising space to the producers of commodities for a teenage market, it could ensure the dissemination of commodity representations amongst a teenage public constituted as such primarily through their role as consumers. *Bravo* readers, the publishers claim, are to be 'taken seriously' as consumers; for it is as such, they say, that teenagers primarily understand themselves.

> Confronted daily with literally hundreds of magazines and newspapers, young people may, it is true, pick up any one of them at any given time. Yet the only medium which will truly appeal to them is one which they feel is meant for and aimed only at them. They want, rightly, to be taken seriously enough for efforts to be made directly on their behalf. This is why *Bravo* has to be the way it is. (DIVO, 1961)

In the face of moral outrage on the part of teachers, parents, academics and other guardians of Culture, Decency and Good Taste, *Bravo* was out to legitimize its own innovations in the field of popular taste. If teenagers were to assert themselves in a hostile world, they needed, it was argued, a mouthpiece through which their grievances could be aired, and it was in this capacity that *Bravo* offered its services, claiming itself to be the only forum in which teenage protest could—and should—find expression. The mode of teenage rebellion was to be, not 'political', but aesthetic: 'We teenagers have our own style. And that's just what makes so many people see red' (Triumph advertisement, 1958). In the opening pages of the DIVO survey, *Bravo* then offered its services as an open site on which new teenage forms could be built and subsequently assembled into smoothly polished consumer lifestyles.

Girls in teenage lifestyle

The discourse of marketing defines lifestyles in terms of the specific configurations of commodity ownership which characterize particular consumer groups. In Germany, the Nürnberg Gesellschaft für Marktforschung was the first marketing institute to develop its own theory of lifestyle; it was not until the mid-fifties that other market research establishments began to look in earnest to sources outside classical economics for more finely differentiated analyses of potential target groups. Taking up the work of Thorstein Veblen, Margaret Mead, Freud, Jung and others, consumption theorists now set about recuperating information gathered in the academic disciplines of cultural anthropology, sociology and psychology to feed the data banks of the capitalist market. Classical political economy had tended to neglect the consumer, or to consider consumption only in relation to the economics of commodity production and distribution. In opposition to this, the new wave of consumption theorists, with Bengler and Vershofen in Nürnberg as their avant-garde, argued consistently for a more sophisticated awareness of the social and aesthetic dimensions of commodity use. Wilhelm Vershofen proposed that the concept of commodity use value should be broken down into three analytical components: basic, or original use value; and social use value, measured against variables such as social prestige; and aesthetic use value, measured against given standards of social taste (Vershofen, 1954, p. 12). Members of the artistic and literary establishment were taken to task for their confinement of Culture to a discrete and autonomous sphere, floating freely above the colourless wasteland of everyday life. The mutual dependence of economy and culture was seen by Vershofen to take active form in the daily exercise of consumer choice, determined as much by aesthetic as by economic or socio-psychological considerations.

The aesthetic principle regulating consumer lifestyles was a unity of form which bound the separate elements through which they were constructed. Part of the function of teenage commodities was to provide aesthetic forms for a cultural 'space' (adolescent leisure culture) which was differently inhabited by female and male consumers. For middle-class and working-class girls, home, the workplace and the street, where they shopped in the daytime and strolled by night, were always simultaneously sites of labour and of leisure. For the female consumer, the focal point of leisure, pleasure and personal freedom is not traditionally any fixed geographical location, but the female body itself. It was therefore the 'image industries'—the female mass media, and fashion and cosmetics industries—which constituted the largest sector of the post-war market in leisure commodities for girls.

The unity of post-war consumer lifestyles demanded new forms, too, for the feminine woman, produced in part on the production lines of the fashion, cosmetics and beauty-care industries. A glance at 1950s fashion images shows designers engaged in the business of sculpting, shaping and moulding ever more imaginative feminine forms: in 1954, the H-line, in spring 1955, the A-line, Dior's 'sack' in 1957, the trapeze line in spring 1958, into 1959 with the Empire line. At the same time, rigorous beauty-care regimes ensured that female bodies slipped smoothly into these new forms. Young girls turning for advice to *Bravo's* beauty-care columnist were taught techniques of body culture and maintenance whereby each part of the body could be separately shaped and trained. When skirt hems rose to just above the knee, attention was focussed on the female leg:

> From Paris comes the news that skirts are getting shorter—and short skirts show more leg! Are your legs in a fit state for public display? Nylon stockings show up every little blemish: do your stockings highlight the soft sheen of your well-cared-for skin . . . or is it the hard rough patches on thighs and knees which show up most? If it is, then something must be done at all costs! (*Bravo*, no. 10, 1958)

Tips on leg maintenance in *Bravo* between 1957 and 1959 included regular gymnastics, massage with 'slimming cream' (sic), visits to the chiropodist for sufferers from flat feet, lukewarm saltwater compresses for fat thighs, cycling for thin legs, trips to the doctor for red and inflamed skin. In conjunction with the beauty column, representations of women in the popular cultural discourses which traversed the pages of *Bravo* (film, television, fashion, rock and pop music and so on) reproduced certain common conventions of pose, gesture and body shape. For the perfect female leg, the general emphasis was on long, sweeping lines, further accentuated by high-heeled shoes tapering down to a pointed toe. Perfection was seen as embodied in particular representative female figures: Marlene Dietrich's legs, like Sophia Loren's hips and Brigitte Bardot's curves, were the talk of fifties beauty columns. Yet *Bravo* did not offer film star pin-ups as models of an ideal to which teenage girls should necessarily aspire; the ideal was displaced from visual representations, and located instead in the masculine gaze. 'Fashion has made skirts shorter,' said the *Bravo* beauty tip in March 1958, 'More than ever, eyes are drawn to your legs'. That these were the eyes of men had been made clear in the same column in an earlier edition of the magazine, which sounded the following note of comfort for girls whose legs, despite hours of tortured beauty treatment, remained stubbornly inelegant.

> A lot of men—for whose sake, after all, we go to all this trouble—don't have anything against legs that are a little stocky. A true man doesn't fall in love with external appearances. And if he does, he's the wrong one for you!' (*Bravo*, no. 44, 1957)

On the one hand, girls were exhorted to invest time and energy into the labour of body maintenance, grooming and careful dressing; on the other, the desired product of their labours remained persistently out of reach. The 'perfect female self' to which girls were urged to aspire was mirrored in the gaze of the men and boys with whom they shared their everyday lives; thus it remained unknowable, not signified in visual or textual representations, but in the ambiguous amorous attentions of men.

'Bravo girls' were offered one route out of this predicament; it led, not directly towards, but around and between the images of women which peopled the pages of the magazine. Mass media icons (film stars, fashion models, pop idols) were mediated to female readers by authoritative experts on fashion and beauty care—'Ilse' in Triumph underwear advertisements, or 'Trixi' in *Bravo*'s own fashion column. The information they filtered down to the female reader concerned, not *what* she should look like, but instructions on *how* to make the best of her own resources. They celebrated, not any single image of femininity, but a set of aesthetic principles as possible instruments for the construction of a more beautiful self. Tailored to the modest resources of the 'Angestellte' who were *Bravo*'s most lucrative market, the mode of aesthetic production propagated here was rule by principles of sobriety, discretion, restraint, moderation and self-control.

> Our 'style' may perhaps tend at times to copy adult fashions. But in general it is still *more restrained, less changeable and less expensive* . . . Slaves to fashion? We're convinced . . . and we hope you are too—that that's the last thing we want to be. (*Triumph* advertisement, *Bravo*, no. 42, 1958; author's emphasis.)

'Consumption' as cultural practice

In the preceding sections of this survey of fifties consumer culture, I have outlined some of the ways in which capital organized commodity markets to expand the boundaries of female consumption. From this analysis of dominant forms, perspectives for future work on gender and consumption now begin to emerge. In the first instance, it is capital which dictates the forms which commodity consumption takes; yet the market remains dependent on the development by the female consumer of specific sets of social competences and skills: from the rational decision-making of the thrifty housewife, to teenage girls' production of themselves as aesthetic objects in the symbolic configurations of teenage lifestyles. The category of 'consumption' covers a multitude of sins: symbolic readings of commodity, representations, processes of sensual gratification, practices of economic and cultural exchange. The so-called 'sphere' of consumption can thus be dismantled into a multiplicity of complex forms, relations and practices, which operate on diverse and discrete market sites. On each of these 'levels' of consumption, female consumers engage differently with the market machine, activating multiple sets of functions, meanings and values in the commodities they consume. Rules and conventions governing these consumer practices are laid down in consumer law, advice and information; thus we have seen *Bravo*'s fashion advisors setting out implicit and explicit rules for the production of teenage style through the consumption of fashion commodities.

Analyses of these rules and conventions are indispensable to, yet at the same time inadequate for feminist research into female practices of consumption. Highlighting the mechanisms of control which capital deploys, they fail to grasp the experiential quality of consumer culture for women and girls. Biographical narratives offer one way of bridging this gap, by tracing the paths whereby social subjects negotiate dominant forms; thus I have chosen to end this series of case studies in gender and consumer culture with two short narratives: a fictional filmic narrative, and a biography taken from an account of ethnographic field-work in the fifties. Positioned within radically different contexts, their common feature is the central significance accorded to one commodity: stockings. By 1961, nylon had swamped the young female market in West Germany; *Bravo's* DIVO survey shows 85 per cent of 'Bravo girls' between the ages of twelve and twenty-four (compared with 80 per cent of non-readers in the same age group) to be wearing seamless stockings; the percentage of female *Bravo* readers who did not possess either Perlon or nylon stockings was nil (DIVO, 1961, p. 137). These figures can neither be read as indicators of girls' blind submission to the dictates of the market, nor do they signify female capitulation to fetishistic 'male' fantasy. The all-pervasiveness of synthetic silk stockings begs different questions: what were the sources of their popularity, and how were they actually 'consumed'?

Ninotchka

In the late fifties, *Bravo* ran a series of half-page advertisements for 'Opal' seamless stockings, depicting crossed female legs, long and sophisticated, emerging from the folds of an elegant black dress. Parallel to the 'Opal' campaign, the magazine carried reports on *Silk Stockings*, Cole Porter's musical remake of Ernst Lubitsch's *Ninotchka* (1939). In the fifties' musical, Wim Sonneveld plays a Russian people's representative in Paris, whose loyalty to the Party is beginning to fade. Three Soviet commissars are ordered from Moscow to Paris: their mission—to rescue their colleague from the clutches of that decadent capital. When they in turn disappear, super-activist Ninotchka (Cyd Charisse) is sent on their trail. She soon recognizes the American, Edwin Canfield (Fred Astaire), as her main adversary; he, meanwhile, is amused, fascinated, but never convinced, by her fervent defence of socialism and the Soviet way of life. He guides her instead down the boulevards of Paris, knowing that no woman—'above all no woman with the charms of Ninotchka'—can withstand the 'democratic temptations' of their dazzling window displays. The 'fortress Ninotchka' finally falls; she succumbs to the charms of Edwin, and of the Western world he represents.

> Moscow—and politics—have lost Ninotchka for ever. Silk stockings may be thin, but in the end and above all, they are more attractive than the best of political convictions. (*Bravo*, no. 4, 1958)

Consumers of 'symbolic commodities' have preferred textual sources from which they draw the meanings with which those commodities are invested. *Bravo* is one such source for teenage consumers, and in 1958 it offered its readers a range of texts ('Opal' advertisements, fashion and beauty tips, reviews of *Silk Stockings*) in which synthetic silk (nylon or Perlon) stockings were encoded into new configurations of meaning. In part, these were drawn from the symbolic field of meanings around genuine silk, with its traditional associations of exoticism, sensuality, luxury and mystery: the legend of the Chinese princess said to have discovered the secret of the silkworm more than five thousand years ago: or the two sixth-century monks reputed to have smuggled the eggs of the silkworm out of China to the court of the Byzantine Emperor Justinian. But the additional glamour of the American nylon has specific origins elsewhere.

On post-1945 black markets, American soldiers were well known as the main purveyors of nylon stockings; by the 1950s, poster graphics were using images of stockinged female legs for comparative representations of rising productivity rates in European countries. In popular representations of the Cold War period, the stocking became a dominant signifier of freedom, democracy and the American way of life; the musical *Silk Stockings* was Hollywood's contribution to this modern myth. In the *Silk Stockings* narrative, real anxieties over a simmering East–West conflict are played out in fantastic form across the female body. Ninotchka first becomes a 'true' woman through romantic association with a Western man—and through her consumption of fashion commodities for the feminine woman. In *Bravo's* review, the resolution of the romantic narrative is couched in terms of military defeat ('the fortress Ninotchka . . . falls'); in the person of Edwin Canfield, America emerges victorious, not only over Ninotchka herself, but over the red threat she represents.

Reconstructing the *Silk Stockings* narrative, *Bravo's* review becomes instrumental in the production of a store of meanings around synthetic silk hose, from which teenage consumers might potentially have drawn. Those meanings cannot, however, simply be read off the *Bravo* text. Post-structuralist studies of narrative as complexly codified systems of representations (Barthes, 1975) have shown meaning to be the product of relationships between reader and text, and thus not an intrinsic characteristic of the narrative itself. In order to make sense of any given narrative, the reader engages differently with each of its multiple 'codes', reproducing in her/his signifying practices the relations of tension and contradiction which exist between those codes. In *Bravo's Silk Stockings* review, the so-called 'hermeneutic' and 'cultural' codes may be seen to produce just such contradictory meanings and values. The 'hermeneutic code' is the one which poses the central questions of the narrative, delaying the answers until the final moment of narrative resolution. The enigma of Ninotchka's narrative is the question of her possible transformation into a 'true' woman—a question answered at the end of the narrative in the language of female submission. Ninotchka capitulates to imperialist drives to colonize enemy continents, drives which are encapsulated here in the sexual passion of Edwin Canfield.

According to Barthes's definition in *S/Z*, the 'cultural code' of narrative refers the reader to meanings and values in the social world beyond the text. The social meaning of synthetic silk stockings is not exhausted in the *Bravo* narrative alone; indeed, connotations from other sources may badly disfigure the patterns of meaning constructed by 'internal' narrative codes (which are, in Barthesian terms, the hermeneutic and the semic codes). The following example of a second 1950s 'stocking narrative' shows one of the forms which these potentially oppositional meanings might take.

Annette

Between 1955 and 1957, a West German social worker, Renate Wald, put together a collection of biographical monographs of working-class factory girls, which were later published in Wurzbacher's *Die Junge Arbeiterin* (1958). She drew on a pool of ethnographic research conducted by a team of participant observers, all of whom had lived and worked as factory employees for a number of months or years.

One of the girls, Annette, works with her mother in a textile factory; an only child, she spends much of her 'leisure time' at home with the family, helping her mother around the house, or enjoying precious moments of lazy conversation when the chores are finally done. Annette's mother, wary of the dangers of possible sexual adventures, is unwilling to allow her to develop close friendships with young people of either sex; even female friendships, she fears, would ultimately lead to perilous encounters with the opposite sex. At the age of fifteen, Annette still amicably complies with her mother's wishes, remaining a model daughter in almost all respects. Even her taste in clothes is dictated by her mother's preferences for careful but unobtrusive dressing:

> She wears plain . . . dark clothes; although she uses powder and lipstick, she does so with care and in moderation; her hair is well-groomed and simply styled. She has an air, not so much of homeliness, as of exceptional respectability. (Wald, in Wurzbacher, 1958, p. 161)

Although mother and daughter rarely clash, there is one niggling point of conflict. The Perlon stockings which Annette wears to work every day cannot stand the rigours of shopfloor labour; inevitably, she wears out two or three pairs a week. Since Annette spends her weekly pocket money on biscuits and sweets, her mother has constantly to replenish her stock of nylons out of the housekeeping money. Her acid comment on her daughter's prodigality: 'She oughtn't to spend so much on titbits to eat. There's plenty of fruit and sweets to be had at home' (Wald, in Wurzbacher, 1958, p. 150). A striking characteristic of Annette's biography is the dreary regularity of her everyday life. Up at six in the morning to snatch a quick breakfast, stack the washing up, air the bedrooms and make the beds before setting out for work: nine hours at the production line: arriving back home at six-thirty in the evening to dust the rooms and clean the stairs before sitting down to eat with the family: retiring to bed by ten o'clock at the latest to recoup energy for the day ahead. Both at home and at the workplace, time, space, experience and action are regulated for Annette by institutions and agents of social control—the family and parents, the factory, overseers and management. In this context, Annette's conflict with her mother over stockings becomes more than a whimsical and inconsequential detail. A moment of disorder and disruption, it marks the displacement of potentially more grandiose demands for self-determination onto the only site where they may realistically be met. Annette is financially and emotionally dependent on the security of family life; she cannot allow herself prolonged struggles over points of generational difference. Repressed from the placid routine of everyday family life, these (inevitable) differences find expression in tangential conflicts and struggles.

It has been suggested that similar processes of displacement were in play in the formation of post-war youth subcultures (Cohen, 1972, p. 26). Yet subcultural resistance was no solution for Annette; isolated as she was from her contemporaries, her struggles necessarily took more minutely personal forms. Her conflicts with her mother centred on practices of day-to-day consumption—the money she wasted on frivolous treats, and her (mis)use of Perlon stockings. Perlon is made to be used and thrown away; mending stocking ladders is difficult, and diminishes aesthetic appeal. The 'built-in obsolescence' of Perlon stockings allowed Annette to use them to express an aberrant disregard for her mother's principle of moderation in all things, a principle to which she otherwise strictly adhered. Mass commodities demand to be consumed to excess: Annette, unconsciously perhaps, took them at their word.

Conclusion

As work on male youth subcultures has traced the 'hidden contradictions' which they 'magically resolve' (Hebdige, 1979, p. 18), so Annette's biography can shed light on some of the ways in which girls may live out the contradictions of their lives through an everyday culture of consumption. Her individual reformulation of the logic of built-in obsolescence took place *within* a teenage consumer culture; for her, hedonic consumption itself became a practice of refusal vis-à-vis dominant codes of social taste.

Feminists have commonly represented the 1950s as an age of repressive quiescence, in which women's disaffection with their feminine lot was successfully obscured and silenced. Since Betty Friedan's *Feminine Mystique* (1963), the blame for a widespread fifties' female malaise has been laid predominantly at the door of capitalist marketeers, to whom is ascribed the ability to dupe and seduce women into slavish submission to the authority of the market. But was 'consumerism' an adequate name for the problems of the female condition? Is there a hidden history of authentic female experience to be unearthed from beneath the glossy façade of fifties' femininity? Or could it not equally be the case that the façade itself 'speaks' the problems (and the delights) of the female condition? Consumerism not only offers, but also continually fulfils its promise of everyday solutions—albeit limited and partial ones—to problems whose origins may lie elsewhere. In post-war West Germany, women were constrained to search beyond national boundaries for female cultural forms untainted by aftertastes of Nazism. To don the accoutrements of an American female ideal—nylon stockings, scarlet lipstick, narrow skirts and high-heeled shoes—was in part to register a public disavowal of fascist images of femininity: scrubbed faces shining with health, sturdy child-bearing hips sporting seamed stockings and sensible shoes. Fifties consumerism, while it held many traps for women, nonetheless offered ways and means of negotiating a cultural history of militaristic discipline and rigorous control. Female 'resistance' of the period was perhaps not so much silenced, as pitched at a different level from earlier campaigns for women's equality (which in the fifties was proclaimed to have been achieved) or later feminist struggles against women's commoditization and objectification on a capitalist market. At specific moments in post-war history, the market has become a target for the rhetoric of a necessary and well-founded feminist opposition; yet in relation to the fifties—and possibly in the eighties too—there was, and is, little to be gained from 'oppositional' postures of aloof distaste.

> For me, the eighties are more than this: love the things that bring you down. I can't change things, I can't think plastic out of my world, so I try to turn the tables on it and see what's actually good about it. Do you see . . . I can drape myself with as much silk and linen as I want, and the plastic still won't go away. So I try to look at it differently. Love the things that bring you down. (Annette Humpe, Ideal)

References and further reading

Barthes, Roland (1970) *S/Z*, London: Jonathan Cape.

Cohen, P. (1972) 'Subcultural conflict and working-class community', *Working Papers in Cultural Studies*, no. 2, Spring.

DIVO/Kindler und Schiermeyer Verlag AG (eds.) (1961) *Bravo-Leser stellen sich vor*, Munich: Kindler und Schiermeyer.

Hall, S. and Jefferson, T. (eds.) (1976) *Resistance Through Rituals: Youth Subcultures in Post-War Britain*, London: Hutchinson.

Hebdige, D. (1979) *Subcultures: The Meaning of Style*, London: Methuen.

Hoggart, R. (1957) *The Uses of Literacy*, Harmondsworth: Penguin.

McRobbie, A. and Garber, J. (1976) 'Girls and subcultures' in S. Hall and T. Jefferson (eds.), *Resistance Through Rituals: Youth Subcultures in Post-War Britain*, London: Hutchinson.

Noelle, E. (1940) *Massenbefragungen über Politik und Presse in USA*, Frankfurt-am-Main: Diesterweg.

Scharmann, D.-L. (1965) *Das Konsumverhalten von Jugendlichen*, Munich: Juventa.

Vershofen, W. (1954) 'Rationalisierung vom Verbraucher her'. *Deutsche Wirtschaft im Querschnitt*, Beilage zu *Der Volkswirt*, no. 28.

Warner, W.L. (1960) *Social Class in America*, Evanston, Illinois: Harper & Row.

Willis, P. (1977) *Learning to Labour: How Working Class Kids get Working Class Jobs*, London: Saxon House.

Woods, W. (1960) 'Psychological dimensions of consumer decision', *Journal of Marketing*, vol. 24, no. 3.

Wurzbacher, G. and Jaide, W. (eds.) (1958) *Die junge Arbeiterin: Beiträge zur Sozialkunde und Jugendarbeit*, Munich: Juventa.

11

Black and white on the dance-floor

Paul Gilroy

From his *There Ain't No Black in the Union Jack* (Hutchinson, 1987).

[. . .] In July 1949, a *Picture Post* feature article by Robert Kee on 'The British colour bar' was illustrated by a photograph of a young couple and their child. The man was black and the woman was white. The caption beneath their picture was headlined 'a marriage that can lead to difficulties'. It revealed that the man, Herman McKay, was earning a living running a dance-band. In fact, the picture shows his wife helping him into his stage costume. The caption explained that he had been forced to adopt the pseudonym 'Alfonso Perez' as an essential part of this musical venture. This picture and its accompanying narrative vividly illustrate the way in which, from the beginning of post-war settlement, blacks were an ambiguous presence inside the popular culture of the 'host society'. Mr McKay was acceptable in the persona of 'Perez' the bandleader. He was welcome as a musician, as a producer of that culture, but the article implies that the informal but widespread colour bar would have excluded him as a customer from many of the places in which he worked as a performer.

The gradual transition from migrant to settler status involved a progression through a medley of different cultural forms. The early settlers were comparatively few in number (Peach, 1968) and beyond the British educations which were their colonial inheritance, they lacked a single cohesive culture which could bind them together. They set about creating it from the diverse influences which were available and which corresponded to their predicament. The dances, parties and social functions in which students, ex-service people and workers enjoyed themselves, reverberated to black musics drawn from the US and Africa as well as Latin America and the Caribbean. They jived and jitterbugged, foxtrotted and quickstepped, moving from one cultural idiom to another as the music changed. Class and occupational conflicts among the settlers as well as ethnic differences and the gender ratio[1] contributed to a degree of fragmentation. The student population concentrated in Bayswater, Kensington and North London diverged sharply from both the new workers who were beginning to make their homes in Brixton and Ladbroke Grove and the older seafaring community centred in the East End. The patterns of leisure generated by each relatively discrete group did not always overlap. Each in its own way combined black cultures from a variety of sources with those of the different white communities into which blacks were being drawn as a replacement population. Dancing was for many a primary leisure activity and, being couple centred, a sequence of conflicts based on whether blacks and whites could fraternize and touch in public began to develop.

Enrico Stennett, a young Jamaican political activist who had moved to Britain during 1947, achieved such notoriety for his prowess in the dance-halls of London that, after first being banned from the Lyceum, the Astoria, the Locarno and the Hammersmith and Wimbledon Palais, he was eventually hired by the management to perform exhibitions of jiving and jitterbugging to the delight of the white working-class crowds. This employment took him to ballrooms throughout the south of England and earned him £25 per week for three nights work. Unable to find a black woman to be his partner, Stennett discovered that dancing with white women provoked intense hostility from the management and sometimes violence. He and his white partner were contracted to leave immediately their exemplary performances ended lest other white women asked him to dance. Operating under the name 'Sugar', he and other young black dancers congregated at the Paramount ballroom in London's Tottenham Court Road. The Paramount rapidly became known as the dance-hall for black teenagers. 'Sugar' and other dance-floor hustlers working under names like 'The Magic Boots' and 'The Gladiator' equally quickly achieved a monopoly of the dance competitions organized by the ballroom owners.

> It was ironic to see, in an area of white people, you could not find one white male dancing. At the Paramount the atmosphere was always electric as the big bands jostled to play for us. . . . At these moments they could really enjoy their playing and by seeing the black people enjoying themselves to the full, it gave them more room for improvisation. . . . Alas there were no black women, but the Paramount was packed with young ladies coming in from the stockbroker belt of Surrey, Essex and Hampshire and other small villages and towns within a 60 mile radius of London.[2]

Stennett's account of the ballroom scene of the early 1950s is particularly valuable if read in conjunction with the autobiography of Leslie Thompson,[3] a black musician who worked in many of the biggest dance-bands during this period. Both testify to the ambiguous penetration of blacks into mainstream working-class leisure space. The contradictory nature of the black presence in those institutions is exemplified by Stennett's tale of the ways in which 'racial' hostility was tempered by the high status that derived from black pre-eminence on the dance-floor.

The different responses of whites along gender lines are also highly significant not only because they fracture the continuity of 'race' but also because of the centrality of miscegenation to the racist ideologies of the time. Stennett describes some of the conflicts which developed when white women were drawn into the unfolding antagonism between their black boyfriends and the police, who were particularly angered by the sight of black and white together. According to his account, both the police and the organized racist groups of the time felt that the association of white women with black men which was a marked feature of the Paramount sub-culture and actively discouraged by its management, degraded Britain as a whole.

Hostile police patrols and groups of racists would wait outside at closing time to assault and intimidate any black man they could find with a white woman.

> On one occasion I had left the Paramount dancehall alone and walked to the no. 1 bus stop in Warren Street. As I stood in a long queue of mostly women, I saw three African men with five English women enter a small café. They were not in the café more than five minutes when a gang of white men entered the café, pulled them outside and set about attacking them. The Africans were badly beaten so I rushed to the telephone to call the police. It was not long before they arrived in their cars and meat wagons. But the arrival of the police did not help the Africans. The leading police car blew his horn repeatedly giving the white men the chance to escape. They then proceeded to arrest the Africans. This did not go down well with the women in the queue. They set about the police attacking them physically with their stiletto heels as weapons. This resulted in many women being arrested along with the three Africans and taken to the police station off the Marylebone Road.[4]

Writing of the relationship between black men and white women at the time, Ras Makonnen (George Griffith) has suggested that a form of proto-feminism was to be found at the roots of women's support for the work of black political activists working in London.

> We recognised that the dedication of some of the girls to our cause was an expression of equal rights for women. One way of rejecting the oppression of men was to associate with blacks. To walk with a negro into a posh club like the Atheneum was to make this point. But many of them were vigorously attacked for this (Makonnen, 1973, p. 147).

It would appear that long before the advent of 'rock n'roll', the rise of soul, disco and reggae, the cultural institutions of the white working class were hosting an historic encounter between young black and white people. This meeting precipitated not only fear of the degeneration of the white 'race' in general and defilement of its womanhood in particular, but also the creation of a youth subculture in which black style and expertise were absolutely central. Indeed black supremacy within this subculture inverted in the most striking manner the relationships of domination and subordination assigned outside the dance-halls on racial lines. Of course, away from the shared spaces in which blacks and whites could interact and overlap, a further layer of exclusively black cultural institutions, clubs and dives was being created. Hiro estimates that during this period there were up to fifty black-owned and managed basement clubs in South London alone (1971). In the centre of London, the 59 Club, the Flamingo, the 77 Club and the Sunset, all in Soho, and the Contemporanean in Mayfair all catered to the needs of black workers. Dances organized by the British Council in its hostel at Hans Crescent in Knightsbridge kept the students occupied.

Sebastian Clarke (1980) has pointed out that 'Melodisc', a specialist label on which 'race' records from various sources could be issued, was operating successfully in this country from 1946 onwards (Cowley, 1985). Early releases on this label included material from the American Savoy catalogue. Melodisc first released calypso records here in 1951, having signed the celebrated troubadour, Lord Kitchener, who had been living in England since 1948.

Daddy Peckings, the proprietor of Peckings's Studio One record shop in West London, was the first person to sell reggae and its antecedents—bluebeat, ska and rocksteady—in this country. He has described the gradual transformation of American musical forms, particularly jazz and jump blues, and their junction with traditional Jamaican musics. This cross-fertilization would eventually lead to modern reggae, the evolution of which can be traced through the development of 'sound systems' (Bradshaw, 1981)—large mobile discos—and their surrounding culture in Jamaica and Britain. According to Peckings, the sound systems playing in the dance-halls of Kingston in the late 1940s and early 1950s—Waldron, Tom 'The Great' Sebastian and Nick—offered a mixture of bepop and swing. The big-band sounds of Duke Ellington and Count Basie were reworked by local musicians: Milton McPherson, Redva Cooke, Steve Dick and Jack Brown. Travelling to England in May 1960, Peckings set up a UK outlet for the product of legendary Jamaican producer and entrepreneur Coxsone Dodd, boss of the legendary Studio One label and the man credited not only with the discovery of modern Jamaica's greatest musical talents—The Heptones, Freddie McGregor, Jackie Mittoo, The Wailers—but with the creation of reggae itself.[5] The fledgling sound system culture of urban Jamaica was transplanted into Britain during the 1950s and on his arrival, Peckings began to supply records to Duke Vin of Ladbroke Grove, the first sound system in this country.

The basic description of a sound system as a large mobile hi-fi or disco does little justice to the specificities of the form. They are, of course, many thousands of times more powerful than a domestic record player but are significantly different from the amplified discos through which other styles of music have been circulated and consumed. The sound that they generate has its own characteristics, particularly an emphasis on the reproduction of bass frequencies, its own aesthetics and a unique mode of consumption. The form of sound systems and the patterns of consumption with which they have become associated will be discussed in detail below. The mark of African elements can be identified on different aspects of sound system culture.

Regardless of their forms and characteristic content, it is necessary to comprehend the importance of the sound systems for both the Jamaican reggae music industry which grew directly out of their activities and for the expressive culture of black Britain in which they remain a core institution. Perhaps the most important effect of the sound systems on the contemporary musical culture of black Britain is revealed in the way that it is centred not on live performances by musicians and singers, though these are certainly appreciated, but on records. Public performance of recorded music is primary in both reggae and soul variants of the culture. In both, records become raw material for spontaneous performances of cultural creation in which the DJ and the MC or toaster who introduces each disc or sequence of discs, emerge as the principal agents in dialogic rituals of active and celebratory consumption. It is above all in these performances that black Britain has expressed the improvization, spontaneity and intimacy which are key characteristics of all new world black musics, providing a living bridge between them and African traditions of music-making which dissolve the distinctions between art and life, artefact and expression which typify the contrasting traditions of Europe (Hoare, 1975; Keil, 1972; Sithole, 1972). As Keil points out, 'outside the West, musical traditions are almost exclusively performance traditions' (1972, p. 85). Sound system culture redefines the meaning of the team performance by separating the input of the artists who originally made the recording from the equally important work of those who adapt and rework it so that it directly expresses the moment in which it is being consumed, however remote this may be from the original context of production. The key to this process is the orality of the artistic forms involved.

The shifting, specialized vocabularies of sound system culture have changed and developed within contradictions generated by wider political and cultural processes—changing patterns of 'race' and class formation in the Caribbean, the US and Britain. The reliance on recorded music takes on even greater significance when it is appreciated that for much of the post-war period, Britain, unlike the US and the Caribbean, lacked both a domestic capacity to produce black musics and any independent means for their distribution. At this stage, the BBC was not interested in including African and Caribbean music in their programmes. When 'pop' charts began to be compiled, black shops and products were structurally excluded from the operations which generated them. This situation contrasts sharply with the position in the US where a well-developed market for 'race records' had grown up (Gillett, 1972), with its own distributors, charts and above all radio stations as a crucial means to spread and reproduce the culture.

Black Britain prized records as the primary resource for its emergent culture and the discs were overwhelmingly imported or licensed from abroad. The dependency of the British music scene on musics pro-duced elsewhere has progressed through several phases. But even as self-consciously British black forms have been constructed, the basic fact of dependency has remained constant. The cultural syncretism that has taken place across the national boundaries that divide the African diaspora has involved relations of unequal exchange in which Britain, for demographic and historical reasons, has until recently had a strictly subordinate place. The importing of music, often in small quantities, encouraged the underground aspects of a scene in which outlets into the dominant culture were already rare. Competition between sound system operators had been an early feature of the Jamaican dance-halls, and was entrenched over here as sound systems jostled for the most up-to-date and exclusive tunes imported from the US as well as the Caribbean. In a major survey of London's black music scene of the early 1970s, Carl Gayle explored the appeal of imported 'pre-release' records on the dance-hall circuit:

> The youngsters today spend more than they can afford on records, but they want the best and the rarest . . . 'We import our records three times a week from Jamaica' said a young guy called Michael . . . 'Pre-release music to me and many people like Sound System men and their followers, is like underground music. As soon as it's released it's commercial music. So you

find the youth of today, the ghetto youth like myself, pre-release music is like medicine.They'll go anywhere to hear it.'⁶

The identification of imported music as free from the commercialization which characterized the British music industry is an important expression of the politics which infused the roots music scene. The supposedly non-commercial status of imported records added directly to their appeal and demonstrated the difference between black culture and the pop-world against which it was defined.

The rivalry between 'sounds' over records was paralleled on the dance-floors by intense competition between their followers. The ritual expressions of both were dance competitions and the occasional fight. In the early 1970s reggae and soul scenes, the formal competitions centred on 'shuffling' and the rivalry between different sound systems was particularly intense where operators from north and south of the river clashed, each operator and toaster striving to match the other tune for tune, rhythm for rhythm, until the system with the best tunes and the weightiest sound emerged as the victor. Carl Gayle identified the level of violence in these encounters as one factor in the decomposition of the scene into sharply differentiated soul and reggae sub-scenes during the 1970s.

> The rivalry which developed between North and South . . . was the foundation for much of the violence of the Ram Jam and other clubs and was perpetrated by the supporters of the Sound Systems—Coxon and Duke Reid in the South and Count Shelly in the North especially. This rivalry, which often erupted into violence, was responsible for the division of the black music scene as a whole. . . . The clubs lost their respectability. Consequently many black youngsters dropped out of the once peaceful reggae-oriented sub-culture, opting for the more tranquil soul scene. Soul had always been popular with West Indians anyway and a lot of people just got scared of the hooliganism.

Gayle tentatively suggests that this violence was something which made reggae attractive to white youth and that it was a significant element in the forging of links between reggae and the skinheads around common conceptions of masculinity and machismo.

At its height, the late 1960s and early 1970s club scene involved alcohol-free daytime sessions completely dominated by dance at some of the best venues. For example, the Sunday afternoon 2–6 p.m. sessions at the Ram Jam in Brixton provided an antecedent for the equally drinkless Saturday lunchtime events organized by DJ Tim Westwood, which were instrumental in the spread of hip-hop in London during the 1980s. Like the hip-hop mixers of the later era, the sound system DJs often removed the labels from the records which they used. This gesture combined the obvious desire to keep the information contained on the labels secret, with a comment on the distance which these subcultures had travelled from their commercialized, overground equivalents. The removal of labels subverted the emphasis on acquisition and individual ownership which the makers of black music cultures identified as an unacceptable feature of pop culture. This simple act suggested alternative collective modes of consumption in which the information essential to purchase was separated from the pleasure which the music created. The record could be enjoyed without knowing who it was by or where it was in a chart. Its origins were r~·   ·secondary to the use made of it in the creative rituals of the c

Depriv<   ~ess to the official charts, the black record sellers began to produce   ~u own alternative indices of roots popularity in specialist publications devoted to black music and in the community's own news and political weeklies. The specialist monthly *Black Music* was launched in December 1973, at exactly the same time as minority programming of black musics was beginning to be introduced into the newly expanded local radio network. The size and distribution of Britain's black populations imposed severe limits on the amount of money which could be made from catering to their leisure needs. The communities remained diverse, small and scattered. These characteristics were important factors in the expansion of black leisure institutions and their partial adaptation to the demands of white Britons. The involvement of whites, particularly young people, in the consumption of black cultures was noted by commentators in the early 1960s. It has been discussed by other authors and by myself elsewhere (Patterson, 1966; Hebdige, 1979; Gilroy and Lawrence, 1982). The centrality of distinctively black forms to white youth cultures was observed by Hamblett and Deverson in 1964:

> The Blue Beat is here to stay. . . . Around the dancehalls and discotheques the Blue Beat has been added to the youngsters' already overstepping dance crazes. . . . Many mods that I have spoken to say that the Mersey Sound is out and this new sound is the big thing at the moment. As one youngster put it to me 'The Beatles have been well and truly squashed and we don't dig their sound anymore'.[7]

This mod's use of black American slang, 'dig', and the Beatles' early reliance on cover versions of material from rhythm and blues artists like Barrett Strong and Larry Williams are probably as significant as the blue beat itself in the history of how popular culture has formed spaces in which the politics of 'race' could be lived out and transcended in the name of youth.

The development of Jamaican popular music in the encounter between folk forms and American R and B picked up from radio stations transmitting in the southern states is well known (Clarke, 1980; Kimberley, 1982). At each stage of its progress through blue beat, ska, rocksteady and reggae it is possible to indicate shifting patterns in the involvement of young whites. For example, a white reggae band 'Inner Mind' was formed in London during 1967 and was considered good enough to back such vintage Jamaican performers as Laurel Aitken, Alton Ellis and Owen Grey.[8] The band played at all the leading black venues of the period—Mr B's, the Q and Colombo's in London, the Santa Rosa in Birmingham and Wolverhampton's Club '67. In *The Empire Strikes Back* (1982) I have indicated some of the elements by means of which this substantial history of white involvement can be periodized. The mass marketing of Caribbean music as a pop form can be traced from Millie Small's 'My Boy Lollipop' through the reggae festival at Wembley Stadium in 1969 and into the selling of

Bob Marley as a 'rebel superstar'. Simon Jones (1986) has pointed out that there were seventeen top twenty hits based on Jamaican music during the period 1969–72. The attempts of white companies to sell the music to whites also relied on the growth of minority programming within the newly established local radio network. The local stations which proliferated between 1970 and 1972 were concentrated in urban areas and each of them featured two or three hours of black music per week. This development was more significant in the history of Caribbean forms, because the pirate radio stations and the American Forces station in Europe already carried a certain amount of soul music to British fans. Radio Luxembourg, a leading pirate, broadcast Dave Christian's 'Soul Bag' early (1.30 a.m.) on Monday mornings. The new local stations made black music available to anyone who was interested enough to tune in to the unpopular slots—usually Sunday lunchtime—in which the minority shows were programmed. In the south-east, Steve Barnard's 'Reggae Time' on Radio London became particularly influential. Having experimented with several presenters for their reggae programme, Capital Radio launched David Rodigan's 'Roots Rockers' in October 1979. This show became the most important in reggae broadcasting, extending its running time from one and a half to three hours. The power of the show and the extent to which the reggae industry depended on it were revealed in 1985 when Rodigan announced that he had been threatened and intimidated by a small minority of record producers who sought to use the show to push their own product and ensure its commercial success regardless of artistic considerations. Rodigan did not name the producers responsible for his harassment, but told his listeners over the air:

> I've reached the point of no return with these hustlers. I'm tired of the threats and I'm standing up to them from now on. I'm going to entertain the public, not the reggae producers. I'm not going to bow down any more. All they can do is kill me now—that's all they can do.[9]

The gradual involvement of large corporations with a broad base in the leisure industries in the selling of reggae stimulated important changes reflecting a conscious attempt to separate the product from its producers and from its roots in black life. Whatever the effect of the reggae film *The Harder They Come* in the Caribbean (Brathwaite, 1984), in Britain, it marked the beginning of a new strategy for white consumption. The film was presented as little more than visual support for the sound-track recording made available by Island Records, an Anglo-Jamaican company. Cinemas showing the film became artificially insulated spaces in which images of black life, in this case as backward, violent, sexist and fratricidal, could be consumed without having to face the difficulties associated with sharing leisure space with real live black people. Island Records, the company who pioneered this ploy, elaborated it further in subsequent films of reggae artists in live performance and in the 'adventure fantasy', *Countryman* in 1982. This last film, a tale of Obeah and adventure, was based on a simple inversion of the Robinson Crusoe myth. 'Friday', recast in the form of a Rasta hermit-fisherman endowed with magical powers that originated in his total harmony with the natural world, saves and protects two young white Americans who fall into his Eden as the result of a plane crash. They are unwittingly involved in the drug business but with his help are reunited with their families and sent back to the US once the villains, the military wing of Michael Manley's socialist government, have been put in their place. This plot is less significant than the fact that the film was billed as 'A tribute to Bob Marley'. This time, the sound-track recording featured his songs.[10]

Island Records was also at the forefront of moves to sign black performers and, having adjusted their music and image to the expectations of white rock audiences, sell them as pop stars. The example of Bob Marley, an Island artist from 1972 until his death in 1981, provides the most acute illustration of a marketing process which was repeated by the company on a smaller, less successful scale with other lesser known (in rock terms) artists like the Heptones and Burning Spear. It was a strategy which was less productive for other rival British companies which lacked Island's roots in the Caribbean. Foremost among these was Virgin, who signed many leading Jamaican performers—the Gladiators, U Roy and the Mighty Diamonds—in the early 1970s. Marley's rise was also significant in that it facilitated the popularization of Rastafari ideology in Britain and throughout the world. The years between 1972 and 1981 saw him rise to outernational prominence and take reggae music forever into the lexicon of pop. There are good reasons to support the view that his foray into pop stardom was a calculated development in which he was intimately involved, having realized that the solidification of communicative networks across the African diaspora was a worthwhile prize. The minor adjustments in presentation and form that rendered his reggae assimilable across the cultural borders of the overdeveloped countries were thus a small price to pay. His incorporation of bluesy guitar playing and 'disco' rhythms can be interpreted not as obvious concessions to the demands of a white rock audience (Wallis and Malm, 1984), but as attempts to utilize the very elements most likely to appeal to the black audiences of North America.

Marley died at the very moment when he had steered reggae to the brink of an organic and overdue encounter with rhythm and blues. His work found considerable support in the new pop markets of Latin America and Africa, where he had performed at the independence ceremonies for Zimbabwe, symbolizing the recovery of Africa for the black peoples of the new world and the recovery of the new world diaspora for Africa. Whatever the ambiguities in Marley's music and mode of presentation, he provided a heroic personality around which the international mass-marketing of reggae could pivot. His 'Exodus' album remained on the British pop chart for fifty-six consecutive weeks in the period 1977–8. Marley acknowledged his newfound white listeners with the release of 'Punky Reggae Party' also in 1977. It signified not so much the confluence of two oppositional impulses—Rasta and punk—as the durability of pop and its capacity to absorb diverse and contradictory elements. The Caribbean was becoming an increasingly important subcultural resource once white British youth began to break free of their own dependency on American images and meanings (Hebdige, 1983). By consolidating reggae's position on the charts outside novelty categories and becoming a star, Marley created a new space in pop. In the period leading up to his death, it was a space filled primarily by the 'two-tone' cult. In this movement, earlier Caribbean forms, particularly ska, which had been exposed by the serious reggae fans' search for musical authenticity behind Marley's obvious compromises, were captured and rearticulated into distinctively British styles and concerns. This fusion took several contrasting paths. The assertively 'white' reggae of London bands like Madness and Bad Manners attracted the support of young racists, whose patriotic nativism had been reborn in the revival of the skinhead style. It contrasted sharply with the work of racially mixed groups from the Midlands. Where Madness simply hijacked ska and declared it white, the Beat, the Specials and other similar outfits sought to display the contradictory politics of 'race' openly in their work. Their best efforts acknowledged the destructive power of racism and simultaneously invited their audience to share in its overcoming, a possibility that was made concrete in the co-operation of blacks and whites in producing the music.

If Marley's excursions into pop had seeded the ground for this two-tone harvest, this era suggests that the lasting significance of his rise to prominence lies not at the flamboyant extremities of youth subculture where punks had reworked the themes and preoccupations of Rastafari around their dissent from and critique of Britishness, but in the youth-cultural mainstream. Here, the posters of Bob, locks flying, which had been inserted into his crossover product by Island, became icons in the bedroom shrines of thousands of young whites. In his egalitarianism, Ethiopianism and anti-imperialism, his critique of law and of the types of work which were on offer, these young people found meanings with which to make sense of their lives in post-imperial Britain. The two-tone bands appreciated this and isolated the elements in Marley's appeal that were most appropriate to the experiences of young, urban Britons on the threshold of the 1980s. They pushed the inner logic of his project to its conclusion by fusing pop forms rooted in the Caribbean with a populist politics. Marley's populism had been focussed by the imperatives of black liberation and overdetermined by the language of Rastafarian eschatology. Theirs was centred instead on pointing to the possibility that black and white young people might discover common or parallel meanings in their blighted, post-industrial predicament. The experience of living side by side in a 'ghost town' had begun to raise this question. The Specials' song, which topped the chart as the rioting of 1981 was at its peak, asked, 'Why must the youth fight against themselves?' and cleverly entangled its pleas against both racism and youth–cultural sectarianism. The two-tone operation depended on being seen to transcend the various prescriptive definitions of 'race' which faced each other across the hinterland of youth culture. With Marley's death equilibrium was lost. One pole of the cultural field in which two-tone had formed ceased functioning. Marley's position was usurped eagerly not by the next generation of Jamaican and British artists who had been groomed by their record companies to succeed him, but by a new wave of post-punk white reggae musicians. The best known of these inverted the preconceptions of Rasta by calling themselves The Police and armed with 'Aryan' good looks and dedication to 'Regatta de Blanc' served, within pop culture at least, to detach reggae from its historic association with the Africans of the Caribbean and their British descendants.

Notes

1 Hiro (1971) periodizes the early settlement and argues that skilled and semi-skilled settlers were in the majority between 1948 and 1955. In the later period between 1955 and 1962 'the "typical" migrant was unskilled or semi-skilled with a rural or semi-rural background' (p. 10).
   Peach, (1968, pp. 41–2) has the figures on the gender difference among the black settler population. According to his tables, women were only an overall majority of immigrants in 1958 and 1959 though the percentage of men and women varied quite widely between the different West Indian territiories. In 1958 for example, 60.6 per cent of Guyanese and 48.3 per cent of Jamaican emigrants were male.
2 *Caribbean Times*, 241, 25 October 1985. I spoke to Mr Stennett in October 1985.
3 See Leslie Thompson's autobiography (1985).
4 *Caribbean Times*, 242, 1 November 1985.
5 The Cables' 'Baby Why' (Studio One) is one of the first discernably 'reggae' recordings, and typifies the Coxsone approach of the period.
6 *Black Music*, 1, no. 8, July 1974.
7 Charles Hamblett and Jane Deverson, *Generation X*, London: *Tandem Books*, 1964.
8 *Black Music*, March 1976.
9 *Time Out*, 16–22 May 1985.
10 The growth of reggae as a form of pop or rock music during the 1970s resulted in a proliferation of pictorial 'coffee table' books about Rastafari, reggae and Jamaica. Soft core porn photographs of black bodies, male and female, were interspersed by journalistic commentary about the brutishness and the hedonism of this Caribbean idyll. Typical manifestations of this genre include Michael Thomas and Adrian Boot's *Jah Revenge*, Eel Pie/Hutchinson, 1982; and Adrian Boot and Vivien Goldman's *Bob Marley Soul Rebel–Natural Mystic*, Eel Pie/Hutchinson, 1981.

Bibliography

Bradshaw, P. (1981) 'A big sound system splashdown', *New Musical Express*, 21 February.
Braithwaite, E.K. (1984) *History of the Voice: The Development of Nation Language in Anglophone Caribbean Poetry*, London: New Beacon Press.
CCCS (1982) *The Empire Strikes Back*, London: Hutchinson.
Clarke, S. (1980) *Jah Music*, London: Heinemann.
Cowley, J. (1985) *West Indian Gramophone Records in Britain: 1927–1950*, ESRC Occasional Papers in Ethnic Relations, no. 1.
Gillett, C. (1972) 'The black market roots of rock' in Denisoff and Peterson (eds.), *The Sounds of Social Change Studies in Popular Culture*, Chicago: Rand McNally.
Gilroy, P. and Lawrence, E. (1982) 'Two-tone Britain, black youth, white youth and the politics of anti-racism', in Bains and Cohen (eds.), *Youth in Multi-racist Britain*, London: Macmillan.
Hebdige, D. (1979) *Subculture: The Meaning of Style*, London: Methuen.

Hebdige, D. (1983), 'Ska Tissue: The Rise and Fall of Two Tone' in Simon and Davis (eds.) *Reggae International*, London: Thames & Hudson.

Hiro, D. (1971) *Black British White British*, London: Eyre & Spottiswoode.

Hoare, I. *et al.* (1975) *The South Book*, London: Methuen.

Jones, S. (1986) *White Youth and Jamaican Culture*, unpublished Ph.D. thesis, University of Birmingham: Centre for Contemporary Cultural Studies.

Keil, C. (1972) 'Motion and feeling through music' in Kochman (ed.), *Rappin' and Stylin' Out*.

Kimberley, N. (1982) 'Ska: how Jamaica found a sound of its own', *The Encyclopaedia of Rock*, 5, issue 49.

Makonnen, R. (1973) [George Griffith] *Pan Africanism from Within*, Nairobi: Oxford University Press.

Patterson, O. (1986) 'The dance invasion', *New Society*, reprinted in *Pressure Drop*, no. 2, undated.

Sithole, E. (1972) 'Black folk music' in Kochman (ed.), *Rappin' and Stylin' Out*.

Thompson, L. (1985) *An Autobiography*, Crawley: Rabbit Press.

12

Minimal selves

Stuart Hall

From *The Real Me—Postmodernism and the Question of Identity* (ICA Documents, 1987).

A few adjectival thoughts only . . .

Thinking about my own sense of identity, I realize that it has always depended on the fact of being a *migrant*, on the *difference* from the rest of you. So one of the fascinating things about this discussion is to find myself centred at last. Now that, in the postmodern age, you all feel so dispersed, I become centred. What I've thought of as dispersed and fragmented comes, paradoxically, to be *the* representative modern experience! This is 'coming home' with a vengeance! Most of it I much enjoy—welcome to migranthood. It also makes me understand something about identity which has been puzzling me in the last three years.

I've been puzzled by the fact that young black people in London today are marginalized, fragmented, unenfranchized, disadvantaged and dispersed. And yet, they look as if they own the territory. Somehow, they, too, in spite of everything, are centred, in place: without much material support, it's true, but nevertheless, they occupy a new kind of space at the centre. And I've wondered again and again: what it is about that long discovery-rediscovery of identity among blacks in this migrant situation, which allows them to lay a kind of claim to certain parts of the earth which aren't theirs, with quite that certainty? I do feel a sense of—dare I say—envy surrounding them. Envy is a very funny thing for the British to feel at this moment in time—to want to be black! Yet I feel some of you surreptitiously moving towards that marginal identity. I welcome you to that, too.

Now the question is: is this centring of marginality really *the* representative postmodern experience? I was given the title 'the minimal self'. I know the discourses which have theoretically produced that concept of 'minimal self'. But my experience now is that what the discourse of the postmodern has produced is not something new but a kind of recognition of where identity always was at. It is in that sense that I want to redefine the general feeling which more and more people seem to have about themselves—that they are all, in some way, *recently migrated*, if I can coin that phrase.

The classic questions which every migrant faces are twofold: 'Why are you here?' and 'When are you going back home?' No migrant ever knows the answer to the second question until asked. Only then does she or he know that really, in the deep sense, she/he's never going back. Migration is a one way trip. There is no 'home' to go back to. There never was. But 'why are you here?' is also a really interesting question, which I've never been able to find a proper answer to either. I know the reasons one is supposed to give: 'for education', 'for the children's sake', 'for a better life, more opportunities', 'to enlarge the mind', etc. The truth is, I am here because it's where my family is not. I really came here to get away from my mother. Isn't that the universal story of life? One is where one is to try and get away from somewhere else. That was the story which I could never tell anybody about myself. So I had to find other stories, other fictions, which were more authentic or, at any rate, more acceptable, in place of the Big Story of the endless evasion of patriarchal family life. Who I am—the 'real' me—was formed in relation to a whole set of other narratives. I was aware of the fact that identity is an invention from the very beginning, long before I understood any of this theoretically. Identity is formed at the unstable point where the 'unspeakable' stories of subjectivity meet the narratives of history, of a culture. And since he/she is positioned in relation to cultured narratives which have been profoundly expropriated, the colonized subject is always 'somewhere else': doubly marginalized, displaced always *other* than where he or she is, or is able to speak from.

It wasn't a joke when I said that I migrated in order to get away from my family. I did. The problem, one discovers, is that since one's family is always already 'in here', there is no way in which you can actually leave them. Of course, sooner or later, they recede in memory, or even in life. But these are not the 'burials' that really matter. I wish they were still around, so that I didn't have to carry them around, locked up somewhere in my head, from which there is no migration. So from the first, in relation to them, and then to all the other symbolic 'others', I certainly was always aware of the self as only constituted in that kind of absent–present contestation with something else, with some other 'real me', which is and isn't there.

If you live, as I've lived, in Jamaica, in a lower-middle-class family that was trying to be a middle-class Jamaican family trying to be an upper-middle-class Jamaican family trying to be an English Victorian family . . . I mean the notion of displacement as a place of 'identity' is a concept you learn to live with, long before you are able to spell it. Living with, living through difference. I remember the occasion when I returned to Jamaica on a visit sometime in the early 1960s, after the first wave of migration to England, my mother said to me: 'Hope they don't think you are one of those immigrants over there!' And of course, at that point I knew for the first time I was an immigrant. Suddenly in relation to that narrative of migration, one version of the 'real me' came into view. I said: 'Of course, I'm an immigrant. What do you think I am?' And she said in that classic Jamaican middle-class way, 'Well, I hope the people over there will shove all the immigrants off the long end of a short pier.' (They've been shoving ever since.)

The trouble is that the instant one learns to be 'an immigrant', one recognizes one can't be an immigrant any longer: it isn't a tenable place to be. I, then, went through the long, important, political education of discovering that I am 'black'. Constituting oneself as 'black' is another recognition of self through difference: certain clear polarities and extremities against which one tries to define oneself. We constantly underestimate the importance, to certain crucial political things that have happened in the world, of this ability of people to constitute themselves, psychically, in the black identity. It has long been thought that this is really a simple process: a recognition—a resolution of irresolutions, a coming to rest in some place which was always there waiting for one. The 'real me' at last!

The fact is 'black' has never been just there either. It has always been an unstable identity, psychically, culturally and politically. It, too, is a narrative, a story, a history. Something constructed, told, spoken, not simply found. People now speak of the society I come from in totally unrecognizable ways. Of course Jamaica is a black society, they say. In reality it is a society of black and brown people who lived for three or four hundred years without ever being able to speak of themselves as 'black'. Black is an identity which had to be learned and could only be learned in a certain moment. In Jamaica that moment is the 1970s. So the notion that identity is a simple—if I can use the metaphor—black or white question, has never been the experience of black people, at least in the diaspora. These are 'imaginary communities'—and not a bit the less real because they are also symbolic. Where else could the dialogue of identity between subjectivity and culture take place?

Despite its fragmentations and displacements, then, 'the self' does relate to a real set of histories. But what are the 'real histories' to which so many at this conference have 'owned up'? How new is this new condition? It does seem that more and more people now recognize themselves in the narratives of displacement. But the narratives of displacement have certain conditions of existence, real histories in the contemporary world, which are not only or exclusively psychical, not simply 'journeys of the mind'. What is that special moment? Is it simply the recognition of a general condition of fragmentation at the end of the twentieth century?

It may be true that the self is always, in a sense, a fiction, just as the kinds of 'closures' which are required to create communities of identification—nation, ethnic group, families, sexualities, etc.—are arbitrary closures; and the forms of political action, whether movements, or parties, or classes, those, too, are temporary, partial, arbitrary. I believe it is an immensely important gain when one recognizes that all identity is constructed across difference and begins to live with the politics of difference. But doesn't the acceptance of the fictional or narrative status of identity in relation to the world also require as a necessity, its opposite—the moment of arbitrary closure? Is it possible for there to be action or identity in the world without arbitrary closure—what one might call the necessity to meaning of the end of the sentence? Potentially, discourse is endless: the infinite semiosis of meaning. But to say anything at all in particular, you do have to stop talking. Of course, every full stop is provisional. The next sentence will take nearly all of it back. So what is this 'ending'? It's a kind of stake, a kind of wager. It says: 'I need to say something, something . . . just now.' It is not forever, not totally universally true. It is not underpinned by any infinite guarantees. But just now, this is what I mean; this is who I am. At a certain point, in a certain discourse, we call these unfinished closures, 'the self', 'society', 'politics', etc. Full stop. OK. There really (as they say) is no full stop of that kind. Politics, without the arbitrary interposition of power in language, the cut of ideology, the positioning, the crossing of lines, the rupture, is impossible. I don't understand political action without that moment. I don't see where it comes from. I don't see how it is possible. All the social movements which have tried to transform society and have required the constitution of new subjectivities, have had to accept the necessarily fictional, but also the fictional necessity, of the arbitrary closure which is not the end, but which makes both politics and identity possible.

Now I perfectly recognize that this recognition of difference, of the impossibility of 'identity' in its fully unified meaning, does, of course, transform our sense of what politics is about. It transforms the nature of political commitment. Hundred-and-one per cent commitment is no longer possible. But the politics of infinitely advancing while looking over the shoulder is a very dangerous exercise. You tend to fall into a hole. Is it possible, acknowledging the discourse of self-reflexivity, to constitute a *politics* in the recognition of the necessarily fictional nature of the modern self, and the necessary arbitrariness of the closure around the imaginary communities in relation to which we are constantly in the process of becoming 'selves'?

Looking at new conceptions of identity requires us also to look at re-definitions of the forms of politics which follow from that: the politics of difference, the politics of self-reflexivity, a politics that is open to contingency but still able to act. The politics of infinite dispersal is the politics of no action at all; and one can get into that from the best of all possible motives (i.e., from the highest of all possible intellectual abstractions). So one has to reckon with the consequences of where that absolutist discourse of postmodernism is pushing one. Now, it seems to me that it is possible to think about the nature of new political identities, which isn't founded on the notion of some absolute, integral self and which clearly can't arise from some fully closed narrative of the self. A politics which accepts the 'no necessary or essential correspondence' of anything with anything, and there has to be *a politics of articulation*—politics as a hegemonic project.

I also believe that out there other identities *do* matter. They're not the same as my inner space, but I'm in some relationship, some dialogue, with them. They are points of resistance to the solipsism of much postmodernist discourse. I have to deal with them, somehow. And all of that constitutes, yes, a politics, in the general sense, a politics of constituting 'unities'-in-difference. I think that is a new conception of politics, rooted in a new conception of the self, of identity. But I do think, theoretically and intellectually, it requires us to begin, not only to speak the language of dispersal, but also the language of, as it were, contingent closures of articulation.

You see, I don't think it's true that we've been driven back to a definition of identity as the 'minimal self'. Yes, it's true that the 'grand narratives' which constituted the language of the self as an integral entity don't hold. But actually, you know, it isn't just the 'minimal selves' stalking out there with absolutely no relation to one another. Let's think about the question of nation and nationalism. One is aware of the degree to which nationalism was/is constituted as one of those major poles or terrains of articulation of the self. I think it is very important the way in which some people now (and I think particularly of the colonized subject) begin to reach for a new conception of ethnicity as a kind of counter to the old discourses of nationalism or national identity.

Now one knows these are dangerously overlapping terrains. All the same they are not identical. Ethnicity *can* be a constitutive element in the most viciously regressive kind of nationalism or national identity. But in our times, as an imaginary community, it is also beginning to carry some other meanings, and to define a new space for identity. It insists on difference—on the fact that every identity is placed, positioned, in a culture, a language, a history. Every statement comes from somewhere, from somebody in particular. It insists on specificity, on conjuncture. But it is not necessarily armour-plated against other identities. It is not tied to fixed, permanent, unalterable oppositions. It is not wholly defined by exclusion.

I don't want to present this new ethnicity as a powerless, perfect universe. Like all terrains of identification, it has dimensions of power in it. But it isn't quite so framed by those extremities of power and aggression, violence and mobilization, as the older forms of nationalism. The slow contradictory movement from 'nationalism' to 'ethnicity' as a source of identities is part of a new politics. It is also part of the 'decline of the west'—that immense process of historical relativization which is just beginning to make the British, at least, feel just marginally 'marginal'.

13

Between holy text and moral void

Bhikhu Parekh

Originally published in *New Statesman and Society* on 24 March 1989, five weeks after the Ayatollah Khomeini issued his *fatwa* against Salman Rushdie and *The Satanic Verses*.

Salman Rushdie's *The Satanic Verses* has become a terrain for many different and interrelated battles. Strange alliances have been formed across different battle lines, and the British cultural, educational and political scene has undergone transformations hardly anyone could have predicted a few weeks ago. *The Satanic Verses* is a dense and highly complex book, articulated at a variety of levels held together by a range of common concerns. It is, therefore, hardly surprising that most of the protesting Muslims haven't read it all, or have not read it with the care it deserves, and throw around passages taken out of context as polemical hand grenades. I wonder how many of the journalists, and even the high-minded literary critics, have understood it either. The book has a distinctly Bombayite ambience, ethos and style of writing, and many of its nuances, allusions and literary mannerisms are likely to be lost upon those who have not lived in that great metropolitan melting pot.

It is also full of colloquial and evocative Hindi words which are not just thrown in as street talk but made to serve strategic literary purposes. A professor of English was surprised when I told him that the word *chamcha* in the name of one of the central characters means a stooge or a hatchet-man, that it is widely used to question a man's integrity and that Rushdie's use of it was highly suggestive. He was surprised, too, when I told him that *chod* was the Hindi equivalent of an English four-letter word, and that *behanchod* meant (but did not have the same emotional force as) 'sister-fucker'.

Again, the chapters dealing with 'Mahound' (Muhammad) and his new religion are suffused with subtle allusions and insinuations likely to be lost on or misunderstood by those who are not well-versed in the history of Islam and have not grown up in a Muslim household. If the much-maligned illiterate peasants of Bradford protest in ignorance of the book, many of those who arrogantly lecture them could also do with a little humility.

Though I am a Bombayite and know something of that city's culture, my knowledge of Islam is limited and distorted by the usual prejudices of a Hindu. Having read the book on my own, I decided to read the relevant chapters again with two Muslim friends. If we are to make sense of the

139

Muslims' fierce and apparently uncompromising protest, we owe them a basic moral obligation to read it with their eyes. What follows is my own construction of the book, based on critical reflections on its different readings, including the Muslim.

Much confusion is created by the view that *The Satanic Verses* is a work of fiction. It is a story of migration and exile, and represents, among other things, an attempt to see the world from the perspective of an immigrant. As such, it deals with contemporary social reality in a highly imaginative manner. Imaginative exploration of reality can take many forms depending on the level of abstraction adopted by the author. Rushdie adopts a relatively low level of abstraction. He fantasises and redefines real, recognizable men and women and does not create wholly new characters and images. His characters are not products of what Kant called 'pure' or 'transcendental' imagination, but real people subjected to the free play of fantasy. *The Satanic Verses* is thus a work of fantasy, not of pure fiction, of an imaginatively reinterpreted but not a radically reconstituted reality.

Many of Rushdie's major 'characters' resemble men and women we know, and some are even given the names they bear in real life. This is also true of his discussion of Islam in the controversial chapters. 'Mahound' is none other than a poorly abstracted and richly fantasized Muhammad. Muhammad *was* called Mahound by the nervous and bewildered Christians in the Middle Ages. Two of the verses in the Koran *were* suspected to be products of Satanic intervention. Pre-Islamic Mecca *was* called the land of *Jahil*, or ignorance. Muhammad did have twelve wives and they were called Ayesha, Khadija and all the other names Rushdie gives them in the book. The first man who answered 'the call of prayer' *was* called Bilal, an emancipated black slave. The promiscuous wife of Abu Suplian, the most powerful chief of Mecca and custodian of the temple, *was* called Hind. Ayesha *did* disappear for two days and that became a subject of much gossip. And so on.

Chapters two and six in *The Satanic Verses* are fantasized history; that is, they are *fantasies*, but fantasies relating to, deeply embedded in and severely hedged in by, *history*.

The frequent use of dreams does not alter its status. They are at best literary stratagems, at worst useful defences against possible attack and even perhaps litigation. Had its author totally abstracted from history and created characters, episodes, symbols and images that applied to all religions and hence to none in particular, the case would have been different.

This approach enables Rushdie to enter into and tease out with great clarity and vividness the structure and inner dynamics of the immigrant's everyday life, including racism, self-alienation, the joys and tortures of harbouring several selves, and the fantasized reality in which he is forced to live. It also helps him to reconstruct the dead world of historical individuals and to offer incisive insights into their dilemmas, struggles and states of mind.

Rushdie's approach, however, has its dangers. If a writer is not careful, he or she can end up treating recognizable men and women as *mere* objects of fantasies, as people whom he knows better than they do themselves, as *manipulable* material for the free play of his imagination. The writer may then become not just disrespectful and irreverent, but supercilious and dismissive, a shade crude, even perhaps exhibitionist, scoring cheap points off half-real characters. Rushdie's approach yields a splendid harvest when applied to politics, business, middle-class social life and other areas which are amenable to it, but it can come to grief when used to explore areas, experiences, activities, relationships and individuals considered holy or at least sacred.

By sacred, I mean that which is beyond utilitarian considerations and has an intrinsic or non-instrumental significance, which transcends and links up individuals with something greater than themselves and gives their lives depth and meaning. The holy represents sacredness anchored in, and defined in, terms of a divine principle. Religion is the realm of the holy *par excellence*, but it does not exhaust sacredness. Even the atheist regards certain relationships, activities, experiences, life and fellow-humans as sacred. Broadly speaking, holiness is a religious category, sacredness a spiritual category, and respect a moral category.

The central life experiences of immigrants cast them in a highly ambiguous relationship with the sacred. Lacking roots in an ongoing way of life, unable to feel in their bones the deepest joys and agonies of their adopted home, cut off from the social well-springs of meaning and value, their lives lack depth and richness, the commonest source of the experiences of sacredness. Their dignity as human beings is constantly mocked by the hostile 'host' society; their sacred family ties are brutally snapped by evil immigration laws; their children leave home every morning and return speaking a language increasingly unintelligible and even hurtful to them. Thanks to all this, their predominant mood is one of doubt and suspicion, a subdued rage at the hypocrisy of a society that says one thing but does the opposite.

Different immigrants respond to these experiences and moods differently and evolve different strategies of physical and moral survival. Of these, two are relevant to our discussion. At one extreme, there is total cynicism. All people stink, are imposters, ruthless, cheats, predators, manipulators. None can be trusted, not even or rather especially not fellow-immigrants. Everything in this world is superficial and crude, and can be mocked, deflated, perverted, turned upside down. At the other extreme, there is a retreat to the familiar certainties of the past.

The meaning of life is deemed to be permanently and incorrigibly revealed in a sacred text, a body of rituals, or a pool of inherited and inviolable traditions. Even if these are perceived to be irrelevant or inapplicable in the new environment, they are uniquely the immigrant's own in a society that has stripped him or her of all else, the only thing that *distinguishes* them, gives them a past, roots in the present and the confidence to face the future. The holy text or traditions give certainty in a world of moral void; they are a sure protection against the dehumanizing impact of cynicism. At one extreme, then, a deep and self-destructive doubt, at the other, an impenetrable and intolerant certainty. One has lost a sense of sacredness, the other has a surfeit of it.

All immigrants, however reflective and introspective they may be, har-
bour bits of both tendencies (and many others), nervously holding them
in a precarious balance, turning to one when the other fails or becomes
unbearable. Rushdie is no exception. He writes about the tension between
these tendencies without fully appreciating that it lies at the very centre
of his being and both enriches and distorts his perception of his subject
matter.

This is evident in *The Satanic Verses*. An immensely daring and persistently probing exploration of the human condition, which only a rootless
immigrant can undertake, lies ill at ease with timid obeisance to the latest
literary and political fashions; profound seriousness lapses suddenly and
without warning into pointless playfulness. The sacred is interlaced with
flippancy, the holy with the profane. Intensely delicate explorations of
human relationships and emotions are shadowed by an almost childlike
urge to shock, hurt and offend.

As an immigrant, Rushdie sometimes seems to resent that everyone
around him is not an immigrant; on other occasions, he is profoundly
pleased that the natives have their roots intact and showers benedic-
tion. At a different level, he is both drawn towards and repelled by his
fellow-immigrants. He both fights them and fights for them; both resents
them and delights in their world of certainties; cares for them but also
tramples on their dearest memories and sentiments. He loves them as real
human beings, yet he also turns them into an abstract cause; and his holy
anti-racism goes hand-in-hand with touches of contempt for them.

It is this that at least partly explains the current tension between him
and the Muslims. The tension is a result of the conflict between two very
different approaches to the predicament of an exile. Unlike the white
onlookers who understand neither, the contestants know that nothing
less than their fundamental existential choices, and even sanity, are at
stake. The vast majority of Muslims have chosen one way of coping with
their predicament; Rushdie another. They give meaning to their poor and
empty lives by holding on to the holy and its rocklike certainties; he doubts
almost everything, including the very search for meaning. Their approach
has little room for doubt; Rushdie's has only a limited space for the holy, or
even the sacred, and he is deeply nervous in its presence. They solace each
other within a common fellowship and lead individually heterogeneous
lives within an autonomous group; Rushdie's quest for personal autonomy
leads to an ambiguous relationship with the white society and especially its
literary establishment. The inescapable conflict between the two exploded
the moment he produced a full-scale exploration of the sacred in *The Satanic
Verses*.

In chapters two and six, as well as elsewhere in the book, Rushdie does
not explore religion *per se* but Islam, not *a* prophet but Muhammad; and
he remains too close to Islamic history to be justified in claiming, or to
succeed in persuading his adversaries, that his account is fictional.

Rushdie's imaginative explorations of the birth of Islam, Muhammad's
'terrifying singularity', the way his new religion came to terms with the
constraints of the contemporary world, and the logic of total submission
are bold and penetrating. Though they might and do offend some of the

faithful, they form part of a legitimate inquiry. To have called Muhammad Mahound rather than by any other historically less evocative name was unwise, and comes close to a deliberate attempt to offend and provoke. Since only two out of several hundred verses were suspected of being inspired by Satan, the title of the book, too, was unnecessarily provocative. Muhammad is often described as a businessman, constantly bargaining and doing 'deals' with the archangel. He is sometimes referred to as 'the Businessman'; his is a 'revelation of convenience'; 'his God is really a businessman'; the archangel was 'businesslike' and 'obliging', and even reduced the initial quota of forty prayers a day to five.

Here, as elsewhere, Rushdie's approach is not only irreverent but mocking, dismissive, angry. It is designed to put Muhammad in his place. Not surprisingly, it has deeply offended Muslim sensibilities. However, this is all part of a legitimate literary inquiry. And if a creative writer were to be hamstrung by the feelings and sentiments of over-sensitive readers, the writer's search for truth would be hampered and humankind would suffer a loss. The offence caused to Muslims could therefore be ignored in the larger interests of truth.

Doubts begin to arise with respect to other parts of *The Satanic Verses*. Muhammad is called a 'smart bastard', a debauchee who, after his wife's death, slept with so many women that his beard turned 'half-white' in a year. Muslims deeply respect Bilal, the emancipated black slave who was the first convert to Islam. Here, he is an 'enormous black monster . . . with a voice to match his size.' Muhammad's three revered colleagues, including Bilal, are 'those goons—those fucking clowns', the 'trinity of scum'. Like any great religious text, the Koran is full of rules and injunctions about forms of worship, helping the poor, concern for those in need, moral purity, self-discipline and surrender to the will of God. *The Satanic Verses* mockingly reduces it to a book 'spouting' rules about how to 'fart', 'fuck' and 'clean one's behind', and why only two sexual positions are legitimate, one of them being sodomy (that tired anti-Muslim canard yet again).

These remarks lack artistic justification. For Muslims, these and other such remarks are not only offensive and distressing; they also take on the character of what lawyers call 'fighting words'. Fighting words are verbal equivalents of the first shoves and pushes in a fight. They insult and provoke the devout; they challenge Muslim men to stand up and fight back if they have any self-respect and a sense of honour. They amount to a declaration of hostility. Even as we all feel not just hurt, but *provoked*, when we, our parents and loved ones or ethnic group are insulted and called obscene names, a Muslim man rightly feels challenged to a fight when those whose venerated memories he holds in sacred trust are ridiculed and abused.

Another passage, which rather surprisingly, Muslim leaders have not highlighted, relates to Mahound's twelve wives. When Ayesha, his young and favourite wife, protested against his taking on so many wives, the novel goes on: *'Who* can blame her? *Finally*, he went into—what else? One of his *trances*, and *out he came* with a message from the archangel. Gibreel had recited verses giving him full divine support. *God's own permission to fuck as many women as he liked. So there:* What could poor Ayesha say against the *verses of God*? *You know* what she did say? This: *Your God* certainly *jumps* to it when you need him to *fix things* up for you.'

Each of the words I have italicized reflects a supercilious and dismissive attitude. The reference to God's permission to fuck is cheap and vulgar. Even if one rejected the Muslim criticism that Muhammad should not have been presented as an imposter and a devious manipulator, they are certainly right to insist that a man whom millions consider holy and who has for centuries given meaning and depth to their lives, deserves to be discussed in a less aggressive manner.

There is also a brothel scene in which twelve whores take the names of Muhammad's wives. Rushdie has argued that it was intended to provide a profane antithesis to (and thus to highlight and accentuate) the holy. But since the holy has been mocked the brothel scene cannot be its antithesis; rather it is a further expression of the same approach.

Unlike Jesus, a divine figure for Christians, Muhammad is a human being chosen as the vehicle of Allah's will. His family is *ahl-al-baith*, the first family, and his wives are invariably referred to as *alwaj-e-mutahire*, the sacred wives of the prophet. The brothel scene represents a gross assault on the tradition. In pretending to be the wives of Muhammad, the prostitutes do not acquire an aura of sacredness; rather the sacred wives are dragged down to the level of prostitutes. They are symbolically violated. Every customer who plays at being a Muhammad vulgarizes and reduces him to the status of an indiscriminate debauchee.

It is not difficult to see why the Muslims feel lacerated. Though they have sometimes called the book blasphemous, the term does not at all convey their basic criticisms. They seem to have adopted it largely because of the British law of blasphemy. Barring a few fundamentalists, most Muslims do not seem terribly worried by the irreverent tone, the questioning of the authenticity of the Koran, and the satirical treatment of Allah and the Archangel Gibreel. Nor are they worried that the book will shake their *faith*. They are *distressed* and *outraged* by what, with some exaggeration, their spokesmen have called the 'obscene', 'indecent', 'most filthy' and 'abominably foul language' in reference to the men whose memories they consider sacred and whose persons they consider holy. They also feel belittled and demeaned in their own and others' eyes, provoked and challenged to a fight by both the language and the 'outrageous liberties' taken with their sacred collective heritage.

These feelings are particularly strong among immigrants who cope with their predicament by holding on to traditionally inherited notions of sacredness. That is why the most uncompromising and tenacious reaction against *The Satanic Verses* came from British Muslims, representing the largest Muslim community in the west. This may also explain why the first generation of Muslims who turned to religion to give some meaning and hope to their empty lives (such as those in Bradford) responded more angrily to the book and more enthusiastically to Ayatollah Khomeini's *fatwa* than the others.

Religion represents the realm of the sacred *par excellence* and calls for an extremely delicate and sensitive handling. Otherwise one not only risks outraging people and provoking them to fight back, but also fails to comprehend the integrity of religion as a distinct form of consciousness. We have taken centuries to learn how to explore sexuality in literature without becoming either puritanical or pornographic. Religion requires a greater degree of sensitivity. While for the most part *The Satanic Verses* meets this requirement and the Muslims are wrong to deny that, it does from time to time become offensive and provocative.

Talking about our fellow human beings in a manner that insults, demeans, distresses or holds them up to contempt in their own or others' eyes betrays a lack of elementary respect for them and is rightly deplored. We do not generally prohibit it by law because of the obvious difficulties, but we do strongly disapprove of it morally.

Recently Sir James Miskin, the recorder of London, was rightly pulled up by the Lord Chancellor and the media for using the words 'nig-nogs'. Even when he apologized, many including the *Sun* (3 March) thought that he should 'hang up his wig; for good'. Several American courts have considered the use of such words as 'black bastards' and 'bloodsucking Jews' unacceptable and condoned their use in literary works *only when* that was shown to serve a literary purpose or to help explore or express literary truths.

This is a persuasive and sensible doctrine and applies to religious communities as well. When a prophet is treated in a supercilious, dismissive or crude manner, what is at stake is not his honour—for he is dead and too big a person to be affected by insults. What is really at stake is the sense of self-respect and integrity of those living men and women who define their identity in terms of their allegiance to the prophet. Their pride, good opinion of themselves, dignity and self-esteem deserve to be protected and nurtured, especially when these are subjected to daily assaults by a hostile society. It is self-contradictory to fight for their future and to undermine their past, to promote their political aspirations and to mock their cultural memories.

Some of the passages in *The Satanic Verses* do demean Muslims in their own and others' eyes. The passages perpetuate prejudices about them and give grounds for a few more into the bargain.

When such lapses occur, it is tempting to turn to the law, to press for a ban, to demand that the offending passages be expunged, and so on. The temptation must be resisted. Once a literary work is published, it is permanently in the public realm. No expedients can prevent its circulation or diminish its impact. Anyway, the law is too blunt an instrument to deal with creative literature, and bans and censorship have always done more harm than good.

The answer lies at the moral and social level. When a creative writer, conducting imaginative experiments and daring to think the unthinkable, outrages, hurts or provokes others, he should be challenged, criticized, asked to explain himself and made to suffer his peers' criticism and the anger of hurt sensibilities. It was a pity that for months Rushdie contemptuously dismissed the protests of the Muslims. However misguided, they were *his* people, or at least fellow-immigrants desperately struggling like him to cope with their predicament. His book was about them, and he owed them an obligation to understand their feelings, to explain his position, to argue with them, to do all in his power to mollify and hopefully win them over to his point of view.

But he treated them the way he had treaded Mahound and his companions and added to their hurt. He enjoyed the uncritical support of a literary establishment obsessed with 'terrifying singularity'. Until the book-burning in Bradford (predictably but inaccurately compared to the Nazi book-burning), no national newspaper published the offending passages, invited Muslim spokesmen to write about the book, or made a sympathetic attempt to read it with their eyes. Liberal opinion came down on Muslims like a ton of bricks, ridiculing them, and asking if such barbarians deserved to be citizens of a 'civilized' society. Liberals rightly remembered the principle of liberty but forgot the equally important principles of fairness, compassion and humanity.

The Muslims had no friends. They felt intensely lonely and helpless. Hence they felt compelled to step up their protest, to seek a place for their grievances on the national agenda and demand a long-denied dialogue.

It is only from such a painful ordeal that new truths, including new tools of exploring them, are born. A dialogue is only possible in a climate of mutual tolerance, free from intimidation and threats. Muslims have made their point, albeit with unacceptable threats of violence. They have highlighted the crucial question about a writer's moral responsibility to his or her fellow human beings as well as to their craft. They should now leave Rushdie alone to ponder over it in peace and security, and hope that he will one day provide an answer that reconciles a creative writer's right to freedom of thought and expression with other people's right to respect and dignity. If any harm were to come to him now, or fifty years hence, they would rightly be condemned for behaving as 'barbarians' and betraying the religion they use to defend such a ghastly deed. The prophet they revere has much to say about good manners and charity of spirit.

14

Technology and tradition—audio-visual culture among south Asian families in west London

Marie Gillespie

From *Cultural Studies*, vol. 3, no. 2 (Methuen, 1989).

This ethnographic account is based on research among south Asian families in Southall, Middlesex.[1] Southall is a 'town', formerly an autonomous London borough, with a population of some 65,000. Its demographic majority is of south Asian origin, predominantly of Sikh religion, but divided along cross-cutting cleavages of national, regional, religious, and caste heritage.

The study evolved over seven years of teaching in two Southall high schools where the popularity of 'Indian' films was evident; and yet various manifestations of resistance to their pleasures seemed to signify a great deal more than mere expressions of taste or preference.

The extensive use of the VCR at home to view 'Indian'[2] films represents a powerful means for grandparents and parents to maintain links with their country of origin. Second-generation children, however, born and educated in Britain, position themselves and are positioned rather differently in relation to notions of 'Asian' and 'British' culture. The legitimation of state racism in postwar Britain has been secured in an important way around particular ideological constructions of south Asian cultures, especially their marriage and family systems. For long, these have been seen to be based on archaic and traditional customs and practices and are presented as an 'alien threat' to the 'British way of life'. But in much of the literature produced by the 'Race Relations Industry' it is 'culture-clash' and inter-generational conflict, low self-esteem and negative self-image, rather than racism, that, paradoxically, have been identified as both 'the problem' and 'the cause'.[3]

Such dominant assumptions went unchallenged as young Asian voices were usually excluded or marginalized from debates which concerned them. This paper therefore is an attempt to re-present 'their voices', concentrating on their interpretations of popular Indian films and the themes and issues arising from their viewing experiences and which they find salient.

The ethnographic data are based on interviews carried out with young people predominantly of Panjabi origin and aged 15–18. A set of basic questions was used to spark off each interview. When do you watch? What do you watch? With whom do you watch? Who chooses what you watch in which situations? The wide range of methodological issues which the study raises will not be dealt with here, and this account will be structured around four main concerns:

First, it will contextualize the shift by briefly outlining the history of Indian cinema in Southall, and the shift from public exhibition to private viewing in the home. Secondly, it will examine the implications of this shift by focussing on the family-viewing context. It will explore questions of choice and preference alongside issues of family power and control. The third part will examine the responses of young people to Indian films and the factors mediating their various interpretations. Finally, it will bring together the diverse strands of the study in order to highlight the different ways in which viewing experiences are used.

Indian cinema in Southall: from public pleasure to private leisure

The first 'Indian' films were shown in Southall in 1953 in hired halls and then in three local cinemas. During the 1960s and 1970s the cinema provided the principal weekend leisure activity in Southall and represented an occasion for families and friends to get together; the social event of the week.

In 1978, when VCRs came on the market, many families were quick to seize the opportunity to extend their choice and control over viewing in the home. Many Asian communities obtained them as early as 1978–9 before most other households in Britain. It is estimated that between 40 and 50 per cent of households in Britain now own or rent a VCR but in Southall the figure is held to be 80 per cent.[4]

Most shops rent popular Hindi (also known as 'Bombay') films and although films in Panjabi and Urdu are also available from shops they lack the broad-based appeal of the popular Hindi movie. In fact the Bombay film has gained something of a cultural hegemony in south Asia and among many 'Asian' settlers across the world. To understand this one has to look to the specific evolution of the popular Hindi genre which, in order to appeal to a mass audience, had to produce films which would cross the linguistic, religious, and regional differences that exist within India, as indeed within Southall.

Many of the films combine a catholicity or universality of appeal with a careful handling of regional and religious differences. A distinctive form of Bombay Hindi, characterized by a certain 'linguistic openness' has evolved which makes most films accessible also to speakers of other south Asian languages. The distinctive visual style, often foregrounded over dialogue, combines with successive modes of spectacle, action and emotion which facilitates cross-cultural understanding.[5] In the light of this we can understand the huge uptake of Hindi films on cassette among the diverse linguistic groups in Southall.

With the arrival of video, the adventure, romance, and drama of the Bombay film was to be enjoyed in domestic privacy. A small piece of home technology brought the cinema hall into the home, or so it appeared. A lot was gained but much was lost. The weekly outing became a thing of the past as the cinemas closed and the big screen image shrunk into the TV box and entered the flow of everyday life in the living room.

In Southall the rapid expansion of the home video market needs to be considered not only as providing an extension to an already important and dynamic film culture but also very much a response on the part of a black community to life in Britain. Southall, like many other black communities, has come into existence in the first instance as a result of racist immigration and housing policies. Such communities have developed as 'sanctuaries' against the racism they experience.[6] The exclusion and marginalization of many people in Southall from mainstream British society, coupled with the failure to provide adequate leisure/culture facilities, has (like among the *Gastarbeiter* (guest worker) Turkish community in West Germany) contributed to the development of an important home video culture.

But the consequences of a decade of video use are perceived in contradictory ways by the youth of Southall. Many young people feel that the VCR has served further to isolate the community from mainstream British society. It is also seen to have specific effects on the lives of women: 'The video has isolated the community even more. They might as well be in India, especially the women.' Others see it as a liberating pleasure, especially for females: 'Some girls can't get out of the house that much so they can get a film and keep themselves occupied within the four walls of the house. It's an advantage for them.'

Such contradictory evaluations need to be seen in the contexts in which they originate.

Domestic viewing contexts

During the course of the study it became possible to construct a broad typology of contexts and associated texts. For the purpose of this account I shall concentrate on weekend family viewing because this situation was so frequently and consistently discussed by all interviewees, and due to the importance given to it within this cultural context.[7]

The VCR is used predominantly at the weekend in most families. Viewing 'Indian' films on video is the principal, regular family leisure activity. Weekend family gatherings around the TV set are a social ritual repeated in many families. The VCR and TV screen become the focus and locus of interaction. Notions of togetherness and communality are stressed: 'It's probably the only time in the week that we are all together so when we're watching a film at least we're all together.'

This togetherness is by no means that of passive viewers: 'No one is silent, we're all talking through the film about what's happening here and there and generally having a chat . . . it sort of brings you closer together.'

The weaving of conversation through the narrative is facilitated by an impressive familiarity with films brought about by repeated viewings. The episodic structure of films which moves the spectator through the different modes of spectacle, song and dance, drama, action, and affect also provides natural breaks for talk, emotion and reflection.

With such large family gatherings the question of power and control over viewing becomes important. The interviews highlight the way in which parents actively set and maintain viewing rules which govern viewing patterns and modes of parent–child interaction.

While the father is usually seen to determine when children are allowed access to the screen by his absence or presence in the home, the mother is perceived as exercising a greater degree of power and control over the choice of what is watched. This was a significant pattern across the interviews, emphasizing the important role mothers play in socializing their children in the domestic context. It also makes clear that the relationship between family power structures and family viewing patterns is not one of simple correspondence.

There are also clear differences in the attentiveness and in the degree of salience of Indian films to various family members, which are obscured by the simple observation that the family all watched the same programme.[8] Many young people say they sit with parents and view parts of the films just to please them, or say that their parents encourage or even 'force' them to watch.

As gender differences are important to understand parental control over viewing they are also a significant factor in understanding young people's viewing preferences and behaviour. Boys tend to experience greater freedom in deciding how they use their leisure time and spend more time engaged in activities outside the home. In contrast, girls are usually socialized to remain within the domestic realm and often participate in strong and supportive female cultures in the home where the viewing of Indian films on video frequently plays an important role. This explains to some extent the generally greater engagement with popular Hindi videos on the part of most girls interviewed. In one interview two boys rather begrudgingly claim: 'It doesn't hurt to watch an Indian film with the parents.' 'No, it kills you.'

In spite of this repeatedly expressed reluctance the way in which the screen can serve social interaction in the family tends to override individual preferences and return young people to the family situation. One boy commented to the general agreement of the group: 'Well we don't usually stay in another room while they're watching, if you've got something to yourself, you isolate yourself, don't you?' It is clear that what might be seen on the one hand as 'enforced' or 'reluctant' viewing can take on pleasurable connotations where the emphasis is on 'being together'. Parents do not have much time for leisure due to long working hours and shift work, so the time when the family is together around the TV set is often much appreciated by all concerned.

Conversely, the family audience is frequently fragmented by English and American films: 'When it's Indian films it's all of us together but when it's English films it's just me and my brother.' This fragmentation is partly due to the texts of English and American films themselves. Given parental reservations about the language, sensuality, and references to sexuality, young people may often prefer to view them on their own to escape parental censure or vigilance.

You may now have the impression that the avid consumption of VCR films falls into two neat categories. While Hindi films tend to be viewed in large family gatherings and to be celebrated by intense social interaction, British and American films tend to be consumed on their own in a more or less assertive circumvention of parental control and preferences. While viewing patterns tend indeed to correspond to this dichotomy, young people's viewing of Hindi films raises further ethnographic questions about perceptions of 'Indianness' and Britain or India and 'Britishness'.

Representations of India

For young people in Southall who have little or no direct experience outside the UK, perceptions of India will be founded on a complex combination of factors. But invariably they will also be influenced by 'Indian' films. Even for those who have lived or spent long periods in India the films provide a counterpoint to their own personal experiences.

Throughout the interviews a series of related binary oppositions frame and structure accounts of how India is perceived through the films:

> Village . . . . City
> Poverty . . . . Wealth
> Communality . . . . . . Individualism
> Tradition . . . . Modernity
> Morality . . . . Vice

The interviewees' accounts are in some measure reconstructions of and responses to patterned social and moral discourses prevalent in popular Hindi films, where a pristine and moral rural India is often constructed by opposing it to an exotic and decadent 'other'—usually signified by symbols of the West and city life.

Thus, across the interviews, village life is frequently contrasted with city life. The village community is seen as one of extended kin where co-operation and communality prevail, notions of individualism are absent. Village life is seen as 'pure' because 'people are so honest there, they never look with the "evil eye", they help each other even though they're poor, they never "skank" [betray] one another.'

Such interpretations contrast with those of city life which, through the films, is perceived as decadent, immoral, and polluted—a place 'where prostitutes hang out and where even pundits [priests] try to rape girls.'

There was considerable criticism of the 'unrealistic' portrayal of village life and an often acute awareness is shown of the selective and ideological nature of representations: 'There's not so much about the landless labourers and the position of women, you know, who spend hours and hours looking for water and fuel . . . in the scorching heat.'

Exploitation of the poor by the rich is another common theme and the plight of the illiterate landless labourers was referred to on several occasions: 'The films show how rich treat poor, how they don't go to school and have to work from when very young, they can't read and so rich people trick them and take their lands and crops.'

Striking gender differences emerge in the framing of accounts. Girls often express their perceptions of India through an exploration of the social and moral values inherent in the films via a 'retelling' of the narratives. In contrast boys seem to be much more concerned with representational issues, particularly 'negative images' and, in many cases, reject Hindi films *per se* on that basis.

Several male respondents see Indian films as offensive in their emphasis on poverty and corruption: 'They should not portray India as if it's really poor and backward even though they're Indians themselves, it's degrading; that's a lot of the reason I don't like Indian films.'

Others ridicule the 'backward image' of 'Indians' in the films because of the different norms associated with fashion and style but they also remark upon the selective nature of images: 'they follow up too late in India, they still wear flares, though I must admit they're not backward in everything they're very advanced in technology but they don't show you those aspects of India.' One boy vehemently rejected the films and wished to dissociate himself from both films and India but not without some irony: 'I didn't learn anything from the films apart from the fact that India is one of the most corrupt countries in the world,' and later, 'that country has nothing to do with me any more.'

Such discussions often provoke comments on representations of India in British media more generally which is seen on the whole to reinforce an 'uncivilized', poverty-stricken image of India: 'Documentaries shown in this country degrade India badly as well.' Strong resentment is expressed at the way India is 'degraded' in the West by the circulation of images of poverty, underdevelopment, death, and disease. Such images are linked to the 'degradation' of Indians in Britain where they 'get racist harassment'.

In identifying 'salient' themes and making selective interpretations, a range of 'meanings' are projected onto the films which undoubtedly derive from experiences of racism in Britain. Such experiences underpin and sensitize responses to constructions of Indian society in Hindi films and in the media generally. Boys, in particular, show an understanding of how Indian films may be rebuked and ridiculed as 'backward', 'foreign' and 'ludicrous' by 'outsiders' (for example, their white peers) but they also, clearly, feel somewhat estranged from the sense of 'Indianness' and from the 'India' represented in the films. At the same time, there is a tacit acknowledgement that the films may be used to confirm what constitute dominant discourses on India in British society, and an underlying awareness of how they function as racist discourses. As a result the boys would appear to occupy shifting and often contradictory positions from which they view and interpret the films—positions which vary according to context.

It would appear that experiences of racism as well as the reading of films are gender specific. A similar connection may be detected between gender and genre.

Genre

For nearly a century Hindi films have been either rebuked or ignored in the West by critics, academics, and film enthusiasts alike. Such institutionalized disdain and ignorance is not only a symptom of racism but feeds directly into it. The fierce rejection of the popular Hindi film, seen as a genre in itself, especially among the boys interviewed, echoes Western critical discourses about the genre. Films are consistently criticized for being 'all the same,' based on 'ideas got from Westerns . . . just a mixture of everything . . . commercial . . . full of songs and running round trees and rose gardens.'

An eighteen-year-old male interviewee in a rather eloquent condemnation of Indian films claims: 'With the standards of media appreciation in the West it's hard to understand the sort of psyche that would appreciate these kinds of film again and again and again. . . . If you've been exposed to a film culture based on plots and detailed cinematography then you'd expect the same from the other culture and if it doesn't match up to that standard you don't want to see it anymore . . . it's like driving a Morris Minor after you've driven a Porsche.'

The widespread condemnation of popular Indian films and the coincidence of views held by both film critics and many of the boys interviewed does not confirm a 'truth' about Hindi cinema but, rather, exposes a common frame of reference which is based on dominant Hollywood and Western film-making practices. Clearly, a cultural experience dominated by Western film-genres will initially militate against an engagement with popular Hindi films, which are likely to disorientate the spectator by subverting generic conventions even where language presents no barrier.

The focus of this study on south Asian families should not exclude consideration of the context of power relations in which this community lives and between Western and 'Third World' countries and cultures. It should, rather, lead us further to consider the nature of white norms and white cultural practices, especially when they entail the abrogation of measures for culturally distinct genres which are clearly incommensurate. Otherwise such a study becomes merely a descriptive exercise, devoid of political responsibility, intent, or analysis.

What becomes clear from the interviews is that for those who do find pleasure in popular Hindi films, the skilful blending of certain generic ingredients is crucial: the screenplay, the music and songs, the emotional appeal, spectacle, production values, and, of course, the stars. But it is above all when narrative is discussed in the interviews that one becomes aware of a deeper engagement with the films. The pleasures involved become apparent but we can also begin to unravel some further causes of resistance to films.

Narrative

According to many writers, the popular Hindi film has evolved from village traditions of epic narration, and the dramas and characters, as well as the structure of the mythological epics, are regularly and openly drawn upon. Film-makers and theorists claim that there are only two stories or 'metatexts', the *Mahabharata* and the *Ramayana*, and that every film can be traced back to these stories.

Vijay Mishra (1985) sees Bombay films as transformations of the narrative structures that may be discovered in these epics. According to him their influence is not limited to narrative form alone since 'these epics were also ideological tools for the expansion of beliefs endorsed by the ruling classes'. In his view the Bombay film legitimates its own existence through a reinscription of its values into those of the *Mahabharata* and the *Ramayana*.

But what seems to distinguish the Hindi film most from its Western counterparts is the form and movement of the narrative. The balance between narrative development, spectacle and emotion is rather different from that in Western films. Spectacle alone risks losing an audience. Skilled narration involves the swift transition between well-balanced modes of spectacle and an emotional involvement invited by the reassuring familiarity of many narratives, structured by discourses, deeply rooted in Indian social, moral, and psychic life (Thomas, 1985).

One of the most common assertions across the interviews is that the films all have the same type of stories. Usually this means that the films are 'totally predictable' and therefore not worth watching: 'who wants to sit and watch a film where you can work out the whole plot in the first five minutes?'

Three basic narrative themes of Hindi cinema particularly popular in the late 1970s and 1980s are repeatedly identified and referred to by interviewees: (1) 'Dostana', where the bond of male friendship overcomes the desire for a woman; (2) 'lost and found' parents and children are separated and reunited years later following the revelation of mistaken identities; and (3) revenge, villains get their just deserts at the hands of the heroes they wronged.

Interviewees frame their accounts with references to the discourses which commonly structure these narratives, which are those of kinship duty, social obligation, solidarity, respect or 'izzat', and trust. A sense of social 'order' and 'ideal social relations' is related to living in harmony with fate and respecting social obligations and ties of friendship and family.

Hindi film aesthetics, it is argued, are based not on cognition, as in the West, but in re-cognition. Like Hindu epics whose familiar stories form part of the fundamental myths of Indian society, the Hindi film is said to have evolved a broad framework of its own. Anil Saari (1985) claims: 'thus one film is like another, each film confirms once again the world as it is and has been and is likely to remain. The very hopelessness created by poverty and social immobility demands that the world and distractions from it remain as they are. That is indeed how the world is for the average Indian who is not a member of the ruling elite.'

Many interviewees analyse the narrative closure of contemporary Hindi films and compare them with the older, black and white, social-realist films prevalent in the 1950s and 1960s, in which there is an upsurge of renewed interest among young and old alike: 'They all have happy endings by the way . . . unlike the older films, tragedies are being solved by lucky, fortunate events that turn everything upside down, if a heroine's about to die these days she's saved by a handsome doctor at the last moment . . . everything turns out all right and people have nothing to think about, nothing to cry about, unlike the older films.'

Certain fundamental differences in the narrative structures of 'Hindi' and 'Western' films are highlighted in the interviews. English films are seen as 'continuous all the way . . . they just continue, no songs, no dances . . . that's why I find them boring'. Pleasure is taken in the non-linear narratives. The intricate and convoluted nature of story-telling becomes apparent through attempts at narrative reconstructions. Hindi films are not tightly linear but build in more or less circular fashion through a number of climaxes which are counterposed with scenes of humour, spectacle, and 'pure' emotional import. It is not so much a question of *what* will happen next that drives the narrative but of *how* it will be framed, not so much an enigma to be solved as a moral disordering to be resolved.

Affective involvement is a crucial component of films and is ensured not only by cinematic techniques which encourage identification and involvement, e.g. the use of close-ups, subjective points of view shots, shot reverse shots, but also through the songs: 'The songs back up everything . . . they have real feeling in them and it's not just any old songs, they relate to the actual situations of the films, they get you emotionally involved and influence you.' As in melodrama, undischarged emotion which cannot be accommodated within the action is expressed in song and music: 'Whenever that song comes on, I cry, I can't control myself . . . it's the father of a girl singing to her before she leaves the family to get married, he sings about how you are leaving us now and saying how when you were young I used to hold you in my arms, how I used to play with you. . . . I can't listen to that song without tears pouring out . . . and I think of my sister when she will be leaving us.'

This passage highlights the way in which the Hindi film tends to address and move its spectator by way of affect. This positioning depends for its full effect on certain kinds of cultural competence, most notably a knowledge of the 'ideal moral universe' of the Hindi film. Such cultural knowledge is acquired by young people to very varying degrees and while clearly lending enormous spectator power to some, disallows others from any deep engagement with the films. Conventions of verisimilitude also affect the relationship between text and viewer.

Fantasy and realism

'When I did watch an Indian film after that I'm in heaven but I don't relate to the real world like I did . . . they're in rose gardens and the music just springs up from nowhere . . . that's why people like watching them to get away from their own lives, what do drugs do? They take you to another world . . . so do Indian films but they are a safer way out of your problems.'

For those who enjoy Hindi films fantasy is a chief source of pleasure. The songs and dances as well as their settings often provide discrete dream-like sequences and 'a moment of escape from reality' for the spectator. In comparing drug-induced euphoria with the sensations provoked by the fantasy sequences in films this young girl gives us some insight into the desire provoked by the fantasy films: 'I wouldn't mind sitting around in rose gardens or deserts being loved and things like that.'

Such anti-realism is seen by some as escapist: 'They're fantasies for the poor, they show them what they cannot afford . . . they're satisfied with the songs . . . they create the dream sequences for them.' They are also seen as exploitative and politically reactionary: 'Most of them are just sheer escapism. . . . I think that this has quite a negative effect because it allows people to ignore the reality of their situation, the political realities of India, the exploitation and oppression of the masses.' Several interviewees compared Hindi films of the 1970s and 1980s to the 'social realist' films of the 1950s: 'I think people could identify their immediate lives with them, they were true to life, if they showed a farmer losing his crops after years of hard labour that was a reflection of life and that used to happen to people and they would sit in the cinema and say "well that's true!" There was nothing magical about it as it is now. After this period, people didn't want tragedies, they wanted fantasies, they wanted a means of escape, they wanted to break out of reality and that's when the "masala" films started coming out.'

However, in spite of such criticisms, many of the interviewees do not ignore the cathartic and therapeutic aspects of films. Indeed they are seen to enable a temporary release from the tensions of everyday life and to help discharge distressful emotions: 'I must admit I'm scared of my parents (finding out I have a boyfriend) but after I've watched a film, and listened to a few songs and calmed myself down, I'm not scared of my parents anymore so they give you courage in a way.'

Selective but contradictory judgements about conventions of realism in films are frequent across the interviews as with this girl who on the one hand claims: 'Indian films don't really relate to reality, they're really sheltered . . . it's just fantasy they make it out so perfect.' And yet later, the film's realistic portrayal of love is endorsed: 'Sometimes we'll just sit there and wonder if there's a thing called love . . . whereas in an Indian film you're so convinced that love is real . . . that it's true, that it's really there.'

It is clear that an exposure to Western conventions of realism influence responses considerably. Attention is paid to *mise-en-scène* and anachronism is not easily tolerated. A determined fidelity to details of period representation and dress is adhered to by young male respondents: 'They'll show a man fighting for Independence and you'll see a man on a motorbike with sunglasses and jeans they should at least have the clothes of the period.'

'They'll be showing a scene in the eighteenth century with horse-drawn carriage and at the back you'll see 1980s taxis, scooters, and high-rise buildings. It spoils everything. If only they [the directors] thought more about what they were doing, it looks as though they hadn't planned it.' Western conventions of realism also provide expectations about the way characters should behave, dress, and act. The reality status of stunt sequences is rebuked where production values are low: 'It's stupid motorbikes crossing lakes when you know it's a cartoon.'

There is in Hindi films an acceptable realism and logic beyond the material which is unbelievable. In fact the criteria of verisimilitude in Hindi cinema appears to refer primarily to the skill demonstrated in manipulating the rules of the film's moral universe. Among regular viewers one is more likely to hear accusations of unbelievability if the codes of ideal kinship are flouted than if the hero performs some outrageously unrealistic feat as is the case with disaffected viewers. In order to acquire a better understanding of the conventions of realism/anti-realism in Hindi cinema one would need to consider much wider issues including concepts and conventions of realism in Indian culture generally. Furthermore, a more detailed study of the important influence of the mythological film genre, essentially moral tales, might shed light on the anti-realist strategies of Bombay cinema.

Social and cultural uses of viewing experiences

The final part of this account concerns the social and cultural uses of viewing experiences, broadening the scope beyond that of contemporary popular Hindi films to include the full range of films viewed.

For the older members of the community, nostalgia is a key element in the pleasure experienced through film. In one particularly moving account by a man in his seventies, tears welled in his eyes as he recounted: 'When we see black-and-white films it reminds us of our childhood, our school days, our school mates, of what we were thinking, of what we did do, of our heroes . . . and I tell you this gives us great pleasure.' The films would appear to act as a form of collective popular memory and some parents are able to convey a sense of their past in India to their children.

With the emergence of second-generation children parents and grandparents have found new uses for films. These uses are primarily defined in terms of linguistic, religious, and socio-cultural learning. In viewing Indian films together, many families are enabled to come together on a 'shared' linguistic basis. Both parents and children see this as a major advantage of watching films: 'They help children get a hold of the language.'

For many children the films provide one of the rare opportunities, outside communication in the family and community, to hear that language used and legitimated: 'They can hear and see how the language is used and should be used.' One boy put it more directly: 'They teach not only the language but how "to be" in an Indian environment.' The notion of language as transmitter of culture is prevalent among parents: 'If the children don't speak the language they lose their culture. Language is a potent symbol of collective identity and often the site of fierce loyalties and emotional power. In the context of a society which constructs linguistic difference as a problem rather than as a tool, the desire to defend and maintain one's linguistic heritage becomes strong.

In a community faced with religious distinctiveness and at times division, it is not surprising that cultural identity is often construed as being based not only on linguistic but also on religious continuity. 'Religious' or mythological films are also watched for devotional purposes, particularly by Hindu families, and often integrated with daily acts of worship: 'When we start fasting we always watch these films, sometimes five times a day . . . you kind of pray to God at the same time you know.'

The films are also used as a form of religious education: 'They help parents teach their children about the Holy Books like the *Ramayana*, the *Mahabharat*, and the *Bhaghavat Gita*. It's the tradition in families to tell the young children the stories but some families don't have the time and so there are children who don't know who is Rama.' In some families viewing devotional films has come to replace reading the holy books. Certainly, the video is seen as a great advantage in familiarizing children with parables and religious stories, largely due to the widespread illiteracy of second- and third-generation children in their mother tongue. Not only are the religious and moral values inherent in the films an important aspect of viewing but the visual representation of the deity plays an extremely important symbolic role in the devotional and ritual acts of worship. This relates to the importance of popular forms of religious iconography in Indian society.

Parents use the films to talk about religious festivals: 'Here we can never really celebrate festivals like Holi which involves the whole village and people smearing each other's faces with colour. No one does that here but when you watch you can really appreciate what it's like in India. Here the kids just know about the fireworks but they don't know the real basic thing about why, they don't know about the religious aspects of the festivals.'

Young people and their parents use the films to negotiate, argue, and agree about a wider range of customs, traditions, values, and beliefs. Together, they often enjoy films which encourage discussion: 'films which bring out the contradictions in families, the arranged marriage system, the caste or class system.' The films function as tools for eliciting attitudes and views on salient themes; family affairs and problems, romance, courtship, and marriage were often discussed. There is a recurrent recognition of the 'influence' and value of the films in the lives of girls in particular. There are frequent references to the 'meanings, the really deep meanings, which reflect the way we think, it's just so . . . so . . . so I don't know, so influential.'

It would appear that Hindi films can serve to legitimate a particular view of the world and at the same time to open up contradictions within it. So while young people sometimes use films to deconstruct 'traditional culture' many parents use them to foster certain 'traditional' attitudes, values and beliefs in their children. Films are expected to have both an entertainment and a didactic function and are seen by parents as useful agents of cultural continuity and as contributing to the (re)-formation of cultural identity.

Various degrees of scepticism are registered among the boys about parents' attempts to 'artificially maintain a culture' through film: 'Parents want their children to maintain certain religious values, beliefs and customs but that doesn't mean that Indian films are necessarily going to educate them in that way. They may well do the opposite . . . I think the moral standards in most recent films is pretty appalling.' But clear distinctions are made between religion and a sense of cultural identity and whilst firmly upholding the Sikh faith one boy claims: 'Parents use the films to represent their culture to their children but that will not work because those are not my roots, that place [India] has nothing to do with me anymore.'

Many parents lament what they see as a process of progressive 'cultural loss' in each generation of children. Looking to the past they attempt to re-create 'traditional culture'. Meanwhile young people, with eyes to the future, are busy re-creating something 'new'. The striving after cultural continuity and the negotiation of cultural identity are thus inescapably dialectical processes and they must, moreover, be seen in the widest possible context. The notion of viewing as a social activity which takes place in families needs to be extended to include more detailed explorations of the wider social, cultural, and ideological contexts and uses of the VCR.

What is clear is that for the young people interviewed a sense of ethnic, national, and cultural identity does not displace or dominate the equally lived and formed identities based on age, gender, peer group, and neighbourhood. Static notions of culture are extremely disabling as are absolutist views of black-and-white cultures as fixed, mutually impermeable expressions of 'racial' or national identity. Notions of national culture with unique customs and practices understood as 'pure' homogeneous nationality need to be challenged.

One is reminded in this context of the arguments put forward by Benedict Anderson (1983) about the use of cultural artefacts in constructing 'imagined communities' based on notions of nation and nationness. The 'imagined communities', constructed and created through the viewing of films on VCR, may link Asian communities across the world. However, these communities, with their origins in history and experience, are not fixed but change, develop and combine, and are in turn redispersed in historic processes.

If cultural practices are detached from their origins they can be used to found and extend new patterns of communication which can give rise to new common identities. Perhaps most of all this study provides a contemporary example of how 'traditional' ties are created and recreated out of present rather than past conditions.

Notes

1 This paper is based on a dissertation submitted for MA Film and Television Studies for Education, University of London Institute of Education, 1987.
2 The term 'Indian' film is used most commonly by interviewees but distinctions between films are also drawn according to language (i.e. Hindi, Panjabi, and Urdu) as well as genre.

3 See, for example, Ballard (1979) and Community Relations Commission (1979), and for a critique of such perspectives see Parmar (1981).
4 This estimated figure is based on surveys carried out in three Southall schools.
5 Lutze (1985).
6 Gundara (1986).
7 Other contexts documented in the research included siblings viewed together in the home, viewing with friends/peers, women/girls-only groups, women solo viewing and male-only viewing.
8 For further accounts of family contexts of viewing see, for example, Morley (1986); Simpson (1987).
9 For a more detailed exploration of narration in the popular Hindi film see Thomas (1985).

References

Anderson, Benedict (1983) *Imagined Communities*, London: Verso.
Ballard, Catherine (1979) 'Conflict, continuity and change: second generation Asians' in V. Saifullah Khan (ed.), *Minority Families in Britain*, London: Macmillan.
Community Relations Commission (1979) *Between Two Cultures: A Study of the Relationship between Generations in the Asian Community*, London: Community Relations Commission.
Gundara, Jagdish (1986) 'Education in a multicultural society' in Gundara *et al.* (eds.), *Racism, Diversity and Education*, London: Hodder & Stoughton.
Lutze (1985) 'From Bharata to Bombay: change and continuity in Hindi film aesthetics' in B. Pfleiderer (ed.), *The Hindi Film: Agent and Re-Agent of Cultural Change*, Manohar: 7.
Mishra, Vijay (1985) 'Towards a theoretical critique of Bombay Cinema', *Screen*, 26 (3–4).
Morley, David (1986) Family Television *Cultural Power and Domestic Leisure*, London: Comedia.
Palmer, Patricia (1986) *The Lively Audience*, London: Allen & Unwin.
Parmar, Pratibha (1981) 'Young Asian women: a critique of the pathological approach', *Multi-Racial Education*, 10 (1).
Saarti, Anil (1985) in B. Pfleiderer (ed.), *The Hindi Film: Agent and Re-Agent of Cultural Change*, Manohar: 23.
Simpson, Philip (ed.) (1987) *Parents Talking*, London: Comedia.
Thomas, Rosie (1985) 'Indian cinema pleasures and popularity', *Screen*, 26 (3–4): pp. 123–35.

15

Just looking for trouble—Robert Mapplethorpe and fantasies of race

Kobena Mercer

From Lynne Segal and Mary McIntosh (eds.), *Sex Exposed—Sexuality and the Pornography Debate* (Virago, 1992).

How does 'race' feature in the politics of anti-pornography? Well, it does and it doesn't. 'Race' is present as an emotive figure of speech in the rhetoric of certain feminist anti-pornography arguments; yet 'race' is also markedly absent, since there appears to be no distinctly black perspective on the contentious issue of sexuality, censorship and representation that underpin the volatile nature of the anti-porn debate. Although Audre Lorde and Alice Walker made important contributions early on in the debate in the United States over a decade ago, the question of pornography has hardly been a top priority on the agenda of black feminist politics in Britain in the 1980s and early 1990s.[1] If it is indeed the case that white and black women have not been equally involved in the anti-porn movement, or have not made it a shared political priority, then we have to ask: What role does 'race' play in the discourse of anti-pornography which has come mainly from white women?

'Race' as an issue in anti-pornography feminism

When 'race' is invoked to mobilize moral support for anti-pornography positions it tends to function as a rhetorical trope enabling a race and gender analogy between violence against women and incitement to racial hatred. In their recent campaigns, Labour MPs Clare Short and Dawn Primarolo have frequently used this analogy to argue that just as black people are degraded by racist speech and hurt by racial violence, so women are harmed and victimized by sexist and misogynist representations which portray, and thus promote, the hatred and fear of women that erupt in all acts of male violence. It follows, so the argument goes, that just as the law is supposedly empowered to prohibit and punish incitement to racial hatred, new regulative legislation is needed to 'protect' women from the harm and danger of male violence that pornography represents. Yet the 1965 Race Relations Act, which sought to prohibit racist speech, has never been particularly beneficial to black people—more often than not it has been used against black people to curtail our civil rights to representation, and was proved to be notoriously useless and ineffective by the rise of new racist and fascist movements in the 1970s. Just as most black people know not to entrust our survival and protection to the state, one ought to question any argument, feminist or otherwise, that seeks to extend the intervention of the state in the form of prohibitionary legislation.

Indeed from a black perspective, the problem lies with the very analogy between racial hatred and male violence because it is based on a prior equation between those sexually explicit words and images labelled 'pornographic' and those acts of violence, brutality and homicide that do indeed take place against women in 'real life'. This equation—that 'pornography is the theory, rape is the practice'—is central to the radical feminist anti-pornography argument that gained considerable influence in the USA during the 1980s and is gaining ground in Britain now. One of the most worrying aspects of these developments is the strange alliance that has evolved between radical feminists demanding censorship in the name of women's freedom, and the anti-obscenity lobby of the New Right whose demands for the prohibition of sexual representations have always been part of the moral agenda of mainstream conservatism. For entirely different reasons, these two groups seek further state regulation of pornography, yet their convergence on this objective has created a wider constituency of support for a policy of cultural censorship. Where do black people stand in relation to this unhappy alliance?

While anti-porn feminists are more likely than their neo-conservative counterparts to observe that pornography itself is violently racist, one has to question the highly emotive way in which 'race' is used only to simplify complex issues and polarize opinion, as if everything were a matter of black and white, as if everything depended on whether you are simply for or against pornography and, by implication, male violence. In a theoretical defence of the radical feminist view that pornography does not merely reflect male violence but is itself a form of violence even as representation, Susanne Kappeler uses 'race' precisely in this way—not only to justify the unproven equation between images of sexual violence and actual violence experienced by women, but to elicit a moral response of horror and outrage that lends further credence to the anti-porn argument. At the beginning of her book *The Pornography of Representation*, by means of a graphic description of photographs depicting a black African man—one Thomas Kasire of Namibia—shown mutilated, tortured, and obliterated for the gratification of his white male European captors, Kappeler hopes to persuade us that, essentially, all pornography entails that women experience the same kind of actual violence as the brutal, sadistic and murderous violence of the colonial racism that resulted in the death of this black man.[2] Not only does this analogy reduce 'race' to rhetoric—whereby the black/white polarity serves to symbolize an absolute morality based on an either/or choice between good and evil—but it offers no analysis of racial representation in pornography, nor of black people's experiences of it, as Kappeler nowhere acknowledges the relative absence of black women in defining the feminist anti-porn agenda or the fact that black feminism, in all its varieties, has certainly not prioritized the issue as a touchstone of revolutionary morality.

Each of these issues concerning race, representation and sexual politics has arisen in the very different context of Robert Mapplethorpe's avowedly homoerotic photography, which was at the centre of a major controversy in the United States during 1989 and 1990. Paradoxically, as a result of the campaign led by Senator Jesse Helms to prevent the National Endowment for the Arts from funding exhibitions of so-called 'indecent and obscene materials', Mapplethorpe's photographs have come to the attention of a far wider audience than at any point in his career before his death, from AIDS, in 1989. Although Helms's proposed amendment to NEA funding criteria was eventually defeated, the virulent homophobia that characterized his campaign against Mapplethorpe's 'immoral trash' has helped to create a climate of popular opinion favourable to cultural repression. Just as self-censorship has become routine among art-world decision-makers, so the policing and prosecution of cultural practitioners—from feminist performance artist Karen Finley to the black rap group 2 Live Crew—has also become commonplace. What is truly disturbing about these trends is both the way in which the New Right has successfully hijacked and appropriated elements of the feminist anti-pornography argument, and the way in which some feminists have themselves joined ranks with the law-and-order state. An instance of this occurred in Cincinnati in 1990 when feminist campaigners aligned themselves with the city police department to close down the touring Mapplethorpe retrospective and prosecute the museum director responsible for the exhibition, Dennis Barrie, for the violation of 'community standards'.

Mapplethorpe's black male nudes

In this context, I would like to offer a contribution to the debate on pornography that is based on my reading of Mapplethorpe's troublesome images of nude black men. Although the attack on Mapplethorpe focussed mainly on his depictions of gay male sadomasochism and portraits of naked children, his black male nudes are equally, if not more, problematic—not only because they explicitly resemble aspects of pornography, but because his highly erotic treatment of the black male body seems to be supported by a whole range of racist myths about black sexuality.

To shock was always the key verb in the modernist vocabulary. Like other audiences and spectators confronted by the potent eroticism of Mapplethorpe's most shocking images, black audiences are not somehow exempt from the shock effect that Mapplethorpe's images so clearly intend to provoke. Indeed, it was this sense of outrage—not at the homoeroticism, but at the potential racism—that motivated my initial critique of the work, from a black gay male perspective. I was shocked by what I saw: the profile of a black man whose head was cropped—or 'decapitated', so to speak—holding his semi-tumescent penis through the Y-fronts of his underpants, which is the first image that confronts you in Mapplethorpe's 1982 publication *Black Males*. Given the relative silence of black voices at the time of Mapplethorpe's 1983 retrospective at the Institute of Contemporary Arts in London, when the art world celebrated his 'transgressive' reputation, it was important to draw critical attention to the almost pornographic flamboyance with which Mapplethorpe, whose trademark is cool irony, seemed to perpetuate the racist stereotype that, essentially, the black man is nothing more than his penis.

Yet, as the context for the reception and interpretation of Mapplethorpe's work has changed, I have almost changed my mind about these photographs, primarily because I am much more aware of the danger of simply hurling the accusation of 'racism' about. It leads only to the closure of debate. Precisely because of the hitherto unthinkable alliance between the New Right and radical feminism on the issue of pornography, there is now every possibility that a critique which stops only with this kind of moralistic closure inevitably plays into an anti-democratic politics of censorship and cultural closure sought by the ascendant forces of the New Right. In what follows, I explain how and why I changed my mind.[3]

Picture this: two reasonably intelligent black gay men pore over Mapplethorpe's 1986 publication *The Black Book*. When a friend lent me his copy, this was exactly how it circulated between us: as an illicit and highly troublesome object of desire. We were fascinated by the beautiful bodies and seduced by the pleasure in looking as we perused the repertoire of images. We wanted to look, but we didn't always find what we wanted to see. This was because we were immediately disturbed by the racial dimension of the imagery and, above all, angered by the aesthetic objectification that reduced these individual black men to purely abstract visual 'things', silenced in their own right as subjects and serving mainly as aesthetic trophies to enhance Mapplethorpe's privileged position as a white gay male artist in the New York avant-garde. In short, we were stuck in a deeply ambivalent structure of feeling. In an attempt to make sense of this experience, I drew on elements of feminist cultural theory.

The first thing to notice about Mapplethorpe's black males—so obvious that it goes without saying—is that all the men are nude. Framed within the generic conventions of the fine-art nude, their bodies are aestheticized and eroticized as 'objects' to be looked at. As such, they offer an erotic source of pleasure in the art of looking. But whose pleasure is being served? Regarding the depiction of women in dominant forms of visual representation, from painting to advertising or pornography, feminist cultural theory has shown that the female image functions predominantly as a mirror-image of what men want to see. As a figment of heterosexual wish-fulfilment, the female nude serves primarily to guarantee the stability of a phallocentric fantasy in which the omnipotent male gaze sees but is itself never seen. The binary opposition of seeing/being seen which informs visual representations of the female nude reveals that looking is never an innocent or neutral activity, but is always powerfully loaded by the gendered character of the subject/object dichotomy in which, to put it crudely, men look and women are there to be looked at.

In Mapplethorpe's case, however, the fact that both artist and model are male sets up a tension of sameness which thereby transfers the *frisson* of 'difference' from gender to racial polarity. In terms of the conventional dichotomy between masculinity as the active control of the gaze, and femininity as its passive visual object, what we see in Mapplethorpe's case is the way in which the black/white duality of 'race' overdetermines the power relations implicit in the gendered dichotomy between subject and object of representation.

In this sense, what is represented in Mapplethorpe's photographs is a 'look', or a certain 'way of looking', in which the pictures reveal more about the absent and invisible white male photographer who actively controls the gaze than they do about the black men whose beautiful bodies we see depicted in his photographs. Insofar as the pictorial space excludes any reference to a social, historical, cultural or political context that might tell us something about the lives of the black models who posed for the camera, Mapplethorpe facilitates the projection of certain racial and sexual fantasies about the 'difference' that black masculinity is assumed to embody. In this way, the photographs are very much about sexual investment in looking, because they disclose the tracing of desire on the part of the I/eye placed at the centre of representation by the male gaze.

Through a combination of formal codes and conventions—the posing and posture of the body in the studio enclosure; the use of strong chiaroscuro lighting; the cropping, framing and fragmentation of the whole body into parts—the 'look' constructed not only structures the viewer's affective disposition towards the image but reveals something of the *mise en scène* of power, as well as desire, in the racial and sexual fantasies that inform Mapplethorpe's representation of black masculinity. Whereas the white gay male sadomasochist pictures portray a subcultural sexuality that consists of 'doing' something, the black men are defined and confined to 'being' purely sexual and nothing but sexual—hence hypersexual. We look through a sequence of individually named African-American men, but we see only sexuality as the sum-total meaning of their black male identity. In pictures like 'Man in a Polyester Suit' (1980), apart from the model's hands, it is the penis, and the penis alone, that identifies him as a black man.

Mapplethorpe's obsessive focus on this one little thing, the black man's genitals, and the way in which the glossy allure of the quality monochrome print becomes almost consubstantial with the shiny, sexy texture of black skin, led me to argue that a certain racial fetishism is an important element in the pleasures (and displeasures) which the photographs bring into play. Such racial fetishism not only eroticizes the most visible aspect of racial difference—skin colour—but also lubricates the ideological reproduction of 'colonial fantasy', in which the white male subject is positioned at the centre of representation by a desire for mastery, power and control over the racialized and inferiorized black Other. Hence, alongside the codes of the fine-art nude, Mapplethorpe seems to make use of the regulative function of the commonplace racist stereotype—the black man as athlete, mugger or savage—in order to stabilize the invisible and all-seeing white subject at the centre of the gaze, and thereby 'fix' the black subject in its place not simply as the Other, but as the object in the field of vision that holds a mirror to the fears and fantasies of the supposedly omnipotent white male subject.

According to literary critic Homi Bhabha, 'an important feature of colonial discourse is its dependence on the concept of "fixity" in the ideological construction of otherness'.[4] Just as Mapplethorpe's photographs of female body-builder Lady Lisa Lyon seem obsessively to pin her down by processing the image of her body through a thousand cultural stereotypes of femininity, so the obsessive undercurrent in his black male nudes would appear to confirm this emphasis on fixity as a sign that betrays anxiety as well as pleasure in the desire for mastery. Mapplethorpe's scopic fixation on the luxurious beauty of black skin thus implies a kind of 'negrophilia', an aesthetic idealization of racial difference that merely inverts and reverses the binary axis of colonial discourse, in which all things black are equated with darkness, dirt and danger, as manifest in the psychic representations of 'negrophobia'. Both positions, whether they overvalue or devalue the visible signs of racial difference, inhabit the shared space of colonial fantasy. These elements for a psychoanalytic reading of fetishism, as it is enacted in the theatre of Mapplethorpe's sex–race fantasy, are forcefully brought together in a photograph such as 'Man in a Polyester Suit'.

The use of framing and scale emphasizes the sheer size of the big black penis revealed through the unzipped trouser fly. As Fanon said, when diagnosing the terrifying figure of 'the Negro' in the fantasies of his white psychiatric patients, 'One is no longer aware of the Negro, but only of a penis: the Negro is eclipsed. He is turned into a penis. He *is* a penis.'[5] By virtue of the purely formal device of scale, Mapplethorpe summons up one of the deepest mythological fears in the supremacist imagination: namely, the belief that all black men have monstrously large willies. In the phantasmic space of the white male imagery, the big black phallus is perceived as a threat not only to hegemonic white masculinity but to Western civilization itself, since the 'bad object' represents a danger to white womanhood and therefore the threat of miscegenation, eugenic pollution and racial degeneration. Historically, in nineteenth-century societies structured by race, white males eliminated the anxiety that their own fantastic images of black male sexuality excited through rituals of aggression in which the lynching of black men routinely involved the literal castration of the Other's strange fruit.

The historical myth of penis size amounts to a 'primal fantasy' in Western culture in that it is shared and collective in nature—and, moreover, a myth that is so pervasive and firmly held as a folk belief that modern sexology repeatedly embarked on the empirical task of actually measuring pricks to demonstrate its untruth. Now that the consensual management of liberal race relations no longer provides available legitimation for this popular belief, it is as if Mapplethorpe's picture performs a disavowal of the wish-fulfilment inscribed in the myth: *I know* (it's not true that all black guys have big willies), *but* (nevertheless, in my photographs they do).

Within the picture, the binary character of everyday racial discourse is underlined by the jokey irony of the contrast between the black man's exposed private parts and the public display of social respectability signified by the three-piece business suit. The oppositions hidden and exposed, denuded and clothed, play upon the Manichaean dualism of nature and culture, savage and civilized, body and mind, inferior and superior, that informs the logic of dominant racial discourse. In this way, the construction of racial difference in the image suggests that sexuality, and nothing but sexuality, is the essential 'nature' of the black man, because the cheap and tacky quality of the polyester suit confirms his failure to gain access to 'culture'. The camouflage of bourgeois respectability fails to conceal the fact that the black man, as the white man's Other, originates, like his dick, from somewhere anterior to civilization.

Conflicting readings of Mapplethorpe

Notwithstanding the problematic nature of Freud's pathologizing clinical vocabulary, his concept of fetishism can usefully be adapted, via feminist cultural theory, to help conceptualize issues of subjectivity and spectatorship in representations of race and ethnicity. Its account of the splitting of levels of belief may illuminate the prevalence of certain sexual fantasies and their role in the reproduction of racism in contemporary culture. The sexual fetish represents a substitute for something that was never there in the first place: the mother's penis, which the little boy expected to see. Despite conscious acknowledgement of sexual difference, the boy's castration anxiety forces the repression of his initial belief, such that it coexists on an unconscious level and finds manifestation, in adult sexuality, in the form of the erotic fetish.[6] One might say that, despite anatomical evidence, the belief symbolized in the fantasy of the big black willy—that black male sexuality is not only 'different' but somehow 'more'—is one many men and women, black and white, straight or gay, cling on to, because it retains currency and force as an element in the psychic reality of the social fantasies in which our racial and gendered identities have been historically constructed.

Yet because Freud's concept of fetishism is embedded in the patriarchal system of sexual difference that it describes, treating sexual perversion or deviation as a symptom which reveals the unconscious logic of the heterosexual norm, it is less useful as a tool for examining the perverse aestheticism of the modern homoerotic imagination which Mapplethorpe self-consciously employs. Moreover, there are limits to the race and gender analogy drawn from feminist cultural theory in the preceding analysis of visual fetishism: it ignores the obvious homoerotic specificity of the work. As a gay male artist whose sexual identity locates him in a subordinate relation to heterosexual masculinity, Mapplethorpe is hardly representative of the hegemonic model of straight, white, bourgeois male identity traditionally privileged in art history as the centred subject and agent of representation. Above all, as the recent exhibition history of his work attests, far from demonstrating the stability of this supposedly centred white male subject, the vitriol and anxiety expressed in hostile attacks on Mapplethorpe's *oeuvre* (such as those of radical neo-conservative art critic Hilton Kramer) would suggest that there is something profoundly troubling and disturbing about the emotional ambivalence experienced by different audiences through the salient shock effect of Mapplethorpe's work.

In the light of the changed context of reception, the foremost question is how different audiences and readers produce different and conflicting readings of the same cultural text. The variety of conflicting interpretations of the value of Mapplethorpe's work would imply that the text does not bear one, singular and unequivocal meaning, but is open to a number of competing readings. Thus Mapplethorpe's photographic text has become the site for a range of antagonistic interpretations. Once we adopt this view, we need to reconsider the relationship between artist and audience, or author and reader, because although we habitually attempt to resolve the question of the ultimate 'meaning' of a text by appealing to authorial intentions, poststructuralist theory has shown, by way of the 'death of the author' argument, that individual intentions never have the last word in determining the meaning or value of a text. This is because readers themselves play an active role in interpreting a multivalent and open-ended modernist cultural text.

One might say, therefore, that the difficult and troublesome question raised by Mapplethorpe's black male nudes—do they reinforce or undermine racist myths about black sexuality?—is strictly unanswerable, since his aesthetic strategy makes an unequivocal yes/no response impossible. The question is left open by the author and is thus thrown back to the spectator. Our recognition of the unconscious sex–race fantasies which Mapplethorpe's images arouse with such perverse precision does not confirm a stable or centred subject position, but is experienced precisely as an emotional disturbance which troubles the viewer's sense of secure identity.

The recent actual death of the author entails a reconsideration of the issue of authorship and intentionality, and the reciprocal role of the reader, because the articulation of race and homosexuality in Mapplethorpe's art can also be seen as a subversive move that begins to unravel the violent ambiguity at the interface of the social and the emotional. To clarify my suggestion that his black male nudes are open to an alternative evaluation from that of my initial reading, I should come clean with regard to the specific character of my own subject position as a black gay male reader.

My angry emphasis on racial fetishism as a potentially exploitative process of objectification was based on the way in which I felt identified with the black men depicted in the photographs, simply by virtue of sharing the same 'categorical' identity as a black man. As the source of this anger, the emotional identification can be best described again in Fanon's words as a feeling that 'I am laid bare. I am overdetermined from without. I am the slave not of the "idea" that others have of me but of my own appearance. I am being dissected under white eyes. I am fixed . . . Look, it's a Negro.'[7] It was my anger at the aestheticizing effect of Mapplethorpe's coolly 'ironic' appropriation of racist stereotypes that informed the description of visual fetishism as a process of reduction, or dehumanization. This argument has many similarities with the early feminist critique of images of women in pornography.[8] But the problem with this view is that it moralizes images in terms of a reductive dichotomy between good and bad, 'positive' and 'negative', and thus fails to recognize the ambivalence of the text. If, on the other hand, we recognize that there is an important difference between saying that an image is racist and saying that it is 'about' racism, then we need a more reflexive approach to the ambiguities set into motion in the destabilizing moment of Mapplethorpe's shock effect.

On this view, the strategic use of visual fetishism is not necessarily a bad thing, as it encourages the viewer to examine his or her own implication in the fantasies which the images arouse. Once I acknowledge my own location in the image reservoir as a gay subject—a desiring subject not only in terms of sharing a desire to look, but in terms of an identical object-choice already there in my own fantasies and wishes—then the articulation of meanings about eroticism, race and homosexuality become a lot more complicated. Indeed, I am forced to confront the rather unwelcome fact that as a spectator I actually occupy the very position in the fantasy of mastery previously ascribed to the centred position of the white male subject! In other words, there was another axis of identification—between white gay male author and black gay male reader—that cut across the identification with the black men in the pictures. Could it not be the case that my anger was also mingled with feelings of jealousy, rivalry or envy? If I shared the same desire to look, which would place me in the position of mastery attributed to the author, the anger in the initial critique might also have arisen from a shared, homosexual identification, and thus a rivalry over the same unobtainable object of desire. Insofar as the anger and envy were effects of my identification with both object and subject of the look, I would say that my specific identity as a black gay reader placed me in two contradictory positions at one and the same time. I am sure that emotions such as these are at issue in the rivalry of interpretations around Mapplethorpe's most contentious work. Black gay male readers certainly do not have a monopoly on the conflicted and ambivalent structures of feeling they create. My point here is not confessional, but to use my own experience as a source of data about the complex operations of identification and desire that position us in antagonistic and contradictory relations of race, gender and power, which are themselves partly constituted in representations. In revising my views, I have sought to reopen the question of ambivalence, because rather than simply project it on the author (by asking whether he either perpetuates or challenges racism) one needs to take into account how different readers derive different meanings not only about race, but about sexuality and desire, in Mapplethorpe's work.

The perverse aesthetic

The whole point about the use of textual ambivalence in the modernist tradition is to foreground the uncertainty of any one, singular meaning —which, in the case of Mapplethorpe's double transgressions across race and homosexuality, is a risky business indeed. This is because the open-ended character of the images can provoke a racist reading as much as an anti-racist one, elicit a homophobic reading as much as arouse a homoerotic one. A great deal depends on the reader and the social identity she or he brings to the text. The same statement—the black man is beautiful, say—retains the same denotative meaning, but acquires different connotational values when enunciated by different groups of subjects: the same sentence, uttered by a white man, a black woman, a black man or a white woman, would inevitably take on a qualitatively different 'sound'. Similarly, once we situate the network of relations between author, text and reader, in the contingent, context-bound circumstances in which Mapplethorpe's work currently stands, then we can examine the way in which the open-ended structure of the text gives rise to antagonistic readings that are informed by the social identity of the audience.

Without returning to a naive belief in the author as a godlike figure of authority, it is necessary to argue that it really does matter who is speaking whenever artists, because of their sexual, gender or racial identity, are assigned 'minority' status in the arts and culture at large. Once we take the biographical dimension of Mapplethorpe's work as a gay artist into account it is possible to reinterpret the black male nudes as the beginning of an inquiry into the archive of 'race' in Western culture and history, which has rendered black men into 'invisible men', in Ralph Ellison's phrase. As Mapplethorpe put it in an interview shortly before his death, 'At some point I started photographing black men. It was an area that hadn't been explored intensively. If you went through the history of nude male photography, there were very few black subjects. I found that I could take pictures of black men that were so subtle, and the form was so photographical.' An awareness of the exclusion of the black subject from one of the most valued canonical genres of Western art—the nude—suggests that it is both possible and necessary to reread Mapplethorpe's work as part of an artistic inquiry into the hegemonic force of a Eurocentric aesthetic which historically rendered invisible not only black people but women, lesbians and gays and others before the radical social transformations of the modern and postmodern period.

By virtue of a perverse aesthetic of promiscuous intertextuality, whereby the overvalued aura of the fine-art nude is contaminated by the filthy and degraded form of the commonplace stereotype, Mapplethorpe transgresses on several fronts to make visible that which is repressed and made invisible in the dominant, and dominating, tradition of the West against the rest. In the contemporary United States, for example, black males constitute one of the 'lowest' social identities in the late-capitalist underclass: disenfranchised, disadvantaged, disempowered. Yet in Mapplethorpe's studio, some of the men who in all probability came from this class are elevated on to the pedestal of the transcendental aesthetic ideal of the male nude in Western culture, which had always excluded the black subject from such aesthetic idealization on account of its otherness. Mapplethorpe's achievement as a postmodern 'society photographer' lies in the way he renders invisible men visible in a cultural system—art photography—that always historically denied or marginalized their existence. One can see in Mapplethorpe's use of homoeroticism a subversive strategy of perversion in which the liberal humanist values inscribed in the idealized fine-art nude are led away from the higher aims of 'civilization' and brought face to face with that part of itself repressed and devalued as 'other' in the form of the banal, commonplace stereotype in everyday culture. What is experienced in the salient shock effect is the disruption of our normative expectations about distinctions that imply a rigid separation between fine art and popular culture, or between art and pornography.

Mapplethorpe's transgressive crossing of such boundaries has the effect of calling into question our psychic and social investment in these cultural separations.

Changing political climates

If I am now more prepared to offer a defence rather than a critique of Mapplethorpe's representations of race, because of the changed ideological context, it is because the stakes have also changed. I am convinced that it was not the death of the author so much as the cause of his death that was a major factor in the timing of the Helms campaign against the NEA. Almost all the discourse surrounding the furore noted that Mapplethorpe died of AIDS. The new-found legitimacy of political homophobia and the creation of new folk devils through the mismanagement of the AIDS crisis has proved fertile ground for the spread of popular authoritarian tendencies across the left/right spectrum. Yet the Mapplethorpe/NEA crisis in the USA was often perceived, like the Rushdie crisis in Britain, simply in terms of a straightforward opposition between censorship and freedom of artistic expression. This model of a crude binary frontier is unfeasible because what was at stake in the conflicting readings of Mapplethorpe was not a neat dichotomy between bigoted Philistines and enlightened cultured liberals but a new configuration of social actors, some of whom have engaged in unexpected alliances which have transformed the terrain of contestation.

In many ways the right's success in organizing a popular bloc of public opinion on issues like pornography derives from these new alliances. Just like the alliance formed between radical feminist anti-porn activists and the local state legislature in the form of the Dworkin–MacKinnon-drafted Minneapolis Ordinance in 1984, or the appropriation of the feminist argument that pornography itself is violence in the official discourse of the Meese Commission in 1986, the Helms campaign has highlighted some significant developments in popular right-wing politics. In his original proposal to regulate public funding of art deemed 'obscene and indecent', Jesse Helms went beyond the traditional remit of moral fundamentalism to add new grounds for legal intervention on the basis of discrimination against minorities. Helms wanted the state to intervene in instances where artistic and cultural materials denigrate, debase or revile a person, group or class of citizens on the basis of race, creed, sex, handicap or national origin'. By means of this rhetorical move, he sought to appropriate the language of liberal anti-discrimination legislation to promote a climate of opinion favourable to new forms of coercive intervention. In making such a move, the strategy is not simply to win support from black people and ethnic minorities, nor simply to modernize the traditional 'moral' discourse against obscenity, but to broaden and extend the threshold of illegitimacy to a wider range of cultural texts. As the moral panic unfolds, more and more cultural forms transgress or come up against the symbolic boundary that such prohibitionary legislation seeks to impose. Consider the way in which parental warning labels on rap and rock albums have become commonplace: the Parents' Music Resource Centre that helped to initiate this trend in the 1980s has also inspired prosecutions of rock musicians on the grounds that their cultural texts do not simply 'deprave and corrupt', as it were, but have actually caused violence, in the form of suicides.

Under these conditions—when, despite its initial emancipatory intentions, elements of the radical feminist anti-porn movement of the 1980s have entered into alliance with neo-conservative forces—it is not inconceivable that a reading of Robert Mapplethorpe's work as racist, however well intended, could serve the ends of the authoritarian trend supported by this new alliance of social actors. The AIDS crisis has also visibly brought to light the way in which homophobia can be used to draw upon conservative forces within minority cultures. In black British communities, the anti-lesbian and gay hostility expressed in the belief that homosexuality is a 'white man's thing', and hence, because of the scapegoating of gay men, that AIDS is a 'white man's disease', has not only helped to cement alliances between black people and the New Right (for example, in the local campaign on 'Positive Images' in Haringey, London, in 1987) but has had tragically self-defeating consequences in the black community itself. Men and women have been dying, but the psychic mechanism of denial and disavowal in such fear of homosexuality has been particularly apparent in many black responses to AIDS.

Yet these contradictory conditions have also shaped the emergence of a new generation of black lesbian and gay cultural activists in Britain and the United States. Their presence is seriously important not only because they contest the repressive precepts of authoritarian politics in both white society and in black communities, but because their creativity points to new ways of making sense of the contemporary situation. Black lesbian and gay artists such as Isaac Julien, Pratibha Parmar, Michelle Parkerson and Marlon Riggs in film and video; or Essex Hemphill, Cheryl Clarke, Barbara Smith and Joseph Beam in writing and critique, or Sunil Gupta, Rotimi Fani-Kayode or Lyle Harris in the medium of photography, have widened and pluralized the political and theoretical debates about eroticism, prohibition, transgression and representation. In films such as Isaac Julien's *Looking for Langston* (1989) some of the difficult and troublesome questions about race and homosexuality that Mapplethorpe raised are taken on in a multifaceted dialogue on the lived experience of black gay desire. In his photographs, Rotimi Fani-Kayode also enters into this dialogue, not through a confrontational strategy but through an invitational mode of address which operates in and against the visual codes and conventions his work shares with Mapplethorpe's. But in this hybrid, Afrocentric, homoerotic image world, significant differences unfold as such artists critically 'signify upon' the textual sources they draw from. In the hands of this new generation of black diaspora intellectuals rethinking sex, such 'signifying' activity simultaneously critiques the exclusions and absences which previously rendered black lesbian and gay identities invisible, and reconstructs new pluralistic forms of collective belonging and imagined community that broaden the public sphere of multicultural society.

Such radical changes in black queer visibility were unthinkable ten or fifteen years ago, and one would hope that their emergence now suggests new possibilities for an alternative set of popular alliances that seek to open up and democratize the politics of desire. In the event that the legislation sought by those opposed to whatever can be called 'pornographic' is ever successful in Britain, it is far more likely that it will first be brought to bear on independent artists such as these rather than on the corporations and businessmen who own the porn industry, edit the tabloids or sell advertising. To propose to outlaw something the definition of which no one seems to agree upon is hardly in the interests of anyone seeking not just the protection of our existing civil rights and liberties (few as they are in Britain) but the necessary changes that would further democratize and deepen new practices of freedom.

Notes and bibliography

1 Audre Lorde, 'Uses of the erotic: the erotic as power' (1978) and Alice Walker, 'Coming apart' (1979), both reprinted in Laura Lederer, (ed.), *Take Back the Night: Women on Pornography*. New York: William Morrow, 1980.
2 Susanne Kappeler, *The Pornography of Representation*, Cambridge: Polity Press, 1986, pp. 5–10.
    One important alternative to the race and gender analogy is to open the debate to include racism in both pornography and in the women's movement. This is an important point, raised in the context of a historical overview of the mutual articulation of gender and sexuality in racial oppression, discussed by Tracey Gardner, 'Racism in pornography and the women's movement' (1978), in Lederer (ed.), *Take Back the Night*.
3 See Kobena Mercer, 'Imaging the black man's sex', in Patricia Holland, Jo Spence and Simon Watney (eds.), *Photography/Politics: Two* (London: Comedia, 1986) and, for the revision of the initial analysis, 'Skin head sex thing: racial difference and the homoerotic imaginary', in Bad Object Choices (ed.), *How Do I Look? Lesbian and Gay Film and Video*, Seattle, DC: Bay Press, 1991. Related work on the cultural politics of black masculinity may be found in Isaac Julien and Kobena Mercer, 'Race, sexual politics and black masculinity: a dossier', in Rowena Chapman and Jonathan Rutherford (eds.), *Male Order: Unwrapping Masculinity*, London: Lawrence & Wishart, 1988.
    The black male nude photographs referred to may be found in Robert Mapplethorpe, *Black Males*, Amsterdam: Gallerie Jurka, 1982; *The Black Book* Munich: Schirme-Mosel, 1986; and Richard Marshall (ed.), *Robert Mapplethorpe*, New York: Bullfinch Press, 1990.
4 Homi Bhabha, 'The other question: colonial discourse and the stereotype', *Screen* **24**, 4 (1983), p. 18.
5 Frantz Fanon, *Black Skin/White Masks*, London: Pluto Press, 1986 (first published 1952), p. 120.
6 Sigmund Freud, 'Fetishism' (1923), in *The Pelican Freud Library*, vol. 7, *On Sexuality*, Harmondsworth: Penguin, 1977.
7 Fanon, *Black Skin/White Masks*, p. 82.
8 The humanist critique of objectification is taken up by Essex Hemphill, 'Introduction', in Essex Hemphill (ed.), *Brother to Brother: New Writings by Black Gay Men*, Boston, MA: Alyson Press, 1991.

Section III

Meaning and power

This section comprises a diverse selection of writings broadly on the theme of meaning and power, representing the critical development of cultural studies, some of its constituencies of interest, and various responses to 'the postmodern condition' as lived in socially and spatially situated environments, rather than merely theorized, in recent work.

Liz Curtis's article, a precursor to her book, *Nothing but the Same Old Story* (1984a), focusses upon meaning and power by reminding us of the painful history of British imperialism in the nearby colony of Ireland. Victorian newspapers blamed the victim and dehumanized the other, colonialist tropes that are still familiar in spite of the decline of empires. Contemporary political cartoons depicted the Irish as not yet human, images consistent with the Social Darwinist ideology of racial difference. Writing in the 1970s, when 'the Irish question' had once again exploded onto the domestic political agenda, Curtis illustrates very sharply how racism and the frequently unconscious ruses of collective guilt are connected together by referring, in addition, to the spate of Irish jokes told in Britain at the time. For British media coverage of the Anglo/Irish conflict during this period, see Curtis's (1984b) book which provides extensively documented criticisms and, for the history of what the early-twentieth-century Irish historian Alice Stopford Green called 'the English extirpation of Irish society', see Curtis (1993).

The inclusion of **Judith Williamson**'s Introduction to her *Decoding Advertisements* is intended to whet the reader's appetite for one of the widely acknowledged and still illuminating classics of cultural studies. Williamson applies structuralist theories of ideology, signification and subjectivity that have been central to the development of textual analysis. Through a series of practical case studies, making up the bulk of the book, she seeks to explore how advertisements produce meaning and offer ideal selves with which to identify, in effect drawing attention to the mediation of psychic and economic processes by ideologies of consumption.

Fredric Jameson's piece is a synthesis of two earlier articles: his original 'Postmodernism and Consumer Society', published in Hal Foster's *The Anti-Aesthetic* (Bay Press, 1983), supplemented by material from Jameson's

175

subsequent formulations in the seminal 'Postmodernism, or the Cultural Logic of Late Capitalism' (*New Left Review*, no. 146, 1984), the same title as his recent monumental book on the topic (Jameson, 1991). The version included here provides the most accessible entry to Jameson's controversial thinking on the articulation of culture and economics under postmodern conditions (see Lyotard, 1984; Harvey, 1989; Kellner, 1989). Jameson links current intellectual, social and spatial disorientations to the technological reinvigoration of capitalism and its globalization. Unlike Jean Baudrillard (1988), the guru of postmodernism and prophet of hyperreality (see Norris, 1992), Jameson views present arrangements with a critical rationality and calls for a demystifying political aesthetic of 'cognitive mapping'. Most importantly, he questions intensified commodification and the rebirth of consumer culture (see Lee, 1993).

The extract from **Paul Willis**'s *Common Culture* reiterates some of the formative themes of British cultural studies: the political project of creating a 'common culture', enunciated by Raymond Williams (1958) after R.H. Tawney, and the Birmingham Centre for Contemporary Cultural Studies' thesis that cultural commodities are appropriated and rearticulated meaningfully by ordinary people, especially the young (Jefferson, 1975). Willis's unconcealed populism concerning the symbolic creativity of market-based cultural consumption runs counter to the social democratic tradition of public arts patronage which either sought to disseminate 'elite' culture to the masses or, in community arts, to engage ordinary people in primary cultural production.

Mike Davis, writing in a personalized mode about the region where he grew up, opens *City of Quartz* by recalling the lost history of socialist utopianism in Southern California. This is where affluent community developments, turning the desert into a garden for the few, serve commuters in flight from the socially polarized and politically tense Los Angeles. However, these places are not entirely secure and safe havens for ex-city dwellers with the money to settle elsewhere. From the vantage point provided by Davis, an urban sociologist, the triumph of a displaced postmodern consumerism over local class and race wars seems far from complete. While there are signs that the critical edge of British cultural studies has been blunted, American writing like that of Mike Davis may remind students of cultural studies of its origins in social critique (see Clarke, 1991).

Writing in a similarly critical vein, **Jan Nederveen Pieterse** challenges the complacent rhetoric of European integration, associated with the introduction of a 'single market' at the end of 1992, by raising questions about the suppression of racial and cultural differences. Rather than the civilizing heritage and economic renewal of a greater Europe, Pieterse stresses the actual inequalities and exclusions of this post-imperial solution, the marginalization of peoples and regions, the construction of a 'European Mexico syndrome' in the wake of fallen communism and resurgent Islam.

Both Davis and Pieterse display a heightened sense of what **Doreen Massey** calls the 'power-geometry' of place This sensibility is consistent with 'postmodern geography' (Soja, 1989), which is to some extent reconstructing the preoccupations of cultural studies (see Jackson, 1989/1992). Appropriating and refining David Harvey's concept of 'time-space compression', Massey here connects a holistic concern with spatial dynamics to everyday lived experience. The transition from a predominantly Fordist system of mass production and consumption to a regime of 'flexible accumulation' brings about a certain 'annihilation of space by time' (Marx) whereby distance no longer delays communication (Harvey, 1989). A sense of 'place', both physical and social, is disconcerted in such a rapidly changing and communicating world. Massey draws our attention to the potential meanings of such obscure forces for ordinary people in their homes and on the street. And she stresses how time-space compression is differentially experienced in terms of class, gender and race. These issues were debated at the 1990 'Futures' conference in London's Tate Gallery (see Bird et al., 1992), from which Massey's incisive piece derives.

Like many other subjects in the humanities and social sciences, cultural studies has in the past tended to neglect spatial dynamics, with some notable exceptions (see Cohen, 1972, in Section II), in favour of temporal dynamics. Historical knowledge is, of course, essential to understanding cultural change. Yet, it is now becoming increasingly evident that the logics of meaning and power operate across socio-cultural space as well as through time, thus creating complex and globalizing interrelations between separate places, mediated by cultural, economic and political power.

References

Baudrillard, J. (1988) *Selected Writings*, Cambridge: Polity Press.

Bird, J., Curtis, B., Putnam, T., Robertson, G. and Teichner, L. (eds.) (1992) *Mapping the Futures*, London/New York: Routledge.

Clarke, J. (1991) *New Times and Old Enemies—Essays on Cultural Studies and America*, London: HarperCollins.

Cohen, P. (1972) 'Subcultural conflict and working class community' in *Working Papers in Cultural Studies 2*, Birmingham Centre for Contemporary Cultural Studies.

Curtis, L. (1984a) *Nothing but the Same Old Story—The Roots of Anti-Irish Racism*, London: Information on Ireland.

Curtis, L. (1984b) *Ireland—The Propaganda War*, London: Pluto Press.

Curtis, L. (1993) *The Cause of Ireland—From United Irishmen to Partition*, Belfast: Beyond the Pale.

Harvey, D. (1989) *The Condition of Postmodernity*, Oxford: Basil Blackwell.

Jackson, P. (1989/1992) *Maps of Meaning—An Introduction to Cultural Geography*, London/New York: Unwyn Hyman/Routledge.

Jameson, F. (1991) *Postmodernism or, The Cultural Logic of Late Capitalism*, London: Verso.

Jefferson, T. (ed.) (1975) *Resistance Through Rituals*, Birmingham Centre for Contemporary Cultural Studies.

Kellner, D. (ed.) (1989) *Postmodernism/Jameson/Critique*, Washington: Maisonneuve Press.

Lee, M. (1993) *Consumer Culture Reborn*, London/New York: Routledge.

Lyotard, J. (1984) *The Postmodern Condition*, University of Minnesota/Manchester University Press.

Norris, C. (1992) *Uncritical Theory—Postmodernism, Intellectuals and the Gulf War*, London: Lawrence & Wishart.

Soja, E. (1989) *Postmodern Geographies*, London: Verso.

Williams, R. (1958) *Culture and Society*, London: Chatto and Windus.

16

Echoes of the present—the Victorian press and Ireland

Liz Curtis

From *Truth: the First Casualty* (Information on Ireland, 1978).

'The cry is now for strong measures. Such is the language which is now held by the English journals, which, in their habitual ignorance and presumption, undertake to supply remedies for a social condition, with whose disturbing elements they are utterly unaquainted. They argue from facts of their own creation, and presuppose a state of things to give colour to their absurdities.'

Freeman's Journal, 30 January 1843

England's largest newspapers, wrote Belgian essayist Gustave de Molinari in 1880, 'allow no occasion to escape them of treating the Irish as an inferior race—as a kind of white negroes—and a glance at *Punch* is sufficient to show the difference they establish between the plump and robust personification of John Bull and the wretched figure of lean and bony Pat.'[1]

By the nineteenth century the native Irish had long since been dispossessed of their land by English and Scottish settlers. Their religious and civil rights had been denied. They were racked by repeated famines and evicted from their holdings by rapacious landlords. They were not surprisingly rebellious.

But the major British papers of the period saw no connection between British rule and Irish poverty and violence. Instead they argued that the Irish condition was the fault of the Irish themselves and resulted from moral failings inherent in the Celtic character.

A contributor to *Fraser's Magazine*, popular with the English middle classes, declared in March 1847,

'The English people are naturally industrious—they prefer a life of honest labour to one of idleness . . . Now of all the Celtic tribes, famous everywhere for their indolence and fickleness as the Celts everywhere are, the Irish are admitted to be the most idle and the most fickle. They will not work if they can exist without it.'

The *Times* asked in the same year, 'What is an Englishman made for but for work? What is an Irishman made for but to sit at his cabin door, read O'Connell's speeches and abuse the English?' (*Times*, 26 January 1847).

Supposed criminal tendencies in the Celtic character were used to explain

179

away successive Irish rebellions—the rising of the United Irishmen in 1798, the peasant unrest in the first part of the nineteenth century, the Fenian rising of 1867 and the Land War of 1879–81.

A small minority of English people, including some working-class radicals in the Midlands and a few prominent intellectuals such as the economists George Poulett Scrope and John Stuart Mill, put forward a different view.

John Stuart Mill pointed out that under the existing system of land tenure

PUNCH, OR THE LONDON CHARIVARI.—March 3, 1866.

THE FENIAN-PEST.

Hibernia. "O MY DEAR SISTER, WHAT *ARE* WE TO DO WITH THESE TROUBLESOME PEOPLE?"
Britannia. "TRY ISOLATION FIRST, MY DEAR, AND THEN———"

'The Fenian Pest.' Britannia stamps on rebellion and protects Hibernia from the Fenians in this cartoon by Tenniel (*Punch*, 3 March 1866).

the peasant had nothing to gain from hard work. 'If he were industrious or prudent, nobody but his landlord would gain; if he is lazy or intemperate, it is at his landlord's expense.'[2]

And in 1834 Scrope urged the government to limit landlords' powers, arguing,

> 'It is impossible . . . to have any doubt as to the real cause of the insurrectionary spirit and agrarian outrages of the Irish peasantry. They are the struggles of an oppressed, starving people for existence!'[3]

But in the 1840s only three major newspapers—the *Morning Chronicle*, the *Westminster Review* and the radical *Northern Star*—shared this perspective. The rest all argued that Irish violence was due to the natural criminality of the Celt.

On 13 October 1846 the *Times* put forward this analysis:

> 'An Irishman commits a murder as a Malay runs a-muck. In certain circumstances it is expected of him, and he would be thought a mean and spiritless wretch if he demurred at it. It is only unfortunate that these circumstances are so indefinite. The conditions under which a Malay draws his krise for the last rush . . . are pretty well known by those conversant with the native character . . . But it is impossible to catalogue the offences which amongst Irishmen entail sudden murder or secret assassination.'

The press discovered yet another side to the Irish character in order to denigrate the non-violent movement for the Repeal of the Union between Britain and Ireland. This movement was highly popular, attracting as many as half a million people to its meetings.

The Repeal leader Daniel O'Connell was described in one *Times* article in 1836 as 'scum condensed of Irish bog' and 'a greedy self-serving Satan' (*Times*, 16 June 1836). And on 24 January 1843 the *Times* had this to say about the Irish people and their support for Repeal,

> 'A people of acute sensibilities and lively passions, more quick in feeling wrongs than rational in explaining or temperate in addressing them . . . such is the people whose virtues and whose vices . . . . O'Connell has so fiendishly exploited.'

Coercion, it was widely argued, was the answer to repeal: establish 'tranquillity' first, then reform could follow. The press greeted Government's repressive measures against the Repealers with delight.

The British presupposed that the Irish were inferior in a number of ways to themselves. This inferiority was manifested in Irish poverty and violence. The cure was a further dose of colonial methods. This is how the *Times* argued in 1846 for a coercive response to the Repealers:

> 'The great obstacle to tranquillity in Ireland is the national character —the character of the masses, of the middle classes of the senators of Ireland . . . When Ireland acts according to the principles of civilised man, then she can be ruled by the laws of civilised man.' (*Times*, 30 March 1846)

So the destitution and rebelliousness of the Irish, which British rule had brought about, were used to justify the continuation of British rule. Colonialism produced its own justification. Jean-Paul Sartre described the process

PUNCH, OR THE LONDON CHARIVARI.—December 31, 1881.

TIME'S WAXWORKS.

(1881 *JUST ADDED TO THE COLLECTION.*)

Mr. P. " HA ! YOU 'LL HAVE TO PUT HIM INTO THE CHAMBER OF HORRORS ! "

'Time's Waxworks.' In 1881 the rebellious Irish join other British 'imperial problems' in Father Time's waxworks collection (Tenniel, *Punch*, 31 December 1881).

thus, 'Terror and exploitation dehumanise, and the exploiter authorises himself with that dehumanisation to carry his exploitation further.'[4]

The Irish were not the only people to be regarded by Victorian Britons as inferior. All the imperial subjects were seen in this light: as, in Kipling's words, 'half devil and half child'. Richard Ned Lebow, who studied colonial attitudes in his book *White Britain and Black Ireland*, points out,

'. . . with almost monotonous regularity colonial natives have been described as indolent and complacent, cowardly but brazenly rash, violent, uncivilised and incapable of hard work. On the more complimentary side, they have been characterised as hospitable, good-natured, possessing a natural talent for song and dance and frequently as curious but incapable of a prolonged span of attention. In short, the image of simple creatures in need of paternal domination emerged very clearly.'[5]

Following Sartre and Albert Memmi, Lebow suggests that the stereotype of the inferior native allows the colonizing nation to apply harsher standards of justice than would be applied at home with a clear conscience. It provides a way out of the liberal dilemma: how to reconcile principles with what you see as political necessity.

In earlier days the subject peoples were not even regarded as inferior humans—instead they were seen as animals or as races born to be slaves.

In the sixteenth century a great debate took place in Spain over whether American Indians were in fact human beings. Most conquistadors argued that despite their human form, the Indians were really animals—a view which justified treating them as beasts of burden. A similar outlook enabled Cromwell and the Pilgrim Fathers to retain a clear conscience as they exterminated, respectively, the indigenous Irish and American peoples.

Victorian cartoonists appropriated the image of the 'inferior and uncivilised' Irish and translated it into powerfully propagandistic images.

At the time of the French Revolution in 1789, rioters, radicals and rebels of all nationalities were drawn with sub-human features, and often with pig-like noses, to suggest that they were part of the primitive 'swinish' mob. And when the United Irishmen rose in 1798 they were immediately caricatured as brutish peasants with snub noses and bulging jaws.

In the 1840s brutish caricatures became increasingly identified with Irish people. The Irish were by now a favourite butt for cartoonists. Thousands of destitute Irish immigrants were pouring into England and Scotland. The Repeal movement had started, and the end of the decade was to see the Young Ireland movement attempt to launch an armed uprising.

Daniel O'Connell was portrayed as Frankenstein—a theme that was to recur—conjuring up a monstrous Irish peasant with horns like the Devil. In 1848 *Punch* repeatedly caricatured John Mitchel, the outstanding Young Ireland leader, as a vicious monkey.

The rise of the revolutionary Fenian movement in the 1860s, dedicated to liberating Ireland through force of arms and to returning the land to the people, sparked off anti-Irish hysteria in England and Scotland. The *Glasgow Herald* even produced a special report entitled, 'A night among the Fenians and other wild animals'.[6]

The Fenian campaign of raids on police stations in Ireland and bombings in Britain coincided with a major debate among British scientists about the origins of mankind: are humans descended from Adam and Eve, or do they share an ancestor with the ape?

Many Victorians took comfort from the idea that other races, such as blacks and Irish, were lower on the evolutionary ladder than themselves. Apes were then believed to be vicious creatures—so it was easy to explain away Irish violence as resulting from Irish affinity with apes. Cartoonists and satirists were not slow to utilize the scientists' ideas, and when the first gorilla arrived in London Zoo in 1860 they had the material to hand.

They were quick to caricature the Fenians as ape-like monsters threatening British civilization. As Lewis P. Curtis puts it in his study of Victorian caricature, *Apes and Angels*, famous illustrators like John Tenniel who drew for *Punch*, 'leaned heavily on the traditional theme of Beauty (Hibernia or Erin) being rescued from the clutches of the Beast (Fenianism) by a handsome Prince or St. George (Law and Order).'[7]

On 18 March 1862 *Punch* published this barbed satire:

'A creature manifestly between the gorilla and the negro is to be met with in some of the lowest districts of London and Liverpool by adventurous explorers. It comes from Ireland, whence it has contrived to migrate; it belongs in fact to a tribe of Irish savages: the lowest species of Irish Yahoo. When conversing with its kind it talks a sort of gibberish. It is, moreover, a climbing animal, and may sometimes be seen ascending a ladder laden with a hod of bricks. The Irish Yahoo generally confines itself within the limits of its own colony, except when it goes out of them to get its living. Sometimes, however, it sallies forth in states of excitement, and attacks civilised human beings that have provoked its fury.'

When the Land War started in 1879 cartoonists made the Irish even more monstrous and brutish than before. A spate of evictions—2,100 families

No. 1.—This is little Chalks sent over by the London Illustrated Smudge to furnish truthful sketches of Irish character.

No. 2.—This is his model.

No. 3.—And this is the sketch he furnishes.

'Setting Down in Malice.' An Irish cartoonist, possibly John O'Hea, mocks the efforts of English artists to depict the Irish as monsters ('Pat', 22 January 1881).

'The Irish Frankenstein,' by Matt Morgan ('The Tomahawk', 18 December 1869)

were evicted in the year 1880 alone—led to increasingly bitter agrarian warfare. The cartoonists responded by portraying the Land League's supporters with ape-like faces, huge mouths and sharp fangs to convey that they had not a shred of humanity.

And as the constitutional agitation of the Irish Home Rule Party in Parliament became more militant, Parnell and his supporters too were depicted as ape-like creatures.

As the debate about the origin of species became less controversial, so did the gorilla-Celt begin to fade from the cartoons. The Irish, however, did not. And when the War of Independence started in 1919 the cartoonists displayed their feelings for the rebels by returning to the image of the pig.

Needless to say, the Irish did not see themselves as their British masters saw them. In the satirical magazines read by Ireland's middle and upper classes from 1870 to 1914 it was the Irish—and especially the Home Rulers—who appeared as handsome, honest and even angelic.

Irish cartoonists did not systematically set out to portray the British as apes. But they knew how to make John Bull and his minions—Orangemen, policemen and officials—look cruel. Serious political cartoonists such as John O'Hea, an advocate of Home Rule, contrasted the honest Irishman Pat with unscrupulous British politicians and showed how cruelly Irish landlords—supported by the Tory government—oppressed their tenants.

Irish cartoonists also delighted in mocking British stereotypes of the Irish, and poked fun at their efforts to turn Paddy into a monster.

Today

Today the press still fosters the belief that the current conflict in Ireland is due to the inherent irrationality of the Irish—their illogical religious passions, their proneness to violence. It follows from this view that only the presence of the more 'rational' Briton prevents the situation degenerating even further. In an article in The *Times* on 23 September 1977—later the subject of a complaint to the Commission for Racial Equality—Bernard Levin invoked the Victorian image of the Irish.

> 'There they go still,' he wrote, 'the Irish "pathriots" (sic), with minds locked and tarred, mouths gaping wide to extrude the very last morsel of folly, and consumed with a wild terror that sense may one day prevail.'

Levin was reacting to widespread calls in Ireland for British withdrawal and he was backing up Conor Cruise O'Brien—who had lost his seat in the June election. Levin considered that O'Brien, who supports the link with Britain, was the only sane Irishman. If Ireland were towed into the sea and sunk, said Levin, the British Government would 'send a helicopter to take Senator O'Brien off at the last minute.'

There are echoes of Victorian days, too, in the view that coercion is a legitimate response to Irish 'irrationality'.

'What do we want at Christmas?' asked the *Daily Express* on Christmas Eve in 1977. 'What do we want for Northern Ireland, that wretched, God-stricken back alley of Europe where they shoot people's kneecaps. As a matter of fact, yes—there *are* prospects for Ulster. She has easily the best, toughest, least tractable and most effective Secretary of State ever in Roy Mason . . .'

Such attitudes are reflected—and reinforced—at a popular level by the prevalent anti-Irish joke, which plays a comparable role to the Victorian cartoons. Such jokes, which portray the target group as 'thick', are common wherever there is tension—or a relationship perceived as one of superiority and inferiority—between two groups of people. Indeed the same stories reappear in Australian anti-Pom jokes, American anti-Polish jokes, Glaswegian jokes about 'teuchters' (country bumpkins) and Dublin jokes about Kerrymen.

The rash of anti-Irish jokes has developed since the upsurge in the conflict in 1969 and has had enormous assistance from television. Virtually no TV comedy show is complete without them. Mike Yarwood, the Two Ronnies, Marti Caine, Dick Emery, Jim Davidson, Spike Milligan, Galton and Speight's Tea Ladies and so on all have their quota.

Irish people in Britain fail to find the jokes funny. Indeed, they are so angered by them that for some time the *Irish Post*, 'The Voice of the Irish Community in Britain', has carried a heated correspondence on the subject. And in 1977 Terry Wogan won the *Post*'s 'Irish Person of the Year' award largely on the strength of his public opposition to anti-Irish jokes.

When English people suggest that Irish people are lacking in a sense of humour if they fail to laugh at the jokes—'everyone should be able to laugh at themselves'—Irish people respond with jokes that English people are reluctant to try out on their friends, and which TV comics ignore.

'Heard the one about the two Englishmen who were trying to have a go at an Irishman in a pub? One of them goes up to the Irishman and says, "Did you know the Pope's a bastard?" The Irishman takes no notice, just goes on drinking. Then the other Englishman goes up to him and says, "Hey Paddy! The Pope's an Englishman!" "I know," says the Irishman, "your mate just told me." '

Irish people recognize that anti-Irish jokes inflame popular prejudice against them and feed on the concept—carefully nurtured by the government and the media—that the current war is due to Irish bloody-mindedness.

For their part Irish people see the war as caused by history not psychology. If anything they see the British as stupid, with their chauvinist narrow-mindedness. 'Heard the one about the Englishman with the inferiority complex? He thought he was the same as everybody else.'

For English people, ill-informed or misinformed about the continuing war in Ireland, anti-Irish jokes provide a way of laughing off a situation which they find frustrating and fail to understand. And anti-Irish jokes also provide a kind of misplaced reassurance that John Bull, after all, knows best.

Notes

This article is particularly indebted to two books: *White Britain and Black Ireland* by Richard Ned Lebow (Institute for the Study of Human Issues, Philadelphia, 1976) and *Apes and Angels* by Lewis P. Curtis Jr. (David and Charles, 1971).

1 Quoted in Curtis op. cit., 1.
2 John Stuart Mill, *Principles of Political Economy with Some of Their Applications to Social Philosophy*, Boston, 1848, vol. II, p. 283.
3 George Poulett Thomason Scrope, *How is Ireland to be Governed*, London, 1834, pp. 20–1.
4 Jean-Paul Sartre, Introduction to Albert Memmi's *The Colonizer and the Colonized*, Souvenir Press, London, 1974, p. xxvi.
5 Lebow op. cit., p. 104.
6 Quoted in Curtis op. cit., p. 98.
7 Curtis op. cit., p. 37.

17

Meaning and ideology

Judith Williamson

Introduction to her *Decoding Advertisements* (Marion Boyars, 1978).

'The process, then, is simply this: The product becomes a commodity,
i.e. a mere moment of exchange. The commodity is transformed into
exchange value. In order to equate it with itself as an exchange value, it
is exchanged for a symbol which represents it as exchange value as such.
As such a symbolized exchange value, it can then in turn be exchanged in
definite relations for every other commodity. Because the product becomes
a commodity, and the commodity becomes an exchange value, it obtains,
at first only in the head, a double existence. This doubling in the idea
proceeds (and must proceed) to the point where the commodity appears
double in real exchange: as a natural product on one side, as exchange value
on the other.'

Karl Marx, Grundrisse

Advertisements are one of the most important cultural factors moulding
and reflecting our life today. They are ubiquitous, an inevitable part of
everyone's lives: even if you do not read a newspaper or watch television,
the images posted over our urban surroundings are inescapable. Pervading
all the media, but limited to none, advertising forms a vast superstructure
with an apparently autonomous existence and an immense influence. It
is not my purpose here to *measure* its influence. To do so would require
sociological research and consumer data drawing on a far wider range
of material than the advertisements themselves. I am simply analysing
what can be *seen* in advertisements. Their very existence in more than
one medium gives them a sort of independent reality that links them
to our own lives; since both share a continuity they constitute a world
constantly experienced as real. The ad 'world' becomes seemingly separate
from the material medium—whether screen, page, etc.—which carries it.
Analysing ads in their *material form* helps to avoid endowing them with a
false materiality and letting the 'ad world' distort the real world around the
screen and page.

It is this ubiquitous quality and its tenacity as a recognizable 'form'
despite the fact that it functions within different technical media and
despite different 'content' (that is, different messages about different
products) that indicates the significance of advertising. Obviously it has

a function, which is to sell things to us. But it has another function, which I believe in many ways replaces that traditionally fulfilled by art or religion. It creates structures of meaning.

For even the 'obvious' functions of advertising—the definition above, 'to sell things to us'—involves a meaning process. Advertisements must take into account not only the inherent qualities and attributes of the products they are trying to sell, but also the way in which they can make those properties *mean something to us*.

In other words, advertisements have to translate statements from the world of things, for example, that a car will do so many miles per gallon, into a form that means something in terms of people. Suppose that the car did a high mpg: this could be translated into terms of thriftiness, the user being a 'clever' saver, in other words, *being a certain kind of person*. Or, if the mpg was low, the ad could appeal to the 'above money pettiness', daredevil kind of person who is too 'trendy' to be economizing. Both the statements in question could be made on the purely factual level of a 'use-value' by the simple figures of '50 mpg' and '20 mpg'. The advertisement translates these 'thing' statements to us as human statements; they are given a humanly symbolic 'exchange-value'.

Thus advertising is not, as might superficially be supposed, a single 'language' in the sense that a language has particular identifiable constituent parts and its words are predetermined. The components of advertisements are variable [. . .] and *not* necessarily all part of one 'language' or social discourse. Advertisements rather provide a structure which is capable of transforming the language of objects to that of people, and vice versa. The first part of this book attempts to analyse the way that structure functions. The second part looks at some of the actual systems and things that it transforms.

But it is too simple to say that advertising reduces people to the status of things, though clearly this is what happens when both are used symbolically. Certainly advertising sets up connections between certain types of consumers and certain products (as in the example above); and having made these links and created symbols of exchange it can use them as 'given', and so can we. For example: diamonds may be marketed by likening them to eternal love, creating a symbolism where the mineral means something not in its own terms, as a rock, but in human terms, as a sign. Thus a diamond comes to 'mean' love and endurance for us. Once the connection has been made, we begin to translate the other way and in fact to skip translating altogether: taking the sign for what it signifies, the thing for the feeling.

So in the connection of people and objects, the two do become interchangeable, as can be seen very clearly in ads of two categories. There are those where objects are made to speak—like people: 'say it with flowers'; 'a little gold says it all', etc. Conversely there are the ads where people become identified with objects: 'the *Pepsi People*' and such like. [. . .] This aspect of advertising's system of meaning is shown in Mick Jagger's lines* [. . .]. The classifications of advertisements rebound like a boomerang, as

* From 'Satisfaction'.

we receive them and come to use them. When 'the man' comes on in one advertisement, the TV watcher (who, it is interesting to note, sees all advertisements as one, or rather, sees their rules as applicable to one another and thus part of an interchangeable system) *uses* the classificatory speech from *another* advertisement and directs this speech back at the screen. 'Well he can't be a man 'cause he doesn't smoke/the same cigarettes as me'. Advertisements are selling us something else besides consumer goods: in providing us with a structure in which we, and those goods, are interchangeable, they are selling us ourselves.

And we need those selves. It is the materiality and historical context of this need which must be given as much attention as that equation of people with things. An attempt to differentiate amongst both people and products is part of the desire to classify, order, and understand the world, including one's own identity. But in our society, while the real distinctions between people are created by their role in the *process* of production, as workers, it is the *products* of their own work that are used, in the false categories invoked by advertising, to obscure the real structure of society by replacing class with the distinctions made by the consumption of particular goods. Thus instead of being identified by what they produce, people are made to identify themselves with what they consume. From this arises the false assumption that workers 'with two cars and a colour TV' are not part of the working class. We are made to feel that we can rise or fall in society through what we are able to buy, and this obscures the actual class basis which still underlies social position. The fundamental differences in our society are still class differences, but use of manufactured goods as means of *creating* classes or groups forms an overlay on them.

This overlay is ideology. Ideology is the meaning *made necessary* by the conditions of society while helping to *perpetuate* those conditions. We feel a need to belong, to have a social 'place'; it can be hard to find. Instead we may be given an imaginary one. All of us have a genuine need for a social being, a common culture. The mass media provide this to some extent and can (potentially) fulfil a positive function in our lives.

But advertising seems to have a life of its own; it exists in and out of other media, and speaks to us in a language we can recognize but a voice we can never identify. This is because advertising has no 'subject'. Obviously people invent and produce adverts, but apart from the fact that they are unknown and faceless, the ad in any case does not claim to speak from them, it is not their speech. Thus there is a space, a gap left where the speaker should be; and one of the peculiar features of advertising is that we are drawn in to fill that gap, so that we become both listener and speaker, subject and object. This works in practice as an anonymous speech, involving a set of connections and symbols directed at us; then on receiving it, we *use* this speech, as shown in the 'diamond' example, or in the use of 'a little gold' to 'say it all'. Ultimately advertising works in a circular movement which once set in motion is self-perpetuating. It 'works' because it feeds off a genuine 'use-value'; besides needing social meaning we obviously *do need* material goods. Advertising gives those goods a social meaning so that two needs are crossed, and neither is adequately filled. Material things that we need are made to represent other, non-material things we need; the point of exchange between the two is where 'meaning' is created.

This outlines and necessarily anticipates ground covered step by step below. By examining the *ideological function* of advertisements' *way of meaning*, Part I, 'Advertising Work', seeks to understand the meaning process: this is where structuralism has been influential and helpful. Part II, 'Ideological Castles', examines the ideological context in which things and people are re-used in that process to create new symbolic systems. These systems are an ideological bric-à-brac of things, people, and people's need for things.

The need for relationship and human meaning appropriated by advertising is one that, if only it was not diverted, could radically change the society we live in.

18

Postmodernism and consumer society[1]

Fredric Jameson

From E. Ann Kaplan (ed.) *Postmodernism and its Discontents* (Verso, 1988).

The concept of postmodernism is not widely accepted or even understood today. Some of the resistance to it may come from the unfamiliarity of the work it covers, which can be found in all the arts: the poetry of John Ashbery, for instance, but also the much simpler talk poetry that came out of the reaction against complex, ironic, academic modernist poetry in the 1960s; the reaction against modern architecture and in particular against the monumental buildings of the International Style, the pop buildings and decorated sheds celebrated by Robert Venturi in his manifesto, *Learning from Las Vegas*; Andy Warhol and Pop art, but also the more recent Photorealism; in music, the moment of John Cage but also the later synthesis of classical and 'popular' styles found in composers like Philip Glass and Terry Riley, and also punk and new-wave rock with such groups as the Clash, Talking Heads and the Gang of Four; in film, everything that comes out of Godard—contemporary vanguard film and video—but also a whole new style of commercial or fiction films, which has its equivalent in contemporary novels as well, where the works of William Burroughs, Thomas Pynchon and Ishmael Reed on the one hand, and the French new novel on the other, are also to be numbered among the varieties of what can be called postmodernism.

This list would seem to make two things clear at once: first, most of the postmodernisms mentioned above emerge as specific reactions against the established forms of high modernism, against this or that dominant high modernism which conquered the university, the museum, the art gallery network, and the foundations. Those formerly subversive and embattled styles—Abstract Expressionism; the great modernist poetry of Pound, Eliot or Wallace Stevens; the International Style (Le Corbusier, Frank Lloyd Wright, Mies); Stravinsky; Joyce, Proust and Mann—felt to be scandalous or shocking by our grandparents are, for the generation which arrives at the gate in the 1960s, felt to be the establishment and the enemy—dead, stifling, canonical, the reified monuments one has to destroy to do anything new. This means that there will be as many different forms of postmodernism as there were high modernisms in place, since the former are at least initially specific and local reactions *against* those models.

That obviously does not make the job of describing postmodernism as a coherent thing any easier, since the unity of this new impulse—if it has one —is given not in itself but in the very modernism it seeks to displace.

The second feature of this list of postmodernisms is the effacement in it of some key boundaries or separations, most notably the erosion of the older distinction between high culture and so-called mass or popular culture. This is perhaps the most distressing development of all from an academic standpoint, which has traditionally had a vested interest in preserving a realm of high or elite culture against the surrounding environment of philistinism, of schlock and kitsch, of TV series and *Reader's Digest* culture, and in transmitting difficult and complex skills of reading, listening and seeing to its initiates. But many of the newer postmodernisms have been fascinated precisely by that whole landscape of advertising and motels, of the Las Vegas strip, of the late show and Grade-B Hollywood film, of so-called paraliterature with its airport paperback categories of the gothic and the romance, the popular biography, the murder mystery and the science fiction or fantasy novel. They no longer 'quote' such 'texts' as a Joyce might have done, or a Mahler; they incorporate them, to the point where the line between high art and commercial forms seems increasingly difficult to draw.

A rather different indication of this effacement of the older categories of genre and discourse can be found in what is sometimes called contemporary theory. A generation ago there was still a technical discourse of professional philosophy—the great systems of Sartre or the phenomenologists, the work of Wittgenstein or analytical or common language philosophy—alongside which one could still distinguish that quite different discourse of the other academic disciplines—of political science, for example, or sociology or literary criticism. Today, increasingly, we have a kind of writing simply called 'theory' which is all or none of those things at once. This new kind of discourse, generally associated with France and so-called French theory, is becoming widespread and marks the end of philosophy as such. Is the work of Michel Foucault, for example, to be called philosophy, history, social theory or political science? It's undecidable, as they say nowadays; and I will suggest that such 'theoretical discourse' is also to be numbered among the manifestations of postmodernism.

Now I must say a word about the proper use of this concept: it is not just another word for the description of a particular style. It is also, at least in my use, a periodizing concept whose function is to correlate the emergence of new formal features in culture with the emergence of a new type of social life and a new economic order—what is often euphemistically called modernization, postindustrial or consumer society, the society of the media or the spectacle, or multinational capitalism. This new moment of capitalism can be dated from the post-war boom in the United States in the late 1940s and early 1950s or, in France, from the establishment of the Fifth Republic in 1958. The 1960s are in many ways the key transitional period, a period in which the new international order (neocolonialism, the Green Revolution, computerization and electronic information) is at one and the same time set in place and is swept and shaken by its own internal contradictions and by external resistance. I want here to sketch a few of the ways in which the new postmodernism expresses the inner truth of that newly emergent social order of late capitalism, but will have to limit the description to only two of its significant features, which I will call pastiche and schizophrenia; they will give us a chance to sense the specificity of the postmodernist experience of space and time respectively.

Pastiche eclipses parody

One of the most significant features or practices in postmodernism today is pastiche. I must first explain this term, which people generally tend to confuse with or assimilate to that related verbal phenomenon called parody. Both pastiche and parody involve the imitation or, better still, the mimicry of other styles and particularly of the mannerisms and stylistic twitches of other styles. It is obvious that modern literature in general offers a very rich field for parody, since the great modern writers have all been defined by the invention or production of rather unique styles: think of the Faulknerian long sentence or of D.H. Lawrence's characteristic nature imagery; think of Wallace Stevens's peculiar way of using abstractions; think also of the mannerisms of the philosophers, of Heidegger for example, or Sartre; think of the musical styles of Mahler or Prokofiev. All of these styles, however different from each other, are comparable in this: each is quite unmistakable; once one is learned, it is not likely to be confused with something else.

Now parody capitalizes on the uniqueness of these styles and seizes on their idiosyncrasies and eccentricities to produce an imitation which mocks the original. I won't say that the satiric impulse is conscious in all forms of parody. In any case, a good or great parodist has to have some secret sympathy for the original, just as a great mimic has to have the capacity to put himself/herself in the place of the person imitated. Still, the general effect of parody is—whether in sympathy or with malice—to cast ridicule on the private nature of these stylistic mannerisms and their excessiveness and eccentricity with respect to the way people normally speak or write. So there remains somewhere behind all parody the feeling that there is a linguistic norm in contrast to which the styles of the great modernists can be mocked.

But what would happen if one no longer believed in the existence of normal language, of ordinary speech, of the linguistic norm (the kind of clarity and communicative power celebrated by Orwell in his famous essay, say)? One could think of it in this way; perhaps the immense fragmentation and privatization of modern literature—its explosion into a host of distinct private styles and mannerisms—foreshadows deeper and more general tendencies in social life as a whole. Supposing that modern art and modernism—far from being a kind of specialized aesthetic curiosity—actually anticipated social developments along these lines; supposing that in the decades since the emergence of the great modern styles society has itself begun to fragment in this way, each group coming to speak a curious private language of its own, each profession developing its private code or idiolect, and finally each individual coming to be a kind of linguistic island, separated from everyone else? But then in that case, the very possibility of any linguistic norm in terms of which one could ridicule private languages and idiosyncratic styles would vanish, and we would have nothing but stylistic diversity and heterogeneity.

That is the moment at which pastiche appears and parody has become impossible. Pastiche is, like parody, the imitation of a peculiar or unique style, the wearing of a stylistic mask, speech in a dead language: but it is a neutral practice of such mimicry, without parody's ulterior motive, without the satirical impulse, without laughter, without that still latent feeling that there exists something *normal* compared to which what is being imitated is rather comic. Pastiche is blank parody, parody that has lost its sense of humour: pastiche is to parody what that curious thing, the modern practice of a kind of blank irony, is to what Wayne Booth calls the stable and comic ironies of, say, the eighteenth century.

The death of the subject

But now we need to introduce a new piece into this puzzle, which may help to explain why classical modernism is a thing of the past and why postmodernism should have taken its place. This new component is what is generally called the 'death of the subject' or, to say it in more conventional language, the end of individualism as such. The great modernisms were, as we have said, predicated on the invention of a personal, private style, as unmistakable as your fingerprints, as incomparable as your own body. But this means that the modernist aesthetic is in some way organically linked to the conception of a unique self and private identity, a unique personality and individuality, which can be expected to generate its own unique vision of the world and to forge its own unique, unmistakable style.

Yet today, from any number of distinct perspectives, the social theorists, the psychoanalysts, even the linguists, not to speak of those of us who work in the area of culture and cultural and formal change, are all exploring the notion that that kind of individualism and personal identity is a thing of the past; that the old individual or individualist subject is 'dead'; and that one might even describe the concept of the unique individual and the theoretical basis of individualism as ideological. There are in fact two positions on all this, one of which is more radical than the other. The first one is content to say: yes, once upon a time, in the classic age of competitive capitalism, in the heyday of the nuclear family and the emergence of the bourgeoisie as the hegemonic social class, there was such a thing as individualism, as individual subjects. But today, in the age of corporate capitalism, of the so-called organization man, of bureaucracies in business as well as in the state, of demographic explosion—today, that older bourgeois individual subject no longer exists.

Then there is a second position, the more radical of the two, what one might call the poststructuralist position. It adds: not only is the bourgeois individual subject a thing of the past, it is also a myth; it *never* really existed in the first place; there have never been autonomous subjects of that type.

Rather, this construct is merely a philosophical and cultural mystification which sought to persuade people that they 'had' individual subjects and possessed this unique personal identity.

For our purposes, it is not particularly important to decide which of these positions is correct (or rather, which is more interesting and productive). What we have to retain from all this is rather an aesthetic dilemma: because if the experience and the ideology of the unique self, an experience and ideology which informed the stylistic practice of classical modernism, is over and done with, then it is no longer clear what the artists and writers of the present period are supposed to be doing. What is clear is merely that the older models—Picasso, Proust, T.S. Eliot—do not work any more (or are positively harmful), since nobody has that kind of unique private world and style to express any longer. And this is perhaps not merely a 'psychological' matter: we also have to take into account the immense weight of seventy or eighty years of classical modernism itself. There is another sense in which the writers and artists of the present day will no longer be able to invent new styles and worlds—they've already been invented; only a limited number of combinations are possible; the unique ones have been thought of already. So the weight of the whole modernist aesthetic tradition—now dead—also 'weighs like a nightmare on the brains of the living,' as Marx said in another context.

Hence, once again, pastiche: in a world in which stylistic innovation is no longer possible, all that is left is to imitate dead styles, to speak through the masks and with the voices of the styles in the imaginary museum. But this means that contemporary or postmodernist art is going to be about art itself in a new kind of way; even more, it means that one of its essential messages will involve the necessary failure of art and the aesthetic, the failure of the new, the imprisonment in the past.

The nostalgia mode

As this may seem very abstract, I want to give a few examples, one of which is so omnipresent that we rarely link it with the kinds of developments in high art discussed here. This particular practice of pastiche is not high-cultural but very much within mass culture, and it is generally known as the 'nostalgia film' (what the French neatly call *la mode rétro*—retrospective styling). We must conceive of this category in the broadest way: narrowly, no doubt, it consists merely of films about the past and about specific generational moments of that past. Thus, one of the inaugural films in this new 'genre' (if that's what it is) was Lucas's *American Graffiti*, which in 1973 set out to recapture all the atmosphere and stylistic peculiarities of the 1950s United States, the United States of the Eisenhower era. Polanski's great film *Chinatown* does something similar for the 1930s, as does Bertolucci's *The Conformist* for the Italian and European context of the same period, the fascist era in Italy; and so forth. We could go on listing these films for some time: why call them pastiche? Are they not rather work in the more traditional genre known as the historical film—work which can more simply be theorized by extrapolating that other well-known form which is the historical novel?

I have my reasons for thinking that we need new categories for such films. But let me first add some anomalies: supposing I suggested that *Star Wars* is also a nostalgia film. What could that mean? I presume we can agree that this is not a historical film about our own intergalactic past. Let me put it somewhat differently: one of the most important cultural experiences of the generations that grew up from the 1930s to the 1950s was the Saturday afternoon serial of the Buck Rogers type—alien villains, true American heroes, heroines in distress, the death ray or the doomsday box, and the cliffhanger at the end whose miraculous resolution was to be witnessed next Saturday afternoon. *Star Wars* reinvents this experience in the form of a pastiche: that is, there is no longer any point to a parody of such serials since they are long extinct. *Star Wars*, far from being a pointless satire of such now dead forms, satisfies a deep (might I even say repressed?) longing to experience them again: it is a complex object in which on some first level children and adolescents can take the adventures straight, while the adult public is able to gratify a deeper and more properly nostalgic desire to return to that older period and to live its strange old aesthetic artifacts through once again. This film is thus *metonymically* a historical or nostalgia film: unlike *American Graffiti*, it does not reinvent a picture of the past in its lived totality; rather, by reinventing the feel and shape of characteristic art objects of an older period (the serials), it seeks to reawaken a sense of the past associated with those objects. *Raiders of the Lost Ark*, meanwhile, occupies an intermediary position here: on some level it is *about* the 1930s and 1940s, but in reality it too conveys that period metonymically through its own characteristic adventure stories (which are no longer ours).

Now let me discuss another interesting anomaly which may take us further towards understanding nostalgia film in particular and pastiche generally. This one involves a recent film called *Body Heat*, which, as has abundantly been pointed out by the critics, is a kind of distant remake of *The Postman Always Rings Twice* or *Double Indemnity*. (The allusive and elusive plagiarism of older plots is, of course, also a feature of pastiche.) Now *Body Heat* is technically not a nostalgia film, since it takes place in a contemporary setting, in a little Florida village near Miami. On the other hand, this technical contemporaneity is most ambiguous indeed: the credits—always our first cue—are lettered and scripted in a 1930s Art-Deco style which cannot but trigger nostalgic reactions (first to *Chinatown*, no doubt, and then beyond it to some more historical referent). Then the very style of the hero himself is ambiguous: William Hurt is a new star but has nothing of the distinctive style of the preceding generation of male superstars like Steve McQueen or even Jack Nicholson, or rather, his persona here is a kind of mix of their characteristics with an older role of the type generally associated with Clark Gable. So here too there is a faintly archaic feel to all this. The spectator begins to wonder why this story, which could have been situated anywhere, is set in a small Florida town, in spite of its contemporary reference. One begins to realize after a while that the small town setting has a crucial strategic function: it allows the film to do without most of the signals and references which we might associate with the contemporary world, with consumer society—the appliances and artifacts, the high rises, the object world of late capitalism. Technically, then, its objects (its cars, for instance) are 1980s products, but everything in the film conspires to blur that immediate contemporary reference and to make it possible to receive this too as nostalgia work—as a narrative set in some indefinable nostalgic past, an eternal 1930s, say, beyond history. It seems to me exceedingly symptomatic to find the very style of nostalgia films invading and colonizing even those movies today which have contemporary settings: as though, for some reason, we were unable today to focus our own present, as though we have become incapable of achieving aesthetic representations of our own current experience. But if that is so, then it is a terrible indictment of consumer capitalism itself — or, at the very least, an alarming and pathological symptom of a society that has become incapable of dealing with time and history.

So now we come back to the question of why nostalgia film or pastiche is to be considered different from the older historical novel or film. (I should also include in this discussion the major literary example of all this, to my mind: the novels of E.L. Doctorow—*Ragtime*, with its turn-of-the-century atmosphere, and *Loon Lake*, for the most part about our 1930s. But these are, in my opinion, historical novels in appearance only. Doctorow is a serious artist and one of the few genuinely left or radical novelists at work today. It is no disservice to him, however, to suggest that his narratives do not represent our historical past so much as they represent our ideas or cultural stereotypes about that past.) Cultural production has been driven back inside the mind, within the monadic subject: it can no longer look directly out of its eyes at the real world for the referent but must, as in Plato's cave, trace its mental images of the world on its confining walls. If there is any realism left here, it is a 'realism' which springs from the shock of grasping that confinement and of realizing that, for whatever peculiar reasons, we seem condemned to seek the historical past through our own pop images and stereotypes about that past, which itself remains forever out of reach.

Postmodernism and the city

Now, before I try to offer a somewhat more positive conclusion, I want to sketch the analysis of a full-blown postmodern building—a work which is in many ways uncharacteristic of that postmodern architecture whose principal names are Robert Venturi, Charles Moore, Michael Graves, and more recently Frank Gehry, but which to my mind offers some very striking lessons about the originality of postmodernist space. Let me amplify the figure which has run through the preceding remarks, and make it even more explicit: I am proposing the notion that we are here in the presence of something like a mutation in built space itself. My implication is that we ourselves, the human subjects who happen into this new space, have not kept pace with that evolution; there has been a mutation in the object, unaccompanied as yet by any equivalent mutation in the subject; we do not yet possess the perceptual equipment to match this new hyperspace, as I will call it, in part because our perceptual habits were formed in that older kind of space I have called the space of high modernism. The newer architecture therefore—like many of the other cultural products I have evoked in the preceding remarks—stands as something like an imperative to grow new organs to expand our sensorium and our body to some new, as yet unimaginable, perhaps ultimately impossible, dimensions.

The Bonaventure Hotel
The building whose features I will very rapidly enumerate in the next few moments is the Bonaventure Hotel, built in the new Los Angeles down-town by the architect and developer John Portman, whose other works include the various Hyatt Regencies, the Peachtree Center in Atlanta, and the Renaissance Center in Detroit. I have mentioned the populist aspect of the rhetorical defence of postmodernism against the elite (and utopian) austerities of the great architectural modernisms: it is gently affirmed, in other words, that these newer buildings are popular works on the one hand; and that they respect the vernacular of the American city fabric on the other, that is to say, that they no longer attempt, as did the masterworks and monuments of high modernism, to insert a different, a distinct, an elevated, a new utopian language into the tawdry and commercial sign-system of the surrounding city, but rather, on the contrary, seek to speak that very language, using its lexicon and syntax as that has been emblematically 'learned from Las Vegas'.

On the first of these counts, Portman's Bonaventure fully confirms the claim: it is a popular building, visited with enthusiasm by locals and tourists alike (although Portman's other buildings are even more successful in this respect). The populist insertion into the city fabric is, however, another matter, and it is with this that we will begin. There are three entrances to the Bonaventure, one from Figueroa, and the other two by way of elevated gardens on the other side of the hotel, which is built into the remaining slope of the former Beacon Hill. None of these is anything like the old hotel marquee, or the monumental *porte-cochère* with which the sumptuous buildings of yesteryear were wont to stage your passage from city street to the older interior. The entryways of the Bonaventure are as it were lateral and rather backdoor affairs: the gardens in the back admit you to the sixth floor of the towers, and even there you must walk down one flight to find the elevator by which you gain access to the lobby. Meanwhile, what one is still tempted to think of as the front entry, on Figueroa, admits you, baggage and all, onto the second-storey balcony, from which you must take an escalator down to the main registration desk. More about these elevators and escalators in a moment. What I first want to suggest about these curiously unmarked ways-in is that they seem to have been imposed by some new category of closure governing the inner space of the hotel itself (and this over and above the material constraints under which Portman had to work). I believe that, with a certain number of other characteristic postmodern buildings, such as the Beaubourg in Paris, or the Eaton Centre in Toronto, the Bonaventure aspires to being a total space, a complete world, a kind of miniature city (and I would want to add that to this new total space corresponds a new collective practice, a new mode in which individuals move and congregate, something like the practice of a new and historically original kind of hyper-crowd). In this sense, then, ideally the mini-city of Portman's Bonaventure ought not to have entrances at all, since the entryway is always the seam that links the building to the rest of the city that surrounds it: for it does not wish to be a part of the city, but rather its equivalent and its replacement or substitute. That is, however, obviously not possible or practical, whence the deliberate downplaying and reduction of the entrance function to its bare minimum. But this disjunction from the surrounding city is very different from that of the great monuments of the International Style: there, the act of disjunction was violent, visible, and had a very real symbolic significance—as in Le Corbusier's great *pilotis* whose gesture radically separates the new utopian space of the modern from the degraded and fallen city fabric which it thereby explicitly repudiates (although the gamble of the modern was that this new utopian space, in the virulence of its Novum, would fan out and transform that eventually by the power of its new spatial language). The Bonaventure, however, is content to 'let the fallen city fabric continue to be in its being' (to parody Heidegger); no further effects, no larger protopolitical utopian transformation, is either expected or desired.

This diagnosis is to my mind confirmed by the great reflective glass skin of the Bonaventure, whose function I will now interpret rather differently than I did a moment ago when I saw the phenomenon of reflexion generally as developing a thematics of reproductive technology (the two readings are, however, not incompatible). Now one would want rather to stress the way in which the glass skin repels the city outside; a repulsion for which we have analogies in those reflector sunglasses which make it impossible for your interlocutor to see your own eyes and thereby achieve a certain aggressivity towards and power over the Other. In a similar way, the glass skin achieves a peculiar and placeless dissociation of the Bonaventure from its neighbourhood: it is not even an exterior, inasmuch as when you seek to look at the hotel's outer walls you cannot see the hotel itself, but only the distorted images of everything that surrounds it.

Now I want to say a few words about escalators and elevators: given their very real pleasures in Portman, particularly these last, which the artist has termed 'gigantic kinetic sculptures' and which certainly account for much of the spectacle and the excitement of the hotel interior, particularly in the Hyatts, where like great Japanese lanterns or gondolas they ceaselessly rise and fall—given such a deliberate marking and foregrounding in their own right, I believe one has to see such 'people movers' (Portman's own term, adapted from Disney) as something a little more than mere functions and engineering components. We know in any case that recent architectural theory has begun to borrow from narrative analysis in other fields, and to attempt to see our physical trajectories through such buildings as virtual narratives or stories, as dynamic paths and narrative paradigms which we as visitors are asked to fulfil and to complete with our own bodies and movements. In the Bonaventure, however, we find a dialectical heighten-ing of this process: it seems to me that the escalators and elevators here henceforth replace movement but also and above all designate themselves as new reflexive signs and emblems of movement proper (something which will become evident when we come to the whole question of what remains of older forms of movement in this building, most notably walking itself). Here the narrative stroll has been underscored, symbolized, reified and replaced by a transportation machine which becomes the allegorical signifier of that older promenade we are no longer allowed to conduct on our own: and this is a dialectical intensification of the autoreferentiality of all modern culture, which tends to turn upon itself and designate its own cultural production as its content.

I am more at a loss when it comes to conveying the thing itself, the experience of space you undergo when you step off such allegorical devices into the lobby or atrium, with its great central column, surrounded by a miniature lake, the whole positioned between the four symmetrical residential towers with their elevators, and surrounded by rising balconies capped by a kind of greenhouse roof at the sixth level. I am tempted to say that such space makes it impossible for us to use the language of volume or volumes any longer, since these last are impossible to seize. Hanging streamers indeed suffuse this empty space in such a way as to distract systematically and deliberately from whatever form it might be supposed to have; while a constant busyness gives the feeling that emptiness is here absolutely packed, that it is an element within which you yourself are immersed, without any of that distance that formerly enabled the perception of perspective or volume. You are in this hyperspace up to your eyes and your body; and if it seemed to you before that that suppression of depth I spoke of in postmodern painting or literature would necessarily be difficult to achieve in architecture itself, perhaps you may now be willing to see this bewildering immersion as the formal equivalent in the new medium.

Yet escalator and elevator are also in this context dialectical opposites; and we may suggest that the glorious movement of the elevator gondolas is also a dialectical compensation for this filled space of the atrium—it gives us the chance at a radically different, but complementary, spatial experience, that of rapidly shooting up through the ceiling and outside, along one of the four symmetrical towers, with the referent, Los Angeles itself, spread out breathtakingly and even alarmingly before us. But even this vertical movement is contained: the elevator lifts you to one of those revolving cocktail lounges, in which you, seated, are again passively rotated about and offered a contemplative spectacle of the city itself, now transformed into its own images by the glass windows through which you view it.

Let me quickly conclude all this by returning to the central space of the lobby itself (with the passing observation that the hotel rooms are visibly marginalized: the corridors in the residential sections are low-ceilinged and dark, most depressingly functional indeed: while one understands that the rooms are in the worst of taste). The descent is dramatic enough, plummeting back down through the roof to splash down in the lake; what happens when you get there is something else, which I can only try to characterize as milling confusion, something like the vengeance this space takes on those who still seek to walk through it. Given the absolute symmetry of the four towers, it is quite impossible to get your bearings in this lobby; recently, colour coding and directional signals have been added in a pitiful and revealing, rather desperate attempt to restore the coordinates of an older space. I will take as the most dramatic practical result of this spatial mutation the notorious dilemma of the shopkeepers on the various balconies: it has been obvious, since the very opening of the hotel in 1977, that nobody could ever find any of these stores, and even if you located the appropriate boutique, you would be most unlikely to be as fortunate a second time; as a consequence, the commercial tenants are in despair and all the merchandise is marked down to bargain prices. When you recall that Portman is a businessman as well as an architect, and a millionaire developer, an artist who is at one and the same time a capitalist in his own right, you cannot but feel that here too something of a 'return of the repressed' is involved.

So I come finally to my principal point here, that this latest mutation in space—postmodern hyperspace—has finally succeeded in transcending the capacities of the individual human body to locate itself, to organize its immediate surroundings perceptually, and cognitively to map its position in a mappable external world. And I have already suggested that this alarming disjunction point between the body and its built environment—-which is to the initial bewilderment of the older modernism as the velocities of spacecraft are to those of the automobile—can itself stand as the symbol and analog of that even sharper dilemma which is the incapacity of our minds, at least at present, to map the great global multinational and decentred communicational network in which we find ourselves caught as individual subjects.

The new machine

But I am anxious that Portman's space not be perceived as something either exceptional or seemingly marginalized and leisure-specialized on the order of Disneyland. I would like in passing to juxtapose this complacent and entertaining (although bewildering) leisure-time space with its analog in a very different area, namely the space of postmodern warfare, in particular as Michael Herr evokes it in his great book on the experience of Vietnam, called *Dispatches*. The extraordinary linguistic innovations of this work may still be considered postmodernism, in the eclectic way in which its language impersonally fuses a whole range of contemporary collective idiolects, most notably rock language and black language: but the fusion is dictated by problems of content. This first terrible postmodernist war cannot be told in any of the traditional paradigms of the war novel or movie—indeed that breakdown of all previous narrative paradigms is, along with the breakdown of any shared language through which a veteran might convey such experience, among the principal subjects of the book and may be said to open up the place of a whole new reflexivity. Benjamin's account of Baudelaire, and of the emergence of modernism from a new experience of city technology which transcends all the older habits of bodily perception, is both singularly relevant here, and singularly antiquated, in the light of this new and virtually unimaginable quantum leap in technological alienation:

> He was a moving-target-survivor subscriber, a true child of the war, because except for the rare times when you were pinned or stranded the system was geared to keep you mobile, if that was what you thought you wanted. As a technique for staying alive it seemed to make as much sense as anything, given naturally that you were there to begin with and wanted to see it close; it started out sound and straight but it formed a cone as it progressed, because the more you moved the more you saw, the more you saw the more besides death and mutilation you risked, and the more you risked of that the more you would have to let go of one day as a 'survivor'. Some of us moved around the war like crazy people until we couldn't see which way the run was taking us anymore, only the war all over its surface with occasional, unexpected penetration. As long as we could have choppers like taxis it took real exhaustion or depression near shock or a dozen pipes of opium to keep us even apparently quiet, we'd still be running around inside our skins like something was after us, ha, ha, La Vida Loca. In the months after I got back the hundreds of helicopters I'd flown in begin to draw together until they'd formed a collective meta-chopper, and in my mind it was the sexiest thing going: saver-destroyer, provider-waster, right hand-left hand, nimble, fluent, canny and human; hot steel, grease, jungle-saturated canvas webbing, sweat cooling and warming up again, cassette rock and roll in one ear and door-gun fire in the other, fuel, heat, vitality and death, death itself, hardly an intruder.[2]

In this new machine, which does not, like the older modernist machinery of the locomotive or the airplane, represent motion, but which can only be represented *in motion*, something of the mystery of the new postmodernist space is concentrated.

The aesthetic of consumer society

Now I must try very rapidly in conclusion to characterize the relationship of cultural production of this kind to social life in this country today. This will also be the moment to address the principal objection to concepts of postmodernism of the type I have sketched here: namely that all the features we have enumerated are not new at all but abundantly character-ized modernism proper or what I call high modernism. Was not Thomas Mann, after all, interested in the idea of pastiche, and are not certain chapters of *Ulysses* its most obvious realization? Can Flaubert, Mallarmé and Gertrude Stein not be included in an account of postmodernist tem-porality? What is so new about all of this? Do we really need the concept of *post*modernism?

One kind of answer to this question would raise the whole issue of periodization and of how a historian (literary or other) posits a radical break between two henceforth distinct periods. I must limit myself to the suggestion that radical breaks between periods do not generally involve complete changes of content but rather the restructuring of a certain number of elements already given: features that in an earlier period or system were subordinate now become dominant, and features that had been dominant again become secondary. In this sense, everything we have described here can be found in earlier periods and most notably within modernism proper: my point is that until the present day those things have been secondary or minor features of modernist art, marginal rather than central, and that we have something new when they become the central features of cultural production.

But I can argue this more concretely by turning to the relationship between cultural production and social life generally. The older or classical modernism was an opposition art; it emerged within the business society of the gilded age as scandalous and offensive to the middle-class public—-ugly, dissonant, bohemian, sexually shocking. It was something to make fun of (when the police were not called in to seize the books or close the exhibitions): an offence to good taste and to common sense, or, as Freud and Marcuse would have put it, a provocative challenge to the reigning reality- and performance-principles of early twentieth-century middle-class society. Modernism in general did not go well with over-stuffed Victorian furniture, with Victorian moral taboos, or with the conventions of polite society. This is to say that whatever the explicit political content of the great high modernisms, the latter were always in some mostly implicit ways dangerous and explosive, subversive within the established order.

If then we suddenly return to the present day, we can measure the immensity of the cultural changes that have taken place. Not only are Joyce and Picasso no longer weird and repulsive, they have become classics and now look rather realistic to us. Meanwhile, there is very little in either the form or the content of contemporary art that contemporary society finds intolerable and scandalous. The most offensive forms of this art—punk rock, say, or what is called sexually explicit material—are all taken in stride by society, and they are commercially successful, unlike the productions of the older high modernism. But this means that even if contemporary art has all the same formal features as the older modernism, it has still shifted its position fundamentally within our culture. For one thing, commodity production and in particular our clothing, furniture, buildings and other artifacts are now intimately tied in with styling changes which derive from artistic experimentation; our advertising, for example, is fed by postmodernism in all the arts and inconceivable without it. For another, the classics of high modernism are now part of the so-called canon and are taught in schools and universities—which at once empties them of any of their older subversive power. Indeed, one way of marking the break between the periods and of dating the emergence of postmodernism is precisely to be found there: in the moment (the early 1960s, one would think) in which the position of high modernism and its dominant aesthetics become established in the academy and are henceforth felt to be academic by a whole new generation of poets, painters and musicians.

But one can also come at the break from the other side, and describe it in terms of periods of recent social life. As I have suggested, non-Marxists and Marxists alike have come around to the general feeling that at some point following World War II a new kind of society began to emerge (variously described as postindustrial society, multinational capitalism, consumer society, media society and so forth). New types of consumption;

planned obsolescence; an ever more rapid rhythm of fashion and styling changes; the penetration of advertising, television and the media generally to a hitherto unparalleled degree throughout society; the replacement of the old tension between city and country, centre and province, by the suburb and by universal standardization; the growth of the great networks of superhighways and the arrival of automobile culture—these are some of the features which would seem to mark a radical break with that older prewar society in which high modernism was still an underground force.

I believe that the emergence of postmodernism is closely related to the emergence of this new moment of late, consumer or multinational capitalism. I believe also that its formal features in many ways express the deeper logic of that particular social system. I will only be able, however, to show this for one major theme: namely the disappearance of a sense of history, the way in which our entire contemporary social system has little by little begun to lose its capacity to retain its own past, has begun to live in a perpetual present and in a perpetual change that obliterates traditions of the kind which all earlier social formations have had in one way or another to preserve. Think only of the media exhaustion of news: of how Nixon and, even more so, Kennedy are figures from a now distant past. One is tempted to say that the very function of the news media is to relegate such recent historical experiences as rapidly as possible into the past. The informational function of the media would thus be to help us forget, to serve as the very agents and mechanisms for our historical amnesia.

But in that case the two features of postmodernism on which I have dwelt here—the transformation of reality into images, the fragmentation of time into a series of perpetual presents—are both extraordinarily consonant with this process. My own conclusion here must take the form of a question about the critical value of the newer art. There is some agreement that the older mechanism functioned against its society in ways which are variously described as critical, negative, contestatory, subversive, oppositional and the like. Can anything of the sort be affirmed about postmodernism and its social moment? We have seen that there is a way in which postmodernism replicates or reproduces—reinforces—the logic of consumer capitalism; the more significant question is whether there is also a way in which it resists that logic. But that is a question we must leave open.

Notes

1 The present text combines elements of two previously published essays: 'Postmodernism and consumer society', in *The Anti-Aesthetic*, Port Townsend, WA: Bay Press, 1983; and 'Postmodernism: the cultural logic of late capitalism', *New Left Review* 146 (July–August 1984).
2 Michael Herr, *Dispatches*, New York: Knopf, 1977, pp. 8–9.

19

Symbolic creativity

Paul Willis

From his *Common Culture* (Open University Press, 1990).

The institutions and practices, genres and terms of high art are currently categories of exclusion more than of inclusion. They have no real connection with most young people or their lives. They may encourage some artistic specializations but they certainly discourage much wider and more general symbolic creativity. The official existence of the 'arts' in institutions seems to exhaust everything else of its artistic contents. If some things count as 'art', the rest must be 'non-art'. Because 'art' is in the 'art gallery', it can't therefore be anywhere else. It is that which is special and heightened, not ordinary and everyday.

The arts establishment, by and large, has done little to dispel these assumptions. It prefers instead to utilize or even promote fears of cultural decline and debasement in order to strengthen its own claims for subsidy, institutional protection and privilege. In general the arts establishment connives to keep alive the myth of the special, creative individual artist holding out against passive mass consumerism, so helping to maintain a self-interested view of elite creativity.

Against this we insist that there is a vibrant symbolic life and symbolic creativity in everyday life, everyday activity and expression—even if it is sometimes invisible, looked down on or spurned. We don't want to invent it or propose it. We want to recognize it—literally recognize it. Most young people's lives are not involved with the arts and yet are actually full of expressions, signs and symbols through which individuals and groups seek creatively to establish their presence, identity and meaning. Young people are all the time expressing or attempting to express something about their actual or potential *cultural significance*. This is the realm of living common culture. Vulgar sometimes, perhaps. But also 'common' in being everywhere, resistant, hardy. Also 'common' in being shared, having things 'in common'. Where 'arts' exclude, 'culture' includes. 'Art' has been cut short of meanings, where 'culture' has not.

As Raymond Williams always insisted, culture is ordinary.[1] It is the extraordinary in the ordinary, which is extraordinary, which makes both into culture, common culture. We are thinking of the extraordinary symbolic creativity of the multitude of ways in which young people use,

humanize, decorate and invest with meanings their common and immediate life spaces and social practices—personal styles and choice of clothes;
selective and active use of music, TV, magazines; decoration of bedrooms;
the rituals of romance and subcultural styles; the style, banter and drama
of friendship groups; music-making and dance. Nor are these pursuits and
activities trivial or inconsequential. In conditions of late modernization and
the widespread crisis of cultural values they can be crucial to the creation
and sustenance of individual and group identities, even to cultural survival
of identity itself. There is work, even desperate work, in their play. [. . .]

Our project is to uncover, explore and present symbolic creativity in
everyday life. Apart from merely asserting its importance and, we hope,
demonstrating its existence, why do we insist on the visceral connection
of symbolic creativity to the everyday? At bottom, what anchors it?

We argue that symbolic creativity is not only part of everyday human
activity, but also a necessary part. This is because it is an integral part of
necessary work—that which has to be done every day, that which is not extra
but essential to ensure the daily production and reproduction of human
existence. It is this which actually guarantees and locks in the relevance of
symbolic creativity. It is this which underlies claims that the real roots of
art lie in the everyday. But of what kind of necessary work do we speak?
What is the basis for including symbolic creativity in it?

Necessary work is taken usually to designate the application of human
capacities through the action of tools on raw materials to produce goods
and services, usually through wage labour, to satisfy physical human
needs. [. . .]

But there is another kind of humanly necessary work—often unrec-
ognized but equally necessary—*symbolic work*. This is the application of
human capacities to and through, on and with symbolic resources and
raw materials (collections of signs and symbols—for instance, the language
as we inherit it as well as texts, songs, films, images and artefacts of
all kinds) to produce meanings. This is broader than, logically prior to
and a condition of material production, but its 'necessariness' has been
forgotten.

Necessary symbolic work is necessary simply because humans are
communicating as well as producing beings. Perhaps they are communicative before they are productive. Whilst all may not be productive,
all are communicative. *All*. This is our species distinction. Nor is this a
merely formal or physiological property that might lie unused in some. Only
through its exercise does communication exist and all of us communicate.
This is how we manifest and produce the social and dynamic nature of our
humanity.

We argue that necessary symbolic work is spread across the whole of
life. It is a condition of it, and of our daily humanity. Those who stress the
separateness, the sublime and quintessential in 'art' have actually assumed
and encouraged a mindlessly vulgar, materialist view of everyday life. They
counterpose this to their view of 'the imaginative'. They thereby view daily
life as a cultural desert. The imagined symbolic deficit of everyday life is
then, in its turn, to be repaired by recourse to a free-floating 'imaginative

realm', to 'useless things', to 'art for art's sake', to the 'socially redundant'. But this is not only circular, it's incoherent. It's like trying to make time go faster by speeding up clocks. 'Art' is taken as the *only* field of qualitative symbolic activity, the one-per-cent transcendental value that preserves humanity. As daily life is drained of its symbolic work, 'art' is grotesquely bloated till its pores leak pure imagination. And only from 'art' can come a cultural mission into the humdrum, a doomed attempt to save the masses. Again 'art' produces culture. Symbolic work starts, not ends, in separate artefacts. The imaginative is self-validating!

We insist, against this, that imagination is not extra to daily life, something to be supplied from disembodied 'art'. It is part of the necessariness of everyday symbolic and communicative work. If declared redundant here, it will certainly not be welcomed back in the finer robes of 'art'.

This point cannot be overstated: where we can't now realistically acknowledge and promote the prospect of symbolic creativity in the sinews of necessary work as material production, we can and must recognize symbolic creativity in the sinews of necessary work as symbolic production.

What are some of the basic elements of necessary symbolic work?

First, language as a practice and symbolic resource. Language is the primary instrument that we use to communicate. It is the highest ordering of our sensuous impressions of the world, and the ultimate basis of our hope and capacity to control it. It enables interaction and solidarity with others and allows us to assess our impact on others and theirs on us. It therefore allows us to see ourselves as others.

Second, the active body as a practice and symbolic resource. The body is a site of somatic knowledge as well as a set of signs and symbols. It is the source of productive and communicative activity—signing, symbolizing, feeling.

Third, drama as a practice and symbolic resource. Communicative interaction with others is not automatic. We do not communicate from head to head through wires drilled into our skulls. Communication is achieved through roles, rituals and performances that we produce with others. Dramaturgical components of the symbolic include a variety of non-verbal communications, as well as sensuous cultural practices and communal solidarities. These include dancing, singing, joke-making, story-telling in dynamic settings and through performance.

Fourth and most importantly, symbolic creativity. Language, the body, dramatic forms are, in a way, both raw material and tools. Symbolic creativity is more fully the practice, the making—or their essence, what all practices have in common, what drives them. This is the production of *new* (however small the shift) meanings intrinsically attached to feeling, to energy, to excitement and psychic movement. This is the basis of confidence in dynamic human capacities as realities rather than as potentials—to be made conscious, through some concrete practice or active mediation, of the quality of human consciousness and how it can further be developed through the exercise and application of vital powers. Symbolic creativity can be seen as roughly equivalent to what an all-embracing and inclusive notion of the living arts might include (counterposed, of course, to the current exclusions of 'art'.) Symbolic creativity may be individual and/or collective. It transforms what is provided and helps to produce specific forms of human identity and capacity. Being human—human be-ing-ness—means to be creative in the sense of remaking the world for ourselves as we make and find our own place and identity.

What exactly is produced by symbolic work and symbolic creativity?

First, and perhaps most important, they produce and reproduce individual identities—who and what 'I am' and could become. These may be diffuse, contradictory or decentred but they are produced through symbolic work including struggles to make meaning. Sensuous human communicative activities are also intersubjective. It is through knowing 'the other', including recognizing the self as an other for some others, that a self or selves can be known at all.

Second, symbolic work and creativity place identities in larger wholes. Identities do not stand alone above history, beyond history. They are related in time, place and things. It is symbolic work and creativity which realize the structured collectivity of individuals as well as their differences, which realize the materiality of context as well as the symbolism of self. This reminds us that locations and situations are not only *determinations* —they're also relations and resources to be discovered, explored and experienced. Memberships of race, class, gender, age and region are not only learned, they're lived and experimented with. This is so even if only by pushing up against the oppressive limits of established order and power.

Third and finally, symbolic work and especially creativity develop and affirm our active senses of our own vital capacities, the powers of the self and how they might be applied to the cultural world. This is what makes activity and identity *transitive* and specifically human. It is the dynamic and, therefore, clinching part of identity. It is the expectation of being able to apply power to the world to change it—however minutely. It is how, in the future, there is some human confidence that unities may be formed out of confusion, patterns out of irregularity. This is to be able to make judgements on who's a friend, who's an enemy, when to talk, when to hold silence, when to go, when to stop. But it's also associated with, and helps to form, overall styles of thinking which promise to make most sense of the world for you. It's also a cultural sense of what symbolic forms—languages, images, musics, haircuts, styles, clothes—'work' most economically and creatively for the self. A culturally learned sense of the powers of the self is what makes the self in connecting it to others and to the world.

In many ways this is directly a question of cultural survival for many young people. Processes of symbolic work and symbolic creativity are very open, contested and unstable under conditions of late modernization. All young people experience one aspect or another of the contemporary 'social condition' of youth: unwilling economic dependence on parents and parental homes; uncertainty regarding future planning; powerlessness and lack of control over immediate circumstances of life; feelings of symbolic as well as material marginality to the main society; imposed institutional and ideological constructions of 'youth' which privilege certain readings and definitions of what young people should do, feel or be.[2]

Many of the traditional resources of, and inherited bases for, social meaning, membership, security and psychic certainty have lost their legitimacy for a good proportion of young people. There is no longer a sense of a 'whole culture' with allocated places and a shared, universal value system. Organized religion, the monarchy, trade unions, schools, public broadcasting, high culture and its intertwinings with public culture no longer supply ready values and models of duty and meaning to help structure the passage into settled adulthood. This is certainly partly a result of much commented-upon wider processes related to late modernization: secularization; consumerism; individualization; decollectivization; weakening respect for authority; new technologies of production and distribution. But it is also the case that these inherited traditions owe their still continuing and considerable power to the stakes they offer and seem to offer to the individual: some graspable identity within a set of relationships to other identities; some notion of citizenship within a larger whole which offers rights, satisfactions and loyalties as well as duty and submission. However, for many young people, made to feel marginal to this society, and without their own material stake in it, these merely symbolic stakes can seem very remote. These public traditions and meanings cannot make good what they offer, because they are undercut at another more basic level by unfulfilled expectations. These things are for parents and adults, for those who have an interest in and make up the civil body. For the young black British they're even more remote—they are for other people's parents. No longer can we be blind to the 'whiteness' of our major traditional public sources of identity.

Young working-class women may experience this youth condition in a special way. On the one hand they are a target consumption group for many home commodities as well as for feminine-style-and-identity products. On the other hand, and with no money recompense and no real power in the consumer market, they may be making partial, early and exploited 'transitions' (often in an imperceptible extension of childhood domestic chores 'naturally' expected of girls but not of boys) into domestic roles of care and maintenance. This may seem to be a destination of sorts and a meaningful, useful activity when labour-market opportunities are scarce or difficult, but it can often be a specific unofficial training and subjective preparation for a lifetime's future of domestic drudgery coupled with job 'opportunities' only in part-time, low-paid, insecure, usually dead-end 'female' service work.

In general the arrival of a new and extended youth stage announces itself through the arrival of new institutional forms, and the adaption of old ones, aimed at its regulation. [In Britain,] the Youth Training Scheme, Employment Training, recent developments in youth work practice and drop-in centres for the unemployed, 'civil disorder' and community policing, changes in benefit rules for the under-25s, are all aimed in some way at controlling and filling the time of youth or at maintaining some promise (and discipline) for future transitions or at preventing and pre-empting alternative uses of time and capacity not devoted to preparation for future transitions.

There is a set of meanings and identities on offer here, highly restricted, applied and focussed. They are unlikely to replace the collapsing traditional ones. Indeed the tasks of symbolic work and creativity may include not only the attempt to retain identity in the face of the erosion of traditional value systems but also to forge new resistant, resilient and independent ones to survive in and find alternatives to the impoverished roles proffered by modern state bureaucracies and rationalized industry. [. . .]

As we have used the term so far, 'symbolic creativity' is an abstract concept designating a human capacity almost in general. It only exists, however, in contexts and, in particular, sensuous living processes. To identify the particular dynamic of symbolic activity and transformation in concrete named situations we propose the term 'grounded aesthetic'. This is the creative element in a process whereby meanings are attributed to symbols and practices and where symbols and practices are selected, reselected, highlighted and recomposed to resonate further appropriated and particularized meanings. Such dynamics are emotional as well as cognitive. There are as many aesthetics as there are grounds for them to operate in. Grounded aesthetics are the yeast of common culture.

We have deliberately used the term 'aesthetic' to show both the differences and the continuities of what we are trying to say with respect to the culture and arts debate. We are certainly concerned with what might be called principles of beauty, but as qualities of living symbolic activities rather than as qualities of things; as ordinary aspects of common culture, rather than as extraordinary aspects of uncommon culture. This is the sense of our clumsy but strictly accurate use of 'grounded'.

Our 'groundedness' for some will seem simply no more than the reckless destruction of flight, potting birds of paradise with sociological lead. For others the strange search for archaic aesthetics in grounded, everyday social relations will seem perverse, un-material and even mystical. We're happy to work on the assumption that 'the truth' lies somewhere, always provisionally, in between, that human be-ing-ness needs both air and earth and, in turn, makes possible our very idea of both.

Within the process of creating meanings from and within the use of symbols there may be a privileged role for texts and artefacts, but a grounded aesthetic can also be an element and a quality of everyday social relations. For instance, there is a dramaturgy and poetics of everyday life, of social presence, encounter and event. It may have become invisible in the routinized roles of adult life, but the young have much more time and they face each other with fewer or more fragile masks. They are the practical existentialists. They sometimes have no choice but to be, often too, absorbed in the moment and to ransack immediate experience for grounded aesthetics. For them some features of social life may not be about the regulation and containment of tension, but about its creation and increase. The 'aimless' life of groups and gangs may be about producing something from nothing, from 'doing nothing'. It may be about building tensions, shaping grounded aesthetics, orchestrating and shaping their release and further build-ups, so that a final 'catharsis' takes with it or changes other tensions and stresses inherent in the difficulties of their condition. Making a pattern in an induced swirl of events can produce strangely still centres of heightened awareness where time is held and unusual control and insight are possible. Grounded aesthetics are what lift and mark such moments.

Grounded aesthetics are the specifically creative and dynamic moments of a whole process of cultural life, of cultural birth and rebirth. To know the cultural world, our relationship to it, and ultimately to know ourselves, it is necessary not merely to be in it but to change—however minutely—that cultural world. This is a making specific—in relation to the social group or individual and its conditions of life—of the ways in which the received natural and social world is made human *to them* and made, to however small a degree (even if finally symbolic), controllable by them.

The possibility of such control is, of course, a collective principle for the possibility of political action on the largest scale. But it also has importance in the individual and collective awareness of the ability to control symbols and their cultural work. Grounded aesthetics produce an edge of meaning which not only reflects or repeats what exists, but transforms what exists —received expressions and appropriated symbols as well as what they represent or are made to represent in some identifiable way.

In so-called 'primitive art' and culture, for instance, a central theme is the naming of fundamental forces as gods and demons, thereby to reveal them, make them somehow knowable and therefore subject to human persuasion or placation. Of course, the urban industrial world is much more complex in its organization than are 'primitive' societies, and our apparent technical control over the threatening forces of nature seems greater and different in kind from theirs. What we seek to control, persuade or humanize through grounded aesthetics may be, in part, the force and expression of other human beings rather than forces emanating directly from nature—if you like the work of culture on culture.

A sense of or desire for timelessness and universality may be part of the impulse of a grounded aesthetic. The natural, obvious and immutable become particular historical constructions capable of variation. Subjectivity, taken to some degree out of the particular, is the force which can change it. But we may equally focus on the particular extracted from its context to make sense of the universal (Blake's grain of sand). Such psychic separation may be part of and/or a condition for some grounded aesthetics.

This is not to say that 'universals' really exist, certainly not internally in 'art-objects'. It is extraordinary how many universals—and contradictory ones—are claimed. Nevertheless, experienced universalism, as a movement out of or reperception of the particular, may well be a universal feature of heightened human awareness. This universalism is also a kind of awareness of the future in terms of what it is possible to become. This is part of heightened aspiration and the quest for wider significance and expanded identity. Universalism also gives some vision of the kind of socialness and human mutuality which might locate better and more expanded identities. Grounded aesthetics provide a motivation towards realizing different futures, and for being in touch with the self as a dynamic and creative force for bringing them about.

The received sense of the 'aesthetic' emphasizes the cerebral, abstract or sublimated quality of beauty. At times it seems to verge on the 'an-aesthetic'—the suppression of all senses. By contrast we see grounded aesthetics as working through the senses, through sensual heightening, through joy, pleasure and desire, through 'fun' and the 'festive'.

Concrete skills, concretely acquired rather than given through natural distinction or gift, are involved in the exercise of grounded aesthetics. 'Economy', and 'skill', for instance, enter into the grounded aesthetics of how the body is used as a medium of expression. A bodily grounded aesthetic enters into personal style and presence, dance and large areas of music and performance.

Although they are not things, grounded aesthetics certainly have uses. Such uses concern the energizing, developing and focussing of vital human powers on to the world in concrete and practical ways, but also in lived connected cognitive ways. This is in producing meanings, explanations and pay-offs in relation to concrete conditions and situations which seem more efficient or adequate than other proffered official or conventional meanings. Such 'useful' meanings may well have moral dimensions in providing collective and personal principles of action, co-operation, soli-darity, distinction or resistance.

But 'useful' meanings can also be very private. There are perhaps especially private, symbolic and expressive therapies for the injuries of life. They 'work', not through their direct musical, literary or philo-sophical forms, but through the ways in which a grounded aesthetic produces meanings and understandings which were not there before. This may involve internal, imaginative and spiritual life. It may be in the realm of dream and fantasy, in the realm of heightened awareness of the constructedness and constructiveness of the self: alienation from obvious givens and values; the sense of a future made in the present changing the present; the fear of and fascination for the 'terra incognita' of the self. The usefulness of grounded aesthetics here may be in the holding and repairing, through some meaning creation and human control even in desperate seas, of the precariousness and fragmentedness of identity whose source of disturbance is outside, structural and beyond the practical scope of individuals to influence.

The crucial failure and danger of most cultural analysis are that dynamic, living grounded aesthetics are transformed and transferred into ontological properties of things, objects and artefacts which may represent and sustain aesthetics but which are, in fact, separate. The aesthetic effect is not *in* the text or artefact. It is part of the sensuous/emotive/cognitive creativities of human receivers, especially as they produce a stronger sense of emotional and cognitive identity as expanded capacity and power—even if only in the possibility of *future* recognitions of a similar kind. These creativities are not dependent on texts, but might be enabled by them.[3]

Surprising meanings and creativities can be generated from unpromising materials through grounded aesthetics. But texts and artefacts can also fail to mediate symbolic meanings for many reasons. Many supply only a narrow or inappropriate (for particular audiences) range of symbolic resources. Others encourage *reification* (literally, making into a thing) rather than the *mediation* and enablement of the possibility of grounded aesthetics. They move too quickly to supply a putative aesthetic. The receivers are simply sent a 'message', the meaning of which is pre-formed and pre-given. Signs are pinned succinctly and securely to their meanings. Human receivers are allowed no creative life of their own. The attempt to encapsulate directly an aesthetic militates against the possibility of its realization through a grounded aesthetic because the space for symbolic work of reception has been written out.

There are many ways in which the 'official arts' are removed from the possibility of a living symbolic *mediation*, even despite their possible symbolic richness and range. Most of them are out of their time and, even though this should enforce no veto on current *mediation*, the possibilities of a relevant structuring of symbolic interest are obviously limited. The institutions and practices which support 'art', however, seem designed to break any living links or possibilities of inducing a grounded aesthetic appropriation. 'Official' art equates aesthetics with artefacts. [. . .] The past as museum, Art as objects! The reverence and distance encouraged by formality, by institutions, and by the rites of liberal-humanist education as 'learning the code', kill dead, for the vast majority, what the internal life of signs might offer through grounded aesthetics to current sensibility and social practice. It is as hard for the 'official arts' to offer themselves to grounded aesthetics, as it is for grounded aesthetics to find recognition in the formal canons.

Commercial cultural commodities, conversely, offer no such impediments. At least cultural commodities—for their own bad reasons—are aimed at exchange and therefore at the possibility of use. In responding to, and attempting to exploit, current desires and needs, they are virtually guaranteed to offer some relevance to the tasks of current socially necessary symbolic work. In crucial senses, too, the modern media precisely 'mediate' in passing back to audiences, at least in the first instance, symbolic wholes they've taken from the streets, dance-halls and everyday life. Along with this they may also take, however imperfectly and crudely, a field of aesthetic tensions from daily life and from the play of grounded aesthetics there.

Of course, part of the same restless process is that cultural commodities, especially style and fashion 'top end down', may become subject overwhelmingly to reification, symbolic rationalization and the drastic reduction of the symbolic resources on offer. But consumers move too. When cultural commodities no longer offer symbolic mediation to grounded aesthetics, they fall 'out of fashion'. And in the cumulative symbolic landscape of consumer capitalism, dead packaged, reified grounded aesthetics are turned back into primary raw material for other processes of inevitable necessary symbolic work, with only the cultural theorists paranoiacally labouring back along their 'meta-symbolic' routes to 'golden age' symbolic homologies. This commercial process may, to say the least, be flawed, but it offers much more to grounded aesthetics than do the dead 'official arts'.

There may well be a better way, a better way to cultural emancipation than through this continuous instability and trust in the hidden—selfish, blind, grabbing—hand of the market. But 'official art' has not shown it yet.

Commercial cultural commodities are all most people have. History may be progressing through its bad side. But it progresses. For all its manifest absurdities, the cultural market may open up the way *to* a better way. We have to make our conditions of life before we can dominate and use them. Cultural pessimism offers us only road-blocks.

Against postmodernist pessimism

The much commented upon incandescence—instability, changeability, luminosity—of cultural commodities ('all that is solid melts into air'[4]) is not some form of spontaneous combustion in commodities or another 'wonder' of capitalist production. It is not without or against meaning. This very incandescence passes through *necessary symbolic work*, changes and enables it. The incandescence is not simply a surface market quality. It produces, is driven by, and reproduces further forms and varieties for everyday symbolic work and creativity, some of which remain in the everyday and in common culture far longer than they do on the market.

The market is the source of a permanent and contradictory revolution in everyday culture which sweeps away old limits and dependencies. The markets' restless search to find and make new appetites raises, wholesale, the popular currency of symbolic aspiration. The currency may be debased and inflationary, but aspirations now circulate, just as do commodities. That circulation irrevocably makes or finds its own new worlds.

The style and media theorists—and terrorists—of the left and right see only market incandescence. They warn us of an immanent semi-otic implosion of all that is real. They call us to a strange rejection of all that glitters and shimmers over the dark landscape, as if it *were* the landscape. But this usually metropolitan neurosis is nothing more than a bad case of idealist theorists' becoming the victims of their own nightmares. Mistaking their own metaphors for reality, they are hoist by their own semiotic petards. They are caught by—defined in pro-fessionally charting—the symbolic life on the surface of things without seeing, because not implicated in, the *necessary* everyday role of sym-bolic work, of how sense is made of structure and contradiction. They then coolly announce that modern culture is all surface in danger of collapse.

We must catch up with the movement of the real world. We must not be satisfied with a phantom history and demonology of its surface movement. Above all, self-deluding and complacent beliefs in aesthetic self-sufficiency and separateness, as sanctuaries in and against an imaginary history, must be firmly rejected.

Commerce and consumerism have helped to release a profane explosion of everyday symbolic life and activity. The genie of common culture is out of the bottle—let out by commercial carelessness. Not stuffing it back in, but seeing what wishes may be granted, should be the stuff of our imagination.

Notes

1 Raymond Williams, 'Culture is ordinary' (1958), reprinted at the beginning of this book and in his *Resources of Hope*, Verso, 1988.
2 For a full account of the 'new social condition of youth' in relation to youth unemployment, see P. Willis *et al.*, *The Youth Review*, Avebury, 1988.
3 It is possible to get into a fine and tautological argument about the distinctions and relationships between 'invisible' internal subjective meanings and external 'visible' signs, symbols and practices. Though we insist that grounded aesthetics are a quality of living processes of meaning-making, not of things, this is not necessarily a wholly invisible internal process, though it can be. Words, signs, symbols and practices as 'things' in the world can certainly be part of the operation of particular grounded aesthetics for particular people. They are also taken in by and made sense of in the meaning-making of others. Also we recognize and, in what follows, give many examples of the possibility of grounded aesthetics becoming properly externalized: formalized, made concrete and public in some way. We argue for this as a process which decisively blurs and questions the conventional distinctions between consumption and production. What's crucial here, though, is not the 'thing-like' qualities of such externalizations, but their capacity both to reflect *and promote* the grounded aesthetics of their producers and of others, individuals and collectivities.

 Our internal subjective meanings will never transcend or make redundant the 'given-ness' of textuality, of things, of forms, of symbols. Indeed, these latter are intrinsic to the possibility and creativity of human meanings, but they should always be seen transitively for their role in the mediation of human meaning. They're humble, malleable things, not the kings and queens of expression and experience. In particular, we should understand that processes of human meaning-making and creativity are stopped dead when aesthetics are attached to things instead of to human activities.
4 The title of a book by Marshall Berman New York: Simon and Schuster, 1982) which helped to launch the many faceted and pervasive postmodern debate.

20

The view from futures past

Mike Davis

From his *City of Quartz: Excavating the Future in Los Angeles* (Verso, 1990).

The best place to view Los Angeles of the next millennium is from the ruins of its alternative future. Standing on the sturdy cobblestone foundations of the General Assembly Hall of the Socialist city of Llano del Rio—Open Shop Los Angeles's utopian antipode—you can sometimes watch the Space Shuttle in its elegant final descent towards Rogers Dry Lake. Dimly on the horizon are the giant sheds of Air Force Plant 42 where Stealth Bombers (each costing the equivalent of 10,000 public housing units) and other, still top secret, hot rods of the apocalypse are assembled. Closer at hand, across a few miles of creosote and burro bush, and the occasional grove of that astonishing yucca, the Joshua tree, is the advance guard of approaching suburbia, tract homes on point.

The desert around Llano has been prepared like a virgin bride for its eventual union with the Metropolis: hundreds of square miles of vacant space engridded to accept the future millions, with strange, prophetic street signs marking phantom intersections like '250th Street and Avenue K'. Even the eerie trough of the San Andreas Fault, just south of Llano over a foreboding escarpment, is being gingerly surveyed for designer home sites. Nuptial music is provided by the daily commotion of ten thousand vehicles hurtling past Llano on 'Pearblossom Highway'—the deadliest stretch of two-lane blacktop in California.

When Llano's original colonists, eight youngsters from the Young Peoples' Socialist League (YPSL), first arrived at the 'Plymouth Rock of the Cooperative Commonwealth' in 1914, this part of the high Mojave Desert, misnamed the Antelope Valley,[1] had a population of a few thousand ranchers, borax miners and railroad workers as well as some armed guards to protect the newly-built aqueduct from sabotage. Los Angeles was then a city of 300,000 (the population of the Antelope Valley today), and its urban edge, now visible from Llano, was in the new suburb of Hollywood, where D.W. Griffith and his cast of thousands were just finishing an epic romance of the Ku Klux Klan, *Birth of a Nation*. In their day-long drive from the Labor Temple in Downtown Los Angeles to Llano over ninety miles of rutted wagon road, the YPSLs in their red Model-T trucks passed by scores of billboards, planted amid beet fields and walnut orchards, advertising the impending subdivision of the San Fernando Valley (owned by the city's richest men and annexed the following year as the culmination of the famous 'water conspiracy' fictionally celebrated in Polanski's *Chinatown*).

Three-quarters of a century later, forty thousand Antelope Valley commuters slither bumper-to-bumper each morning through Soledad Pass on their way to long-distance jobs in the smog-shrouded and overdeveloped San Fernando Valley. Briefly a Red Desert in the heyday of Llano (1914–18), the high Mojave for the last fifty years has been pre-eminently the Pentagon's playground. Patton's army trained here to meet Rommel (the ancient tank tracks are still visible), while Chuck Yeager first broke the sound barrier over the Antelope Valley in his Bell X-1 rocket plane. Under the 18,000-square-mile, ineffable blue dome of R-2508—'the most important airspace in the world'—ninety thousand military training sorties are still flown every year.

But as developable land has disappeared throughout the coastal plains and inland basins, and soaring land inflation has reduced access to new housing to less than 15 per cent of the population, the militarized desert has suddenly become the last frontier of the Southern California Dream. With home prices $100,000 cheaper than in the San Fernando Valley, the archetypical suburban fringe of the 1950s, the Antelope Valley has nearly doubled in population over the last decade, with another quarter million new arrivals expected by 2010. Eleven thousand new homes were started in 1988 alone. But since the Valley's economic base, not counting real-estate agents, consists almost entirely of embattled Cold War complexes—Edwards Air Force Base and Plant 42 (altogether about eighteen thousand civilian jobs)—most of the new homebuyers will simply swell the morning commute on the Antelope Valley Freeway.

The pattern of urbanization here is what design critic Peter Plagens once called the 'ecology of evil'.[2] Developers don't grow homes in the desert —this isn't Marrakesh or even Tucson—they just clear, grade and pave, hook up some pipes to the local artificial river (the federally subsidized California Aqueduct), build a security wall and plug in the 'product'. With generations of experience in uprooting the citrus gardens of Orange County and the San Fernando Valley, the developers—ten or twelve major firms, headquartered in places like Newport Beach and Beverly Hills—regard the desert as simply another abstraction of dirt and dollar signs. The region's major natural wonder, a Joshua tree forest containing individual specimens often thirty feet high and older than the Domesday Book, is being bulldozed into oblivion. Developers regard the magnificent Joshuas, unique to this desert, as large noxious weeds unsuited to the illusion of verdant homesteads. As the head of Harris Homes explained: 'It is a very bizarre tree. It is not a beautiful tree like the pine or something. Most people don't care about the Joshuas.'[3]

With such malice toward the landscape, it is not surprising that developers also refuse any nomenclatural concession to the desert. In promotional literature intended for homebuyers or Asian investors, they have started referring to the region euphemistically as 'North Los Angeles County'. Meanwhile they christen their little pastel pods of Chardonnay lifestyle, air-conditioned and over-watered, with scented brand-names like Fox Run,

Mardi Gras, Bravo, Cambridge, Sunburst, New Horizons, and so on. The most hallucinatory are the gated communities manufactured by Kaufman and Broad, the homebuilders who were famous in the 1970s for exporting Hollywood ramblers to the suburbs of Paris. Now they have brought back France (or, rather, California homes in French drag) to the desert in fortified mini-*banlieus*, with lush lawns, Old World shrubs, fake mansard roofs and *nouveaux riches* titles like 'Chateau'.

But Kaufman and Broad only expose the underlying method in the apparent madness of L.A.'s urban desert. The discarded Joshua trees, the profligate wastage of water, the claustrophobic walls, and the ridiculous names are as much a polemic against incipient urbanism as they are an assault on an endangered wilderness. The *eutopic* (literally no-place) logic of their subdivisions, in sterilized sites stripped bare of nature and history, masterplanned only for privatized family consumption, evokes much of the past evolution of tract-home Southern California. But the developers are not just repackaging myth (the good life in the suburbs) for the next generation; they are also pandering to a new, burgeoning fear of the city.

Social anxiety, as traditional urban sociology likes to remind us, is just maladjustment to change. But who has anticipated, or adjusted to, the scale of change in Southern California over the last fifteen years? Stretching now from the country-club homes of Santa Barbara to the shanty *colonias* of Ensenada, to the edge of Llano in the high desert and of the Coachella Valley in the low, with a built-up surface area nearly the size of Ireland and a GNP bigger than India's—the urban galaxy dominated by Los Angeles is the fastest growing metropolis in the advanced industrial world. Its current population of fifteen million, encompassing six counties and a corner of Baja California, and clustered around two super-cores (Los Angeles and San Diego–Tijuana) and a dozen major, expanding metro-centres, is predicted to increase by another seven or eight million over the next generation. The overwhelming majority of these new inhabitants will be non-Anglos, further tipping the ethnic balance away from WASP hegemony toward the polyethnic diversity of the next century. (Anglos became a minority in the city and county of Los Angeles during the 1980s, as they will become in the state before 2010).[4]

Social polarization has increased almost as rapidly as population. A recent survey of Los Angeles household income trends in the 1980s suggests that affluence (incomes of $50,000 plus) has almost tripled (from 9 per cent to 26 per cent) while poverty ($15,000 and under) has increased by a third (from 30 per cent to 40 per cent); the middle range, as widely predicted, has collapsed by half (from 61 per cent to 32 per cent).[5] At the same time the worst popular fears of a generation ago about the consequences of market-driven overdevelopment have punctually come true. Decades of systematic under-investment in housing and urban infrastructure, combined with grotesque subsidies for speculators, permissive zoning for commercial development, the absence of effective regional planning, and ludicrously low property taxes for the wealthy have ensured an erosion of the quality of life for the middle classes in older suburbs as well as for the inner-city poor.

Ironically the Antelope Valley is both a sanctuary from this maelstrom of growth and crisis, and one of its fastest growing epicentres. In the desperate reassurance of their gated subdivisions, the new commuter population attempts to recover the lost Eden of 1950s-style suburbia. Older Valley residents, on the other hand, are frantically trying to raise the gangplanks against this ex-urban exodus sponsored by their own pro-growth business and political elites. In their increasingly angry view, the landrush since 1984 has only brought traffic jams, smog, rising crime, job competition, noise, soil erosion, a water shortage and the attrition of a distinctively countrified lifestyle.

For the first time since the Socialists left the desert (in 1918 for their New Llano colony in Louisiana) there is wild talk of a 'total rural revolution'. The announcement of several new mega-projects—instant cities ranging from 8,500 to 35,000 units, designed to be plugged into the Valley's waiting grid—have aroused unprecedented populist ire. On one recent occasion, the representative of the Ritter Ranch project in rustic Leone Valley was 'ambushed by an angry mob . . . screaming and bitching and threatening to kill [him]'. In the Valley's two incorporated municipalities of Lancaster (the international headquarters of the Flat Earth Society) and Palmdale (the fastest growing city in California for most of the 1980s), more than sixty different homeowners' associations have joined together to slow down urbanization, as well as to contest the state's plan for a new 2,200-bed prison for Los Angeles drug and gang offenders in the Mira Loma area.[6]

Meanwhile the myth of a desert sanctuary was shattered shortly after New Year's Eve 1990 when a stray bullet from a gang member's gun killed a popular high-school athlete. Shortly afterwards, the trendy Quartz Hill area, advertised as the emergent 'Beverly Hills' of the desert, was wracked by a gun-battle between the local 5 Deuce Posse and some out-of-town Crips. The *grand peur* of L.A. street gangs suddenly swept the high desert. While sheriffs hunted fugitive teenagers with dogs—like escapees from a Georgia chain-gang—local businessmen formed the semi-vigilante Gangs Out Now (GON). Intimidated by official warnings that there were six hundred and fifty 'identified gang members' in the Valley, the local high school attempted to impose a draconian dress code banning 'gang colours' (blue and red). Outraged students, in turn, protested in the streets.[7]

While the kids were 'doin' the right thing', the local NAACP was demanding an investigation of three suspicious killings of non-whites by sheriffs' deputies. In one case the deputies gunned down an unarmed Asian college student while in another a Black man accused of wielding a three-pronged garden tool was shot eight times. The most egregious incident, however, was the slaying of Betty Jean Aborn, a homeless middle-aged Black woman with a history of mental illness. Confronted by seven burly sheriffs after stealing an ice-cream from a convenience store, she supposedly brandished a butcher's knife. The response was an incredible volley of twenty-eight rounds, eighteen of which perforated her body.[8]

As the desert thus announced the arrival of the *fin de siècle* with a staggering overture of bulldozers and gunfire, some old-timers—contemplating the rapidly diminishing distance between the solitude of the Mojave and the gridlock of suburban life—began to wonder out loud whether there was any alternative to Los Angeles after all.

The May Pole

Class war and repression are said to have driven the Los Angeles Socialists into the desert. But they also came eagerly, wanting to taste the sweet fruit of cooperative labour in their own lifetime. As Job Harriman, who came within a hair's-breadth of being Los Angeles's first Socialist mayor in 1911, explained: 'It became apparent to me that a people would never abandon their means of livelihood, good or bad, capitalistic or otherwise, until other methods were developed which would promise advantages at least as good as those by which they were living.' What Llano promised was a guaranteed $4 per day wage and a chance to 'show the world a trick they do not know, which is how to live without war or interest on money or rent on land or profiteering in any manner'.[9]

With the sponsorship not only of Harriman and the Socialist Party, but also of Chairman W.A. Engle of the Central Labor Council and Frank McMahon of the Bricklayers' Union, hundreds of landless farmers, unemployed labourers, blacklisted machinists, adventurous clerks, persecuted IWW soapbox orators, restless shopkeepers, and bright-eyed bohemians followed the YPSLs to where the snow-fed Rio del Llano (now Big Rock Creek) met the edge of the desert. Although they were 'democracy with the lid off . . . democracy rampant, belligerent, unrestricted', their enthusiastic labour transformed several thousand acres of the Mojave into a small Socialist civilization.[10] By 1916 their alfalfa fields and modern dairy, their pear orchards and vegetable gardens—all watered by a complex and efficient irrigation system—supplied the colony with 90 per cent of its own food (and fresh flowers as well). Meanwhile, dozens of small workshops cobbled shoes, canned fruit, laundered clothes, cut hair, repaired autos, and published the *Western Comrade*. There was even a Llano motion picture company and an ill-fated experiment in aviation (the homemade plane crashed).

In the spirit of Chautauqua as much as Marx, Llano was also one big Red School House. While babies (including Bella Lewitzky, the future modern dancer) played in the nursery, children (among them Gregory Ain, the future modern architect) attended Southern California's first Montessori school. The teenagers, meanwhile, had their own Kid Kolony (a model industrial school), and adults attended night classes or enjoyed the Mojave's largest library. One of the favourite evening pastimes, apart from dancing to the colony's notorious ragtime orchestra, was debating Alice Constance Austin's design for the Socialist City that Llano was to become.

Although influenced by contemporary City Beautiful and Garden City ideologies, Austin's drawings and models, as architectural historian Dolores Hayden has emphasized, were 'distinctively feminist and California'. Like Llano kid Gregory Ain's more modest 1940s plans for cooperative housing, Austin attempted to translate the specific cultural values and popular enthusiasms of Southern California into a planned and egalitarian social landscape. In the model that she presented to colonists on May Day 1916, Llano was depicted as a garden city of ten thousand people housed in graceful Craftsman apartments with private gardens but communal kitchens and laundries to liberate women from drudgery. The civic centre, as befitted a 'city of light', was composed of 'eight rectangular halls, like factories, with sides almost wholly of glass, leading to a glass-domed assembly hall'. She crowned this aesthetic of individual choice within a fabric of social solidarity with a quintessentially Southern California gesture: giving every household an automobile and constructing a ring road around the city that would double 'as a drag strip with stands for spectators on both sides'.[11]

If Austin's vision of thousands of patio apartments radiating from the Bonaventure Hotel-style Assembly Hall, surrounded by socially owned orchards, factories and a monumental drag strip sounds a bit far-fetched today, imagine what Llanoites would have made of a future composed of Kaufman and Broad *chateaux* ringed by mini-malls, prisons and Stealth Bomber plants. In any event, the nine hundred pioneers of the Socialist City would enjoy only one more triumphant May Day in the Mojave.

> The May Day festivities of 1917 commenced at nine o'clock in the morning with intra-community athletic events, including a Fat Women's Race. The entire group of colonists then formed a Grand Parade and marched to the hotel where the Liberty Program followed. The band played from a bunting-draped grandstand, the choral society sang appropriate revolutionary anthems like the 'Marseillaise', then moved into the Almond Grove for a barbecue dinner. After supper a group of young girls injected the English into the radical tradition by dancing about the May Pole. At 7:30 the dramatic club presented 'Mishaps of Minerva' with newly decorated scenery in the assembly hall. Dancing consumed the remainder of the evening.[12]

Despite an evident sense of humour, Llano began to fall apart in the later half of 1917. Plagued by internal feuding between the General Assembly and the so-called 'brush gang', the colony was assailed from the outside by creditors, draft boards, jealous neighbours, and the Los Angeles *Times*. After the loss of Llano's water rights in a lawsuit—a devastating blow to its irrigation infrastructure—Harriman and a minority of colonists relocated in 1918 to Louisiana, where a hard-scrabble New Llano (a pale shadow of the original) hung on until 1939. Within twenty-four hours of the colonists' departure, local ranchers ('who precariously represented capitalism in the wilderness') began to demolish its dormitories and workshops, evidently with the intention of erasing any trace of the red menace. But Llano's towering silo, cow byre, and the cobblestone foundation and twin fireplaces of its Assembly Hall, proved indestructible: as local patriotic fury subsided, they became romantic landmarks ascribed to increasingly mythic circumstances.

Now and then, a philosophical temperament, struggling with the huge paradox of Southern California, rediscovers Llano as the talisman of a future lost. Thus Aldous Huxley, who lived for a few years in the early 1940s in a former Llano ranch house overlooking the colony's cemetery, liked to meditate 'in the almost supernatural silence' on the fate of utopia. He ultimately came to the conclusion that the Socialist City was a 'pathetic little Ozymandias', doomed from the start by Harriman's 'Gladstone collar' and his 'Pickwickian' misunderstanding of human nature—whose history 'except in a purely negative way . . . is sadly uninstructive'.[13]

Llano's other occasional visitors, lacking Huxley's vedic cynicism, have generally been more charitable. After the debacle of 1960s–70s communitarianism (especially the deadly trail that led into the Guyanese jungle), the pear trees planted by this ragtime utopia seem a more impressive accomplishment. Moreover, as its most recent historians point out, Huxley grossly underestimated the negative impact of wartime xenophobia and the spleen of the Los Angeles *Times* upon Llano's viability. There but for fortune (and Harry Chandler), perhaps, would stand a brave red *kibbutz* in the Mojave today, canvassing votes for Jesse Jackson and protecting Joshuas from bulldozers.[14]

The developers' millennium?

But, then again, we do not stand at the gates of Socialism's New Jerusalem, but at the hard edge of the developers' millennium. Llano itself is owned by an absentee speculator in Chicago who awaits an offer he cannot refuse from Kaufman and Broad. Setting aside an apocalyptic awakening of the neighbouring San Andreas Fault, it is all too easy to envision Los Angeles reproducing itself endlessly across the desert with the assistance of pilfered water, cheap immigrant labour, Asian capital and desperate homebuyers willing to trade lifetimes on the freeway in exchange for $500,000 'dream homes' in the middle of Death Valley.

Is this the world-historic victory of Capitalism that everyone is talking about?

On May Day 1990 (the same day Gorbachev was booed by thousands of alienated Muscovites) I returned to the ruins of Llano del Rio to see if the walls would talk to me. Instead I found the Socialist City reinhabited by two twenty-year-old building labourers from El Salvador, camped out in the ruins of the old dairy and eager to talk with me in our mutually broken tongues. Like hobo heroes out of a Jack London novel, they had already tramped up and down California, but following a frontier of housing starts, not silver strikes or wheat harvests. Although they had yet to find work in Palmdale, they praised the clear desert sky, the easy hitchhiking and the relative scarcity of La Migra. When I observed that they were settled in the ruins of a *ciudad socialista*, one of them asked whether the 'rich people had come with planes and bombed them out'. No, I explained, the colony's credit had failed. They looked baffled and changed the subject.

We talked about the weather for a while, then I asked them what they thought about Los Angeles, a city without boundaries, which ate the desert, cut down the Joshua and the May Pole, and dreamt of becoming infinite. One of my new Llano *compañeros* said that L.A. already was everywhere. They had watched it every night in San Salvador, in endless dubbed reruns of *I Love Lucy* and *Starsky and Hutch*, a city where everyone was young and rich and drove new cars and saw themselves on television. After ten thousand daydreams like this, he had deserted the Salvadorean Army and hitchhiked two thousand five hundred miles to Tijuana. A year later he was standing at the corner of Alvarado and Seventh Streets in the MacArthur Park district near Downtown Los Angeles, along with all the rest of yearning, hardworking Central America. No one like him was rich or drove a new car—except for the coke dealers—and the police were as mean as back home. More importantly no one like him was on television; they were all invisible.

His friend laughed. 'If you were on TV you would just get deported anyway and have to pay some *coyote* in Tijuana $500 to sneak you back to L.A.' He argued that it was better to stay out in the open whenever possible, preferably here in the desert, away from the centre. He compared L.A. and Mexico City (which he knew well) to volcanoes, spilling wreckage and desire in ever-widening circles over a denuded countryside. It is never wise, he averred, to live too near a volcano. 'The old gringo *socialistas* had the right idea.'

I agreed, even though I knew it was too late to move, or to refound Llano. Then, it was their turn to interrogate me. Why was I out here alone, among the ghosts of May Day? What did *I* think of Los Angeles? I tried to explain that I had just written a book. . . .

Notes

1 Despite the incautious claims of Lynne Foster in her recent Sierra Club guide (*Adventuring in the California Desert*, San Francisco, 1987), there is absolutely no evidence that 'many thousands of pronghorn antelope roamed the area' in the nineteenth century. On the contrary, small numbers of pronghorn were introduced in the Space Age, partially to allow the Valley to live up to its name!
2 'Los Angeles: The ecology of evil', *Artforum*, December 1972.
3 Los Angeles *Times*, 3 January 1988; Antelope Valley *Press*, 29 October 1989.
4 For demographic projections, see Southern California Association of Governments (SCAG), *Growth Management Plan*, Los Angeles, February 1989. To the rather arbitrary five-country SCAG area I have added projections for San Diego and Tijuana.
5 County research quoted on KCET-TV's, 'A class by itself', May 1990.
6 Los Angeles *Business Journal*, 25 December 1989; *Press*, 14 and 19 January 1990.
7 Ibid., 17 and 19 January.
8 *Daily News*, 4 June 1989. (It was months before the Los Angeles *Times* reported the Aborn murder in its main edition.)
9 Harriman quoted in Robert Hine, *California's Utopian Colonies*, San Marino, Calif. 1953, p. 117; and Dolores Hayden, *Seven American Utopias*, Cambridge, Mass., 1976, pp. 289–90.
10. Llano chronicler Ernest Wooster quoted in Nigey Lenon, Lionel Rolfe, and Paul Greenstein, *Bread and Hyacinths: Job Harriman and His Political Legacy*, unpublished manuscript, Los Angeles, 1988, p. 21.
11 Cf. Hayden, pp. 300–1 (on Austin's design); and Sam Hall Kaplan, *L.A. Lost and Found*, New York, 1987, p. 137 (on Ain's attempts to design for cooperative living).
12 Hines, p. 127.
13 'Ozymandias, The utopia that failed', in *Tomorrow and Tomorrow and Tomorrow . . .* , New York, 1956, pp. 84–102.
14 Of course I deliberately beg the question of the Joshuas ploughed away to build Llano (ominously they have never grown back), not to mention what would have come of Austin's car in every red garage or where the water for 10,000 singing tomorrows would have been 'borrowed' from.

21

Fictions of Europe

Jan Nederveen Pieterse

From *Race and Class*, vol. 32, no. 3 (January–March 1991).

'European culture'

It is not difficult to find a definition of 'European culture'. For instance:

> What determines and characterises European culture? . . . Europe is formed
> by the . . . community of nations which are largely characterised by the
> inherited civilisation whose most important sources are: the Judaeo-Christian
> religion, the Greek-Hellenistic ideas in the fields of government, philosophy,
> arts and science, and finally, the Roman views concerning law.[1]

This is a definition so average that it is almost official. In fact, it is official,
because it is given by the Netherlands Ambassador for International
Cultural Cooperation, Mr M. Mourik. We are taken past the familiar
stations of Europe: Greece—Rome—Christianity. This is a well-known
entity in the United States also, where it is often referred to as 'Western
civilisation', which may be summed up as 'from Plato to Nato'.[2]

This is the usual façade of Europe, so familiar that it is boring. This is
the Europe that is now being resurrected in the discourses of the official
magisters of culture. The problem, however, is not just that it is boring.
The problem is that, in addition to being chauvinistic, elitist, pernicious
and alienating, it is wrong.

It is wrong as regards the origins of European culture; it is wrong in
so representing European culture that European regional cultures and
subcultures are overlooked; it is wrong in representing elite culture as
culture *tout court* and in denying popular culture; it is wrong in defining
European culture in terms of the past ('inherited civilization') and in totally
ignoring Europe's contemporary multicultural realities.

This old culture is presently being revived in the context of the 'new
Europe'. Many of the political and economic negotiations and virtually
all of the debate on culture focus on *Europe and the nations*. The usual
questions are whether the Europe of '1992' will be dominated by the largest
national European cultures, Germany and France. What about Britain?
What about the identities of the smaller European cultures? What about

central Europe, Mitteleuropa? Will European cultures be steamrollered into a continent-wide pattern of uniformity, propelled by market forces and media magnates and directives from a few Europe metropoles?

The continent that pioneered nationalism pioneers the transcendence of nationalism, and in this context these questions are very meaningful. Yet, this is essentially a discussion about 'Europe and Europe'. There is another question on the horizon which is both larger and potentially more incisive in its implications, and that is *Europe and the continents*. This is infrequently talked about, except in the context of decolonization and the critique of eurocentrism, topics which are not particularly high on the agenda.

We are living in a post-imperial Europe which still maintains an imperial culture. Official European culture, reproduced in declarations, textbooks, media programmes, continues to be the culture of imperial Europe.

Another issue is that Europe, from the point of view of the many migrants in Europe of non-European origin, is now a New World, yet its self-image, its dominant culture, is still that of an Old World—that is a world from which people emigrate.

Certain key experiences are missing from this new old European culture: the experience of decolonization, of migrations, post-imperial ('we are here because you were there') and otherwise, and of globalization.

Walk in any street of any European city and ask yourself—is this 'European culture'? Is this 'Greece—Rome—and Judaeo-Christianity'? Ask contemporary citizens of Europe about their ancestors, their origins—how many of you hail from non-European worlds? Or, to use nineteenth-century racist language, how many of you are half-caste? How many of you were never represented in this elite European project in the first place—as members of the working class or living in the countryside, or in regional cultures such as the 'Celtic fringe'? What is being recycled as 'European culture' is nineteenth-century elite imperial myth-formation. Is it not high time then to open up the imperial façade of European culture, to place it under an X-ray and ask, what here is really Europe and what is not?

Fortress Europe

Europe 1992 means that, as internal borders become lower, the external borders become higher, both in terms of the 'Zollverein Europe' of the internal market and in terms of 'European identity'. Concretely, it refers to the plans for a 'European visum' and to the Schengen Accord, which is to regulate immigration and asylum on a European basis.

Each European country thereby assumes a double identity, national and as member of a United States of Europe, each a gateway towards, or a ramparts of, the European world. As the physical frontier with Africa and the Middle East, Mediterranean Europe occupies a special place in this constellation. There are writings on the wall.

Spain, Portugal and Greece have recently become immigration countries—now more people come from the south than leave for the north. Italy had already held this status for some time. Thus, the Italian and French patterns of racism and racial attacks on minorities of non-European origin, mainly from North and West Africa, may be becoming a Mediterranean pattern. Spanish sociologist Alberto Moncada speaks of 'Spain functioning as a southern European police over the human mass from the Maghreb and Latin America'.[3] In news reports, Greece and also Bulgaria are already talked about as 'frontline states with fundamentalist Islam'.

What is developing in these areas is a European Mexico syndrome—a border-zone where economic, political, cultural, religious and demographic differences accumulate to create a gap between worlds, a zone of confrontation. Like Hong Kong, Europe will, and indeed already does, face refugees, boat people, and police hunting for illegal foreigners.[4]

NATO is also shifting its sights towards the south.[5] With the Cold War past, this is where the 'new enemy' lurks. 'Islamic fundamentalism', poverty and high population growth are identified as the main problems in classified and not-so-classified documents. Over recent years, we have seen the enemy images shifting and new Hitlers paraded on the front pages—Arafat, Khadafi, Khomeini, Assad, and now Saddam Hussein.

Thus, Fortress Europe is becoming a reality. The situation is primarily identified as a security problem, although it is also, secondarily, acknowledged as an economic and humanitarian problem. Europe's historic frontier of confrontation with the world of Islam is being reactivated. The question of Europe and the south, Africa, Asia and Latin America, is acquiring new dimensions. We may sum up this set of problems as: *Europe and the continents.*

These problems also reflect on migrants of non-European origin within Europe, so they also run *through* Europe. We may sum up this question as: *Europe and the minorities.* Thus, the problems of Europe and the continents are reproduced locally throughout Europe, interacting with the problem of Europe and the minorities. Local frontiers, of status and neighbourhood, colour and education, intersect with global frontiers. How minorities of non-European origin are viewed is affected by how Europe views itself in relation to the continents.

The prospect is that of Europe as a fort, with the Straits of Gibraltar and the Bosphorus for moats, and parts of the Third World as hinterlands, optional labour reserves. Gradually, a discreet neo-Malthusianism is becoming a way of thinking about Africa in particular: famine and starvation as the means of re-establishing equilibrium between population and resources.

The inauguration of 'Europe 1992' will coincide with the 1992 Columbus celebrations in Spain and Portugal and the Americas—500 years since the Old World spawned the New World, 500 years of modernization, 500 years to contemplate the paradoxes of progress. . . . In Spain and Portugal, this will be an occasion to erect monuments to commemorate the 'Discoveries' and to celebrate the Conquista, thereby reaffirming and reproducing in their claim to fame the very dualism of the Americas, where Columbus Day is a day of celebration for Europeans and a day of mourning for native Americans.

European identity is no longer an imperial, expansionist identity in the old sense. The era of imperialism is past: The era of decolonization is past and Third Worldism is no longer *à la mode.* European chauvinism now is prosperous, complacent, aloof. Fortress Europe, in its cultural uniform, is not expansionist but critical.

Many 'progressives', intellectuals and left-wing people included, share this kind of definition of the situation. Europe is their castle. Europe is the fortress of their mind. And much as they identify with the Europe of the Enlightenment, they abhor 'Islamic fundamentalism', and, since 'Third Worldism' is out of fashion, they look down, if they look at all, on the poor in the Third World, and find shelter in a self-image of Europe as a world of modernity. The discourse of postmodernism, busy critiquing modernity, turns its back on the 'pre-modern' world.

This situation is an open door to the European Right, culture-baiting minorities as 'aliens'. This creates the danger of a new European consensus of exclusion, a right-to-centre political and cultural coalition that may turn Europe into a complacent shelter of conservatism—in the name of Enlightenment.

One of the European projects waiting in the wings is that of a Europe-wide coalition of right-wing parties, a continental chain of 'national fronts'. It is ironical to realize that, for all their 'national' posturing, several of these organizations are being funded and supported from foreign sources, ranging from American right-wing foundations to the Unification Church of Rev Moon.

The deconstruction of Europe

Rather than recycling the illusions of imperial Europe, we should address and welcome the multicultural realities and opportunities of post-imperial Europe. Recreating Europe in '1992' means to relocate Europe's place in world history, in terms of the real relationship between Europe and the continents and not according to the great walls of empire.

The familiar stations of Europe are: Greece—Rome—Christendom —Renaissance—Enlightenment—industrialization—colonialism. The two main definitions of European identity derived from this are, in shorthand, Christianity and the Enlightenment.

From Santiago de Compostella, Pope John Paul II calls out to a 'Christian Europe'. This historical field mattered to Catholic statesmen Schuman, Adenauer, de Gasperi, who came together for the Treaty of Rome in 1956. The notion of Christian Europe matters to Christian Democrats and to many on the Right, from Otto von Habsburg to Jean Marie le Pen.[6]

There is no question that the histories of Europe and Christianity are interwoven. Yet, indeed, there are many problems with defining European identity in terms of Christianity. What about the Renaissance, the humanists, the anticlericals, the Enlightenment? And what about the great schisms in Christianity—between Greek and Latin Christianity, between Constantinople and Rome, between Europe east and west, and between Roman Catholicism and Protestantism, between Europe south and north? Indeed, Christianity is Asian in origin, and on many medieval maps we find Jerusalem depicted as the centre of the world, an Asian site as the centre of the Christian world—this is the dominant depiction on *mappae mundi* from the seventh to the thirteenth centuries and occurs frequently on maps from 1200 to 1500.

Much more pervasive and more formidable as a definition of Europe is the legacy of the Renaissance/Enlightenment. The characteristic feature of the Europe of the Enlightenment, as Jack Lively has argued, is the Enlightenment itself: European identity was discovered 'in the modernity of Europe'.

> The European personality was distinct and its role was unique, not because its traditionally rooted society marked it out from other cultures, but because it had moved sufficiently far along a path of development to serve as an example for the rest of humanity. The emphasis was now on time rather than space, promise rather than achievement, the future rather than the past. . . . Moreover . . . the modernity of Europe consisted in the Enlightenment itself.[7]

Europe equals modernity, or the critical spirit, its attitude of self-criticism, its tolerance and openness to other views. From Kant to Raymond Aron, this is a recurrent theme.

It relates closely to another European topos: the 'autonomy of the spirit' as a European characteristic, the tension and friction between faith and reason, the aversion to dogma. This is Nietzsche's tradition of the free thinkers, the *libres penseurs*.

This, in turn, overlaps with a discourse which finds the specificity of Europe in the autonomy of its cities, hence the development of its burghers, its citizens and, over time, civil society.

Again we hear the echo of a classic theme: Europe as the land of liberty, as against Asia, the land of despotism and oppression—in a word, oriental despotism and occidental liberty. This is a thesis that harks back to the Greeks: to the east in Persia, despotism; to the north in Europe, the free barbarians; and in the middle, Greece, that is civilization.

These overtones—autonomy, liberty—still play a part in Europe's self-definition but drawn into the background since the experiences with Nazism, fascism, European totalitarianism. The keynote in the self-assessments of Europe remains that of modernity. That is essentially the Europe of the Enlightenment, also as the dapper antidote to totalitarian Europe.

This is the most prominent rhetoric of difference between Europe and non-European worlds, in particular, between Europe and the world of Islam —the common European interpretation of 'fundamentalist Islam' is as a revolt against modernity (that is, against Europe), a countermodernization and the International of '*Unvernunft*'.[8]

'Identity' implies a relationship to what is different and thus a statement of boundaries. Both these European identities—Christianity and the Enlightenment—are such statements of boundaries, border flags which serve as internal as much as external boundaries—protection from the 'barbarians' both within and outside the gates. They are projects rather than realities, mirrors of power and rhetorics of control.

European paradoxes

Why deconstruct Europe? It's not fair. It's hardly been constructed. Americans would say the same thing, why deconstruct Europe? We like Europe, it means a lot to us, it is the prototype of Disneyland.

It is true that European identity is weak. First, because Europeanism is recent. It dates, by and large, from after 1700. Before that, Christendom was the predominant identity. The humanists of the Renaissance looked towards Greece and Rome as the centres of culture. Moreover, until 1683 when the Turks stood before Vienna, Europe was still under threat from the east.

Second, European development has not known a single centre. There has been a continual shift of centres, and with the centre also the peripheries shifted. The Renaissance, the Enlightenment and French Revolution, industrialization and colonial expansion, unfolded in different parts of Europe and spread in different directions. There was never a centre which embodied European identity.

Third, from 1700, European development has taken place by means of single rival states. Already, from the sixteenth century, Europe existed in the form of a 'European balance of power', that is as a polycentric world. From 1700, the keynote of political development were the different monarchies, while from 1800, the keynote of development was *national* development.

Also, outward expansion was undertaken by single rival states. Europe's 'new imperialism' of the late nineteenth century and the scramble for Africa was a pre-emptive imperialism—both in concert with European competitors and aiming to outmanoeuvre them. This is one of the paradoxes of European imperialism: it implied and brought forth both European unity (as in the Berlin Conference on the division of Africa) and European divisions.

Another paradox. The backdrop to nineteenth-century European expansion in Asia and Africa was a concept of 'European civilization'. This was implied in the *'mission civilisatrice'*, even if this was executed primarily by means of national missions. It correlated with racial thinking. 'European civilization' made for a certain affinity among Europeans of different countries even while they were rivals for overseas territory and influence. This European civilization, the bedrock of European superiority and arrogance, received a deadly blow with the First World War. The long conflict from 1914 to 1945 shook the foundations of Europe's overseas imperialism and ushered in the era of decolonization.

Then 'Europe' was born—born out of the contraction of empire: thrown back upon themselves the European nations began to discover each other. 'Europe' was born in the shadow of the superpowers, not as the world's Queen, as she had been in eurocentric iconography since the sixteenth century, but merely as a buffer zone between the superpowers. Now the superpowers themselves are waning and new centres are emerging.

Notes

1 M. Mourik, 'European cultural co-operation', in A. Rijksbaron, W.H. Roobol, M. Weisglas (eds.), *Europe from a Cultural Perspective: Historiography and Perceptions*, The Hague, 1987, p. 19.
2 Elissa McBride, 'Western civilisation: from Plato to Nato', *The Activist* (no. 21, summer 1988), p. 7.
3 Information Bulletin XIIth World Congress of Sociology, Madrid, July 1990, no. 1.
4 Plans are under way to 'manage' and control this problem zone. Spain, France, Italy and Portugal seek the establishment of a Conference for Security and Cooperation in the Mediterranean, a 'Mediterranean Helsinki', modelled on the European Conference for Security and Cooperation. Already they have established a Forum for Regional Cooperation in the Mediterranean, together with Morocco, Algeria, Tunisia, Libya and Mauretania—five countries united in the Arab Maghreb Union. *Volksrant*, 4 August 1990.
5 Mariano Aguirre, 'Looking southwards', in Dan Smith (ed.), *European Security in the 1990s*, London, 1989.
6 Although another section of the Right, notably GRECE in France, rather identifies with 'pagan Europe'.
7 Jack Lively, 'The Europe of the Enlightenment', *History of European Ideas*, vol. I, no. 2, 1981, p. 93. 'Europe's distinction lay in its possessions of truths which, while applicable to all humanity, were not presently available to all humanity', p. 98.
8 T. Meyer (ed.), *Fundamentalismus in der modernen Welt*, Frankfurt, 1989.

22

A global sense of place

Doreen Massey

From *Marxism Today* (June 1991).

This is an era—it is often said—when things are speeding up, and spreading out. Capital is going through a new phase of internationalization, especially in its financial parts. More people travel more frequently and for longer distances. Your clothes have probably been made in a range of countries from Latin America to South East Asia. Dinner consists of food shipped in from all over the world. And if you have a screen in your office, instead of opening a letter which—care of Her Majesty's Post Office—has taken some days to wend its way across the country, you now get interrupted by e-mail.

This view of the current age is one now frequently found in a wide range of books and journals. Much of what is written about space, place and postmodern times emphasizes a new phase in what Marx once called 'the annihilation of space by time'. The process is argued, or—more usually—asserted, to have gained a new momentum, to have reached a new stage. It is a phenomenon which has been called 'time-space-compression'. And the general acceptance that something of the sort is going on is marked by the almost obligatory use in the literature of terms and phrases such as speed-up, global village, overcoming spatial barriers, the disruption of horizons, and so forth.

One of the results of this is an increasing uncertainty about what we mean by 'places' and how we relate to them. How, in the face of all this movement and intermixing, can we retain any sense of a local place and its particularity? An (idealized) notion of an era when places were (supposedly) inhabited by coherent and homogeneous communities is set against the current fragmentation and disruption. The counterposition is anyway dubious, of course; 'place' and 'community' have only rarely been coterminous. But the occasional longing for such coherence is nonetheless a sign of the geographical fragmentation, the spatial disruption, of our times. And occasionally, too, it has been part of what has given rise to defensive and reactionary responses—certain forms of nationalism, sentimentalized recovering of sanitized 'heritages', and outright antagonism to newcomers and 'outsiders'. One of the effects of such responses is that place itself, the seeking after a sense of place, has come to be seen by some as necessarily reactionary.

But is that necessarily so? Can't we re-think our sense of place? Is it not possible for a sense of place to be progressive; not self-enclosing and defensive, but outward-looking? A sense of place which is adequate to this era of time-space-compression? To begin with, there are some questions to be asked about time-space-compression itself. Who is it that experiences it, and how? Do we all benefit and suffer from it in the same way?

For instance, to what extent does the currently popular characterization of time-space-compression represent very much a Western, colonizer's, view? The sense of dislocation which some feel at the sight of a once well-known local street now lined with a succession of cultural imports—the pizzeria, the kebab house, the branch of the Middle-Eastern bank – must have been felt for centuries, though from a very different point of view, by colonized peoples all over the world as they watched the importation, maybe even used the products, of, first, European colonization, maybe British (from new forms of transport to liver salts and custard powder), later US, as they learned to eat wheat instead of rice or corn, to drink Coca Cola, just as today we try out enchiladas.

Moreover, as well as querying the ethnocentricity of the idea of time-space-compression and its current acceleration, we also need to ask about its causes: what is it that determines our degrees of mobility, that influences the sense we have of space and place? Time-space-compression refers to movement and communication across space, to the geographical stretching-out of social relations, and to our experience of all this. The usual interpretation is that it results overwhelmingly from the actions of capital, and from its currently increasing internationalization. On this interpretation, then, it is time space and money which make the world go round, and us go round (or not) the world. It is capitalism and its developments which are argued to determine our understanding and our experience of space.

But surely this is insufficient. Among the many other things which clearly influence that experience, there are, for instance, race and gender. The degree to which we can move between countries, or walk about the streets at night, or venture out of hotels in foreign cities, is not just influenced by 'capital'. Survey after survey has shown how women's mobility, for instance, is restricted—in a thousand different ways, from physical violence to being ogled at or made to feel quite simply 'out of place'—not by 'capital', but by men. Or, to take a more complicated example, Birkett, reviewing books on women adventurers and travellers in the nineteenth and twentieth centuries, suggests that 'it is far, far more demanding for a woman to wander now than ever before'.[1] The reasons she gives for this argument are a complex mix of colonialism, ex-colonialism, racism, changing gender-relations, and relative wealth. A simple resort to explanation in terms of 'money' or 'capital' alone could not begin to get to grips with the issue. The current speed-up may be strongly determined by economic forces, but it is not the economy alone which determines our experience of space and place. In other words, and put simply, there is a lot more determining how we experience space than what 'capital' gets up to.

What is more, of course, that last example indicated that 'time-space-compression' has not been happening for everyone in all spheres of activity.

Birkett again, this time writing of the Pacific Ocean: 'Jumbos have enabled Korean computer consultants to fly to Silicon Valley as if popping next door, and Singaporean entrepreneurs to reach Seattle in a day. The borders of the world's greatest ocean have been joined as never before. And Boeing has brought these people together. But what about those they fly over, on their islands five miles below? How has the mighty 747 brought them greater communion with those whose shores are washed by the same water? It hasn't, of course. Air travel might enable businessmen to buzz across the ocean, but the concurrent decline in shipping has only increased the isolation of many island communities . . . Pitcairn, like many other Pacific islands, has never felt so far from its neighbours.'[2]

In other words, and most broadly, time-space-compression needs differentiating socially. This is not just a moral or political point about inequality, although that would be sufficient reason to mention it; it is also a conceptual point.

Imagine for a moment that you are on a satellite, further out and beyond all actual satellites; you can see 'planet earth' from a distance and, rarely for someone with only peaceful intentions, you are equipped with the kind of technology which allows you to see the colours of people's eyes and the numbers on their numberplates. You can see all the movement and tune-in to all the communication that is going on. Furthest out are the satellites, then aeroplanes, the long haul between London and Tokyo and the hop from San Salvador to Guatemala City. Some of this is people moving, some of it is physical trade, some is media broadcasting. There are faxes, e-mail, film-distribution networks, financial flows and transactions. Look in closer and there are ships and trains, steam trains slogging laboriously up hills somewhere in Asia. Look in closer still and there are lorries and cars and buses, and on down further, somewhere in sub-Saharan Africa, there's a woman on foot who still spends hours a day collecting water.

Now, I want to make one simple point here, and that is about what one might call the *power-geometry* of it all; the power-geometry of time-space-compression. For different social groups, and different individuals, are placed in very distinct ways in relation to these flows and interconnections. This point concerns not merely the issue of who moves and who doesn't, although that is an important element of it; it is also about power in relation *to* the flows and the movement. Different social groups have distinct relationships to this anyway differentiated mobility: some people are more in charge of it than others; some initiate flows and movement, others don't; some are more on the receiving-end of it than others; some are effectively imprisoned by it.

In a sense at the end of all the spectra are those who are both doing the moving and the communicating and who are in some way in a position of control in relation to it—the jet-setters, the ones sending and receiving the faxes and the e-mail, holding the international conference calls, the ones distributing the films, controlling the news, organizing the investments and the international currency transactions. These are the groups who are really in a sense in charge of time-space-compression, who can really use it and turn it to advantage, whose power and influence it very definitely increases.

On its more prosaic fringes this group probably includes a fair number of Western academics and journalists – those, in other words, who write most about it.

But there are also groups who are also doing a lot of physical moving, but who are not 'in charge' of the process in the same way at all. The refugees from El Salvador or Guatemala and the undocumented migrant workers from Michoacan in Mexico, crowding into Tijuana to make a perhaps fatal dash for it across the border into the US to grab a chance of a new life. Here the experience of movement, and indeed of a confusing plurality of cultures, is very different. And there are those from India, Pakistan, Bangladesh, the Caribbean, who come half way round the world only to get held up in an interrogation room at Heathrow.

Or—a different case again—there are those who are simply on the receiving end of time-space-compression. The pensioner in a bed-sit in any inner city in this country, eating British working-class-style fish and chips from a Chinese take-away, watching a US film on a Japanese television; and not daring to go out after dark. And anyway the public transport's been cut.

Or—one final example to illustrate a different kind of complexity—there are the people who live in the favelas of Rio, who know global football like the back of their hand, and have produced some of its players; who have contributed massively to global music, who gave us the samba and produced the lambada that everyone was dancing to last year in the clubs of Paris and London; and who have never, or hardly ever, been to downtown Rio. At one level they have been tremendous contributors to what we call time-space-compression; and at another level they are imprisoned in it.

This is, in other words, a highly complex social differentiation. There are differences in the degree of movement and communication, but also in the degree of control and of initiation. The ways in which people are placed within 'time-space-compression' are highly complicated and extremely varied.

But this in turn immediately raises questions of politics. If time-space-compression can be imagined in that more socially formed, socially evaluative and differentiated way, then there may be here the possibility of developing a politics of mobility and access. For it does seem that mobility and control over mobility both reflects and reinforces power. It is not simply a question of unequal distribution, that some people move more than others, and that some have more control than others. It is that the mobility and control of some groups can actively weaken other people. Differential mobility can weaken the leverage of the already weak. The time-space-compression of some groups can undermine the power of others.

This is well established and often noted in the relationship between capital and labour. Capital's ability to roam the world further strengthens it in relation to relatively immobile workers, enables it to play off the plant at Genk against the plant at Dagenham. It also strengthens its hand against struggling local economies the world over as they compete for the favour of some investment. The 747s that fly computer scientists across the Pacific are part of the reason for the greater isolation today of the island of Pitcairn. But also, every time someone uses a car, and thereby increases their personal mobility, they reduce both the social rationale and the financial viability of the public transport system—and thereby also potentially reduce the mobility of those who rely on that system. Every time you drive to that out-of-town shopping centre you contribute to the rising prices, even hasten the demise, of the corner shop. And the 'time-space-compression' which is involved in producing and reproducing the daily lives of the comfortably-off in First World societies—not just their own travel but the resources they draw on, from all over the world, to feed their lives—may entail environmental consequences, or hit constraints, which will limit the lives of others before their own. We need to ask, in other words, whether our relative mobility and power over mobility and communication entrenches the spatial imprisonment of other groups.

But this way of thinking about time-space-compression also returns us to the question of place and a sense of place. How, in the context of all these socially-varied time-space-changes do we think about 'places'? In an era when, it is argued, 'local communities' seem to be increasingly broken up, when you can go abroad and find the same shops, the same music as at home, or eat your favourite foreign-holiday food at a restaurant down the road—and when everyone has a different experience of all this—how then do we think about 'locality'?

Many of those who write about time-space-compression emphasize the insecurity and unsettling impact of its effects, the feelings of vulnerability which it can produce. Some therefore go on from this to argue that, in the middle of all this flux, people desperately need a bit of peace and quiet—and that a strong sense of place, of locality, can form one kind of refuge from the hubbub. So the search after the 'real' meanings of places, the unearthing of heritages and so forth, is interpreted as being, in part, a response to desire for fixity and for security of identity in the middle of all the movement and change. A 'sense of place', of rootedness, can provide—in this form and on this interpretation—stability and a source of unproblematical identity. In that guise, however, place and the spatially local are then rejected by many progressive people as almost necessarily reactionary. They are interpreted as an evasion; as a retreat from the (actually unavoidable) dynamic and change of 'real life', which is what we must seize if we are to change things for the better. On this reading, place and locality are foci for a form of romanticized escapism from the real business of the world. While 'time' is equated with movement and progress, 'space'/'place' is equated with stasis and reaction.

There are some serious inadequacies in this argument. There is the question of why it is assumed that time-space-compression will produce insecurity. There is the need to face up to—rather than simply deny—people's need for attachment of some sort, whether through place or anything else. Nonetheless, it is certainly the case that there is indeed at the moment a recrudescence of some very problematical senses of place, from reactionary nationalisms, to competitive localisms, to introverted obsessions with 'heritage'. We need, therefore, to think through what might be an adequately progressive sense of place, one which would fit in with the current global-local times and the feelings and relations they give rise to, *and* which would be useful in what are, after all, political struggles often inevitably based on place. The question is how to hold on to that notion of geographical difference, of uniqueness, even of rootedness if people want that, without it being reactionary.

There are a number of distinct ways in which the 'reactionary' notion of place described above is problematical. One is the idea that places have single, essential, identities. Another is the idea that identity of place—the sense of place—is constructed out of an introverted, inward-looking history based on delving into the past for internalized origins, translating the name from the Domesday Book. Thus Wright recounts the construction and appropriation of Stoke Newington and its past by the arriving middle class (the Domesday Book registers the place as 'Newtowne' . . . 'There is land for two ploughs and a half . . . There are four villanes and thirty seven cottagers with ten acres', pp. 227 and 231), and contrasts this version with that of other groups—the white working class and the large number of important minority communities.[3] A particular problem with this conception of place is that it seems to require the drawing of boundaries. Geographers have long been exercised by the problem of defining regions, and this question of 'definition' has almost always been reduced to the issue of drawing lines around a place. I remember some of my most painful times as a geographer have been spent unwillingly struggling to think how one could draw a boundary around somewhere like the 'East Midlands'. But that kind of boundary around an area precisely distinguishes between an inside and an outside. It can so easily be yet another way of constructing a counterposition between 'us' and 'them'.

And yet, if one considers almost any real place, and certainly one not defined primarily by administrative or political boundaries, these supposed characteristics have little real purchase.

Take, for instance, a walk down Kilburn High Road, my local shopping centre. It is a pretty ordinary place, north-west of the centre of London. Under the railway bridge the newspaper stand sells papers from every county of what my neighbours, many of whom come from there, still often call the Irish Free State. The postboxes down the High Road, and many an empty space on a wall, are adorned with the letters IRA. Other available spaces are plastered this week with posters for a special meeting in remembrance: Ten Years after the Hunger Strike. At the local theatre Eamon Morrissey has a one-man show; the National Club has the Wolfe Tones on, and at the Black Lion there's Finnegan's Wake. In two shops I noted this week's lottery ticket winners: in one the name is Teresa Gleeson, in the other, Chouman Hassan.

Thread your way through the often almost stationary traffic diagonally across the road from the newsstand and there's a shop which as long as I can remember has displayed saris in the window. Four life-sized models of Indian women, and reams of cloth. On the door a notice announces a forthcoming concert at Wembley Arena: Anand Miland presents Rekha, live, with Aamir Khan, Salman Khan, Jahi Chawla and Raveena Tandon. On another ad, for the end of the month, is written 'All Hindus are cordially invited'. In another newsagents I chat with the man who keeps it, a Muslim unutterably depressed by events in the Gulf, silently chafing at having to sell *The Sun*. Overhead there is always at least one aeroplane—we seem to be on a flight-path to Heathrow and by the time they're over Kilburn you can see them clearly enough to tell the airline and wonder as you struggle with your shopping where they're coming from. Below, the reason the traffic is snarled up (another odd effect of time-space-compression!) is in part because this is one of the main entrances to and escape-routes from London, the road to Staples Corner and the beginning of the M1 to the North.

This is just the beginnings of a sketch from immediate impressions but a proper analysis could be done, of the links between Kilburn and the world. And so it could for almost any place.

Kilburn is a place for which I have a great affection; I have lived there many years. It certainly has 'a character of its own'. But it is possible to feel all this without subscribing to any of the static and defensive—and in that sense reactionary—notions of 'place' which were referred to above. First, while Kilburn may have a character of its own, it is absolutely not a seamless, coherent identity, a single sense of place which everyone shares. It could hardly be less so. People's routes through the place, their favourite haunts within it, the connections they make (physically, or by phone or post, or in memory and imagination) between here and the rest of the world vary enormously. If it is now recognized that people have multiple identities then the same point can be made in relation to places. Moreover, such multiple identities can either be a source of richness or a source of conflict, or both.

One of the problems here has been a persistent identification of place with 'community'. Yet this is a misidentification. On the one hand communities can exist without being in the same place—from networks of friends with like interests, to major religious, ethnic or political communities. On the other hand, the instances of places housing single 'communities' in the sense of coherent social groups are probably—and, I would argue, have for long been—quite rare. Moreover, even where they do exist this in no way implies a single sense of place. For people occupy different positions within any community. We could counterpose to the chaotic mix of Kilburn the relatively stable and homogeneous community (at least in popular imagery) of a small mining village. Homogeneous? 'Communities' too have internal structures. To take the most obvious example. I'm sure a woman's sense of place in a mining village—the spaces through which she normally moves, the meeting places, the connections outside—are different from a man's. Their 'senses of the place' will be different.

Moreover, not only does 'Kilburn', then, have many identities (or its full identity is a complex mix of all these) it is also, looked at in this way, absolutely *not* introverted. It is (or ought to be) impossible even to begin thinking about Kilburn High Road without bringing into play half the world and a considerable amount of British imperialist history (and this certainly goes for mining villages too). Imagining it this way provokes in you (or at least in me) a really global sense of place.

And finally, in contrasting this way of looking at places with the defensive reactionary view, I certainly could not begin to, nor would I want to, define 'Kilburn' by drawing its enclosing boundaries.

So, at this point in the argument, get back in your mind's eye on a satellite; go right out again and look back at the globe. This time, however, imagine not just all the physical movement, nor even all the often invisible communications, but also and especially all the social relations, all the links between people. Fill it in with all those different experiences of time-space-compression. For what is happening is that the geography of social relations is changing. In many cases such relations are increasingly stretched out over space. Economic, political and cultural social relations, each full of power and with internal structures of domination and subordination, stretched out over the planet at every different level, from the household to the local area to the international.

It is from this perspective that it is possible to envisage an alternative interpretation of place. In this interpretation, what gives a place its specificity is not some long internalized history but the fact that it is constructed out of a particular constellation of social relations, meeting and weaving together at a particular locus. If one moves in from the satellite towards the globe, holding all those networks of social relations and movements and communications in one's head, then each 'place' can be seen as a particular, unique, point of their intersection. It is, indeed, a *meeting* place. Instead then, of thinking of places as areas with boundaries around, they can be imagined as articulated movements in networks of social relations and understandings, but where a large proportion of those relations, experiences and understandings are constructed on a far larger scale than what we happen to define for that moment as the place itself, whether that be a street, or a region or even a continent. And this in turn allows a sense of place which is extroverted, which includes a consciousness of its links with the wider world, which integrates in a positive way the global and the local.

This is not a question of making the ritualistic connections to 'the wider system'—the people in the local meeting who bring up international capitalism every time you try to have a discussion about rubbish-collection —the point is that there are real relations with real content—economic, political, cultural—between any local place and the wider world in which it is set. In economic geography the argument has long been accepted that it is not possible to understand the 'inner city', for instance its loss of jobs, the decline of manufacturing employment there, by looking only at the inner city. Any adequate explanation has to set the inner city in its wider geographical context. Perhaps it is appropriate to think how that kind of understanding could be extended to the notion of a sense of place.

These arguments, then, highlight a number of ways in which a progressive concept of place might be developed. First of all, it is absolutely not static. If places can be conceptualized in terms of the social interactions which they tie together, then it is also the case that these interactions themselves are not motionless things, frozen in time. They are processes. One of the great one-liners in Marxist exchanges has for long been 'ah, but capital is not a thing, it's a process'. Perhaps this should be said also about places; that places are processes, too.

Second, places do not have to have boundaries in the sense of divisions which frame simple enclosures. 'Boundaries' may of course be necessary, for the purposes of certain types of studies for instance, but they are not necessary for the conceptualization of a place itself. Definition in this sense does not have to be through simple counterposition to the outside; it can come, in part, precisely through the particularity of linkage to that 'outside' which is therefore itself part of what constitutes the place. This helps get away from the common association between penetrability and vulnerability. For it is this kind of association which makes invasion by newcomers so threatening.

Third, clearly places do not have single, unique 'identities'; they are full of internal conflicts. Just think, for instance, about London's Docklands, a place which is at the moment quite clearly *defined* by conflict: a conflict over what its past has been (the nature of its 'heritage'), conflict over what should be its present development, conflict over what could be its future.

Fourth, and finally, none of this denies place nor the importance of the uniqueness of place. The specificity of place is continually reproduced, but it is not a specificity which results from some long, internalized history. There are a number of sources of this specificity—the uniqueness of place.[4] There is the fact that the wider social relations in which places are set are themselves geographically differentiated. Globalization (in the economy, or in culture, or in anything else) does not entail simply homogenization. On the contrary, the globalization of social relations is yet another source of (the reproduction of) geographical uneven development, and thus of the uniqueness of place. There is the specificity of place which derives from the fact that each place is the focus of a distinct *mixture* of wider and more local social relations. There is the fact that this very mixture together in one place may produce effects which would not have happened otherwise. And finally, all these relations interact with and take a further element of specificity from the accumulated history of a place, with that history itself imagined as the product of layer upon layer of different sets of linkages, both local and to the wider world.

In her portrait of Corsica, *Granite Island*, Dorothy Carrington travels the island seeking out the roots of its character.[5] All the different layers of peoples and cultures are explored; the long and tumultuous relationship with France, with Genoa and Aragon in the thirteenth, fourteenth and fifteenth centuries, back through the much earlier incorporation into the Byzantine Empire, and before that domination by the Vandals, before that being part of the Roman Empire, before that the colonization and settlements of the Carthaginians and the Greeks . . . until we find . . . that even the megalith builders had come to Corsica from somewhere else.

It is a sense of place, an understanding of 'its character', which can only be constructed by linking that place to places beyond. A progressive sense of place would recognize that, without being threatened by it. What we need, it seems to me, is a global sense of the local, a global sense of place.

Notes

1 D. Birkett, *New Statesman And Society*, 13 June 1990, pp. 41–2.
2 D. Birkett, *New Statesman And Society*, 15 March 1991, p. 38.
3 P. Wright, *On Living In An Old Country*, Verso, 1985.
4 D. Massey, *Spatial Divisions of Labour: Social Structures and The Geography Of Production*, Macmillan, 1984.
5 D. Carrington, *Granite Island: A Portrait of Corsica*, Penguin.

Index